THE HAUNTED BOOKSTORE

Gateway to a Parallel Universe

Vol. 2

ART BY
MEDAMAYAKI

STORY BY
SHINOBUMARU

CHARACTER DESIGN BY
MUNASHICHI

The Story So Far

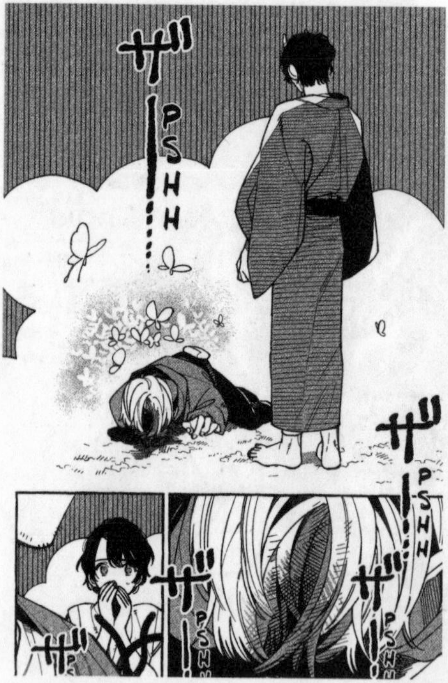
ザー
PSHH...
ザー
PSHH...
ザー
ザー

Ever since she was lost in the spirit realm as a child, Muramoto Kaori has lived in a haunted bookstore with her slob of an adoptive father, Shinonome, and her best friend/sister-figure, Nyaa-san, a talking cat. One day, Shinonome discovered a young man who'd collapsed in the spirit realm. The young man, Suimei, was an exorcist in the human realm, but he's moved in with Kaori and Shinonome in order to find his missing partner.

While helping Kaori with the bookstore, Suimei has had the opportunity to interact with several spirits, allowing him to see a different side of them than he did as an exorcist. After watching Kaori's emotional goodbye to a pair of cicada spirits who live for just a week before they die and are reborn again, Suimei has discovered new feelings blossoming inside of him...

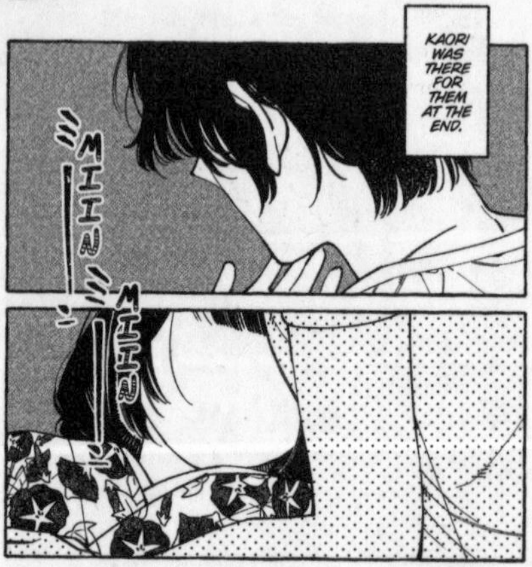
KAORI WAS THERE FOR THEM AT THE END.
ミーン
MIIIN
ミーン
MIIIN

[redacted]

Humans and Spirits

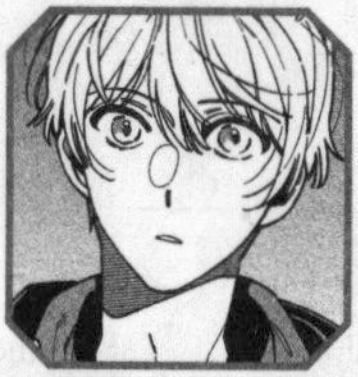

Shirai Suimei

A young man who collapsed in the spirit realm, only to be rescued by Kaori and Shinonome. He works as an exorcist and is searching the spirit realm for a specific spirit. He's also incredibly wealthy.

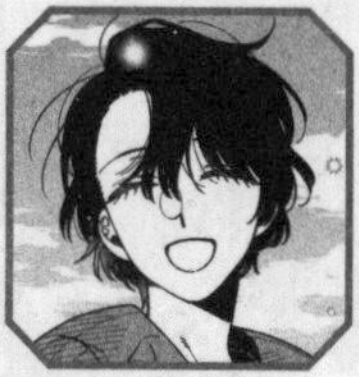

Muramoto Kaori

The only human living in the spirit realm. She was taken in by Shinonome, the bookstore owner, when she was little. She has a part-time job in the human realm, since her father doesn't have a stable salary.

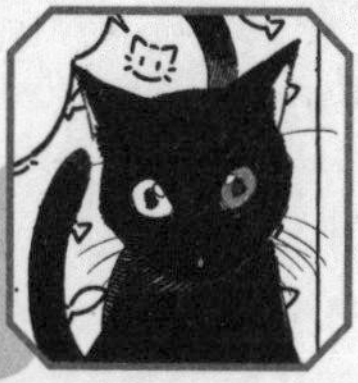

Nyaa

Nyaa-san is a Kasha spirit—a three-tailed black cat who is capable of changing her size. She's Kaori's best friend, and is always by her side. Though she's a bit bossy, she watches over Kaori like an older sister.

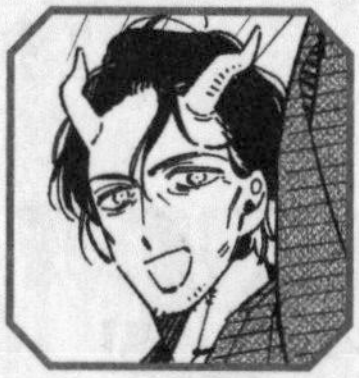

Shinonome

Kaori's adoptive father. He's a writer—an unusual profession for a spirit—but he's also a slob, something Kaori scolds him for frequently.

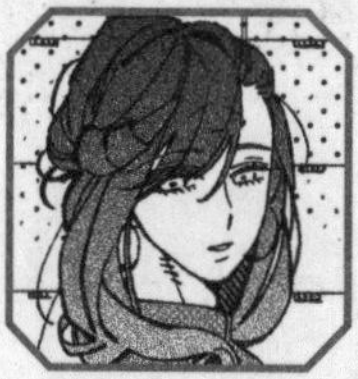

Noname

A spirit who has lived for a very long time, Noname now runs an apothecary in the spirit realm. She's old friends with Shinonome, and is a mother figure to Kaori.

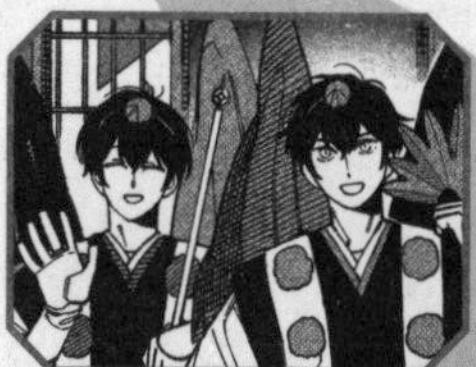

Kinme and Ginme

A pair of Tengu spirits Kaori saved when they were young. The calm one with sloping eyes is Kinme, the eldest. The unruly one with sharp eyes is Ginme, the youngest. Kinme loves his younger brother more than anything, while Ginme has romantic feelings toward Kaori.

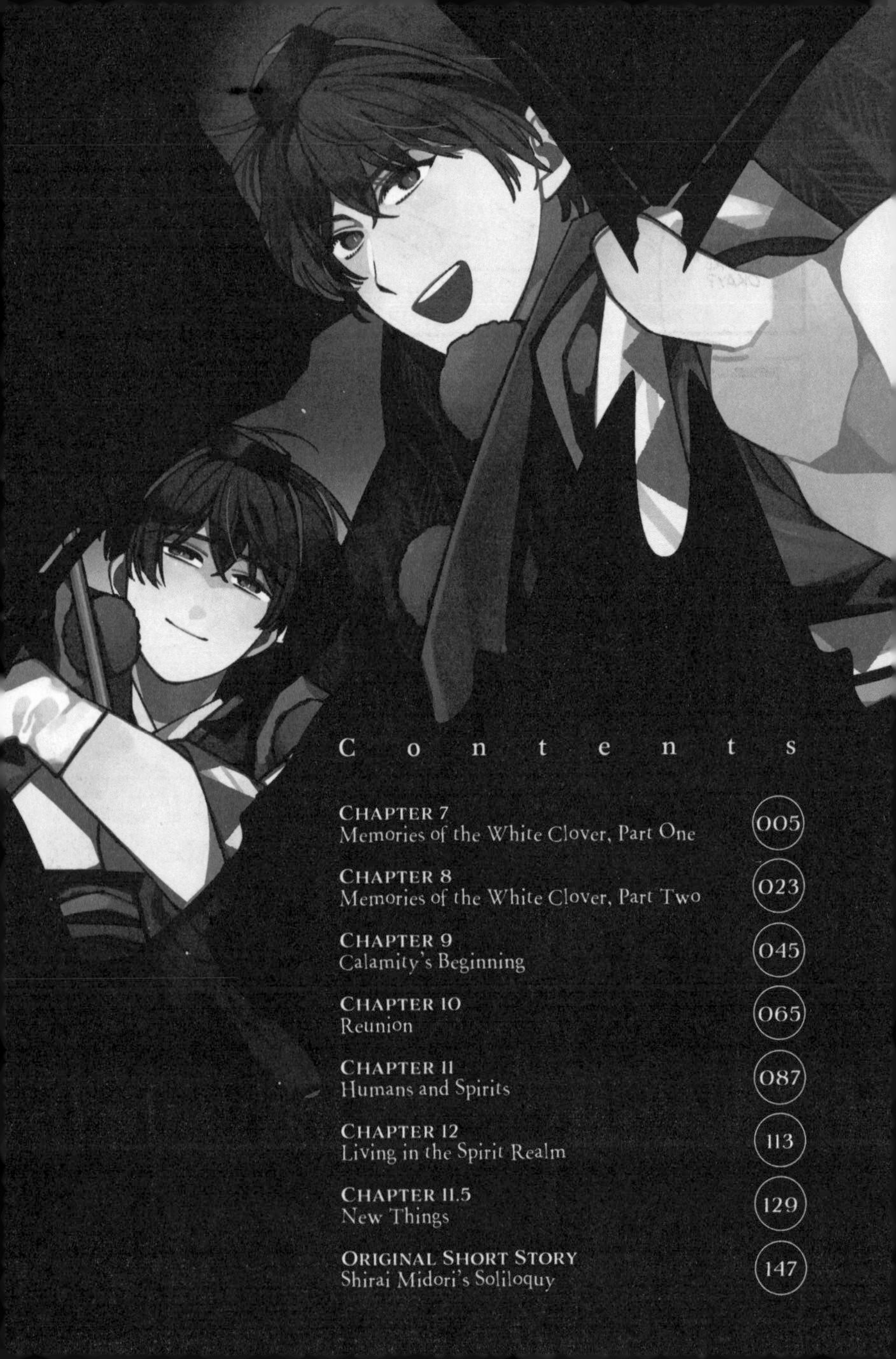

C o n t e n t s

HEY, KAORI.
KAOOORI!
ARE YOU SURE YOU'RE OKAY?
I TOLD YOU, I'M FINE.
YEAH, BUT...
GAAH! YOU'RE SO ANNOY-ING!
SHOCK
A-ANNOY-ING?!

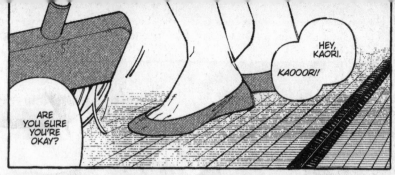

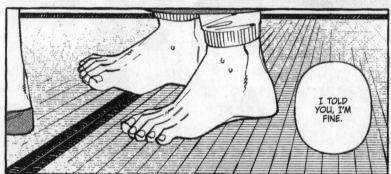

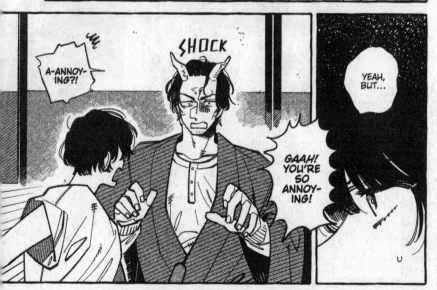

CHAPTER 7

Memories of the White Clover, Part One

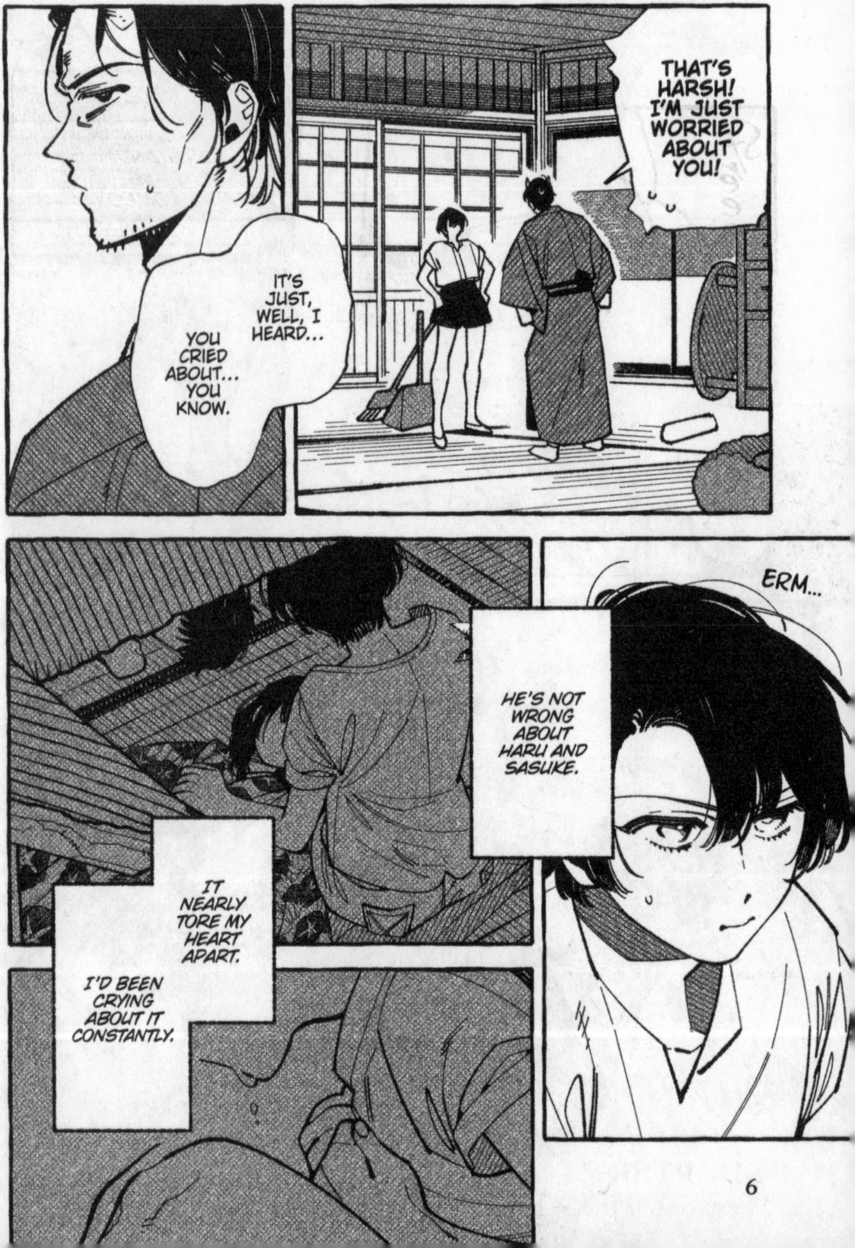
THAT'S HARSH! I'M JUST WORRIED ABOUT YOU!
IT'S JUST, WELL, I HEARD...
YOU CRIED ABOUT... YOU KNOW.
ERM...
HE'S NOT WRONG ABOUT HARU AND SASUKE.
IT NEARLY TORE MY HEART APART.
I'D BEEN CRYING ABOUT IT CONSTANTLY.

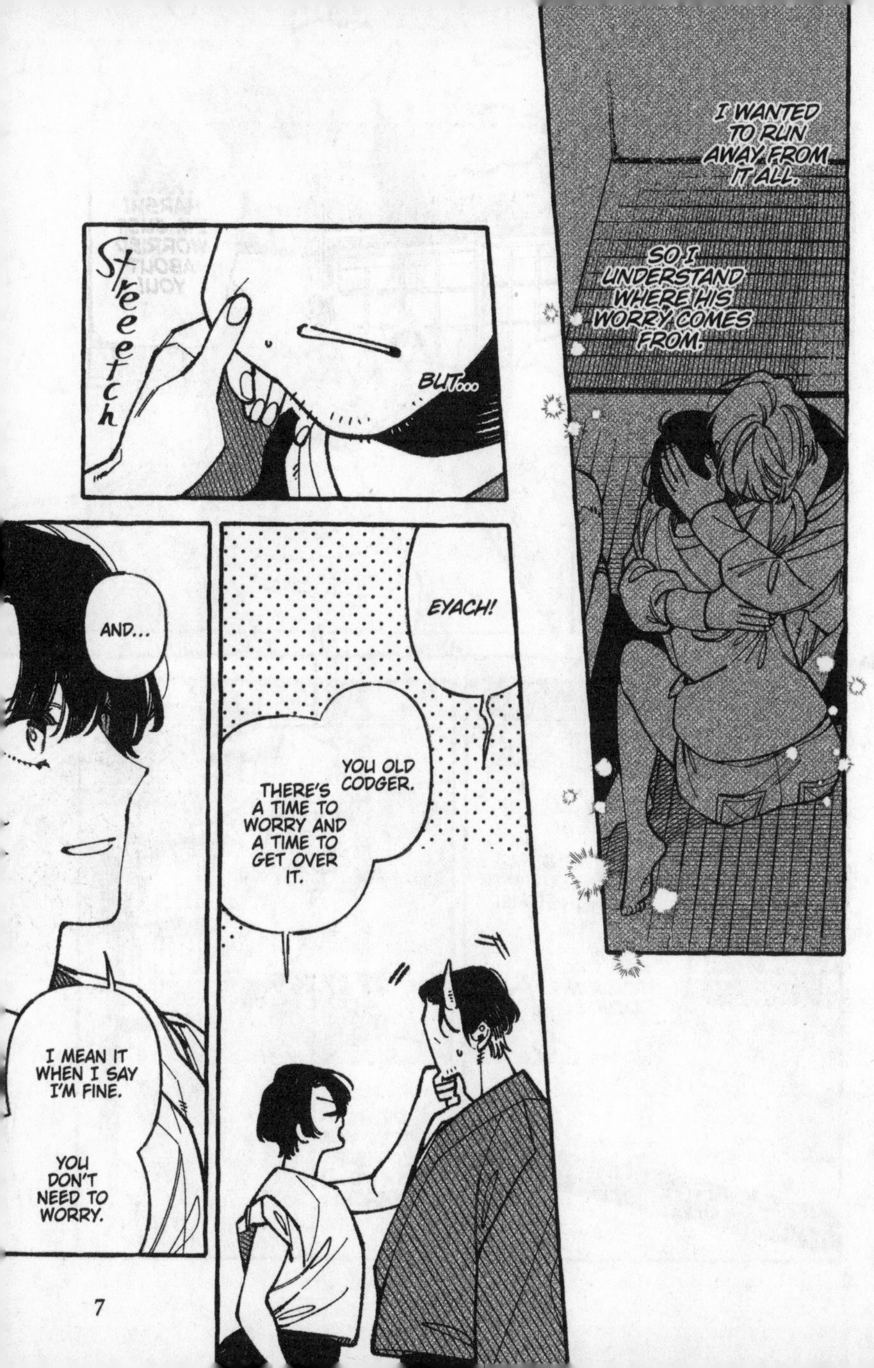

I WANTED TO RUN AWAY FROM IT ALL.
SO I UNDERSTAND WHERE HIS WORRY COMES FROM.
Streeetch
BUT...
EYACH!
YOU OLD CODGER.
THERE'S A TIME TO WORRY AND A TIME TO GET OVER IT.
AND...
I MEAN IT WHEN I SAY I'M FINE.
YOU DON'T NEED TO WORRY.

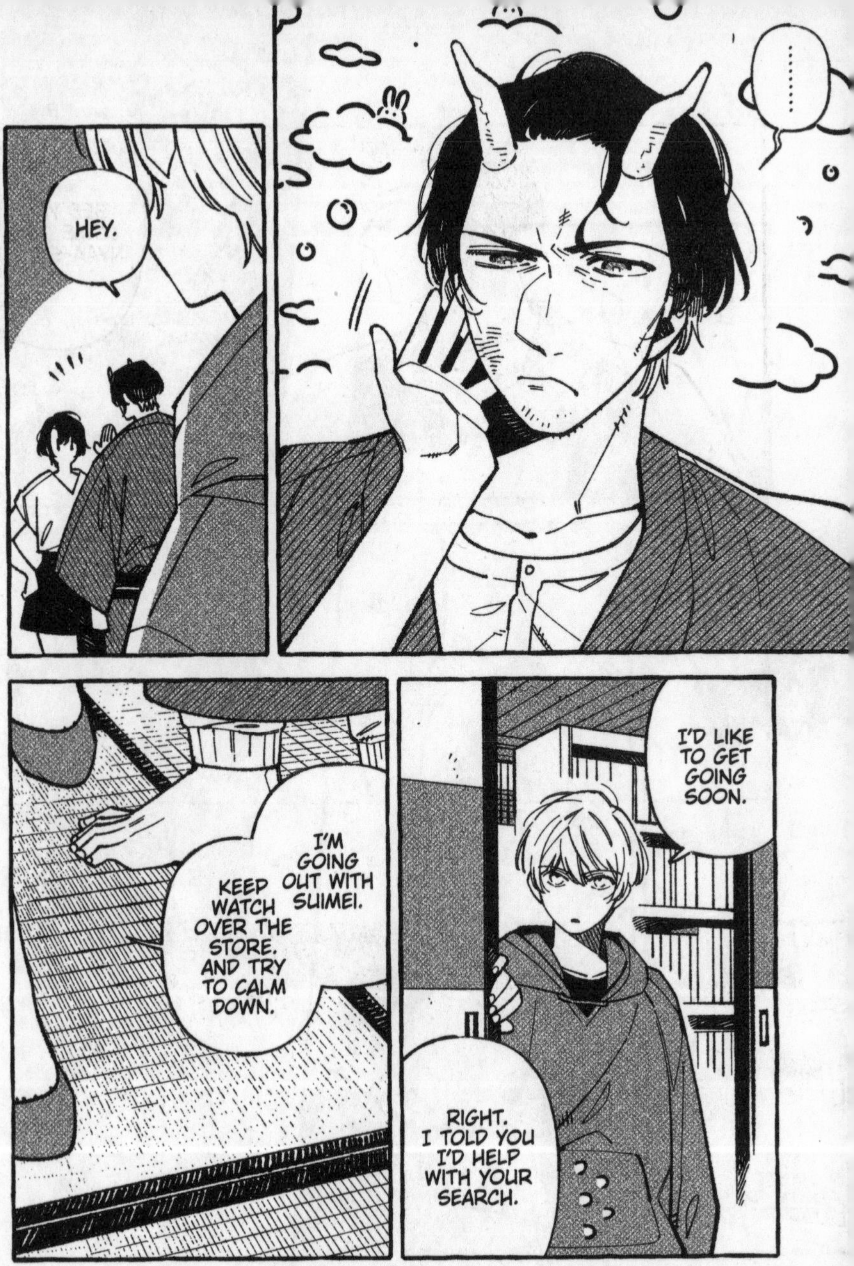
......
HEY.
I'D LIKE TO GET GOING SOON.
RIGHT. I TOLD YOU I'D HELP WITH YOUR SEARCH.
I'M GOING OUT WITH SUIMEI.
KEEP WATCH OVER THE STORE. AND TRY TO CALM DOWN.

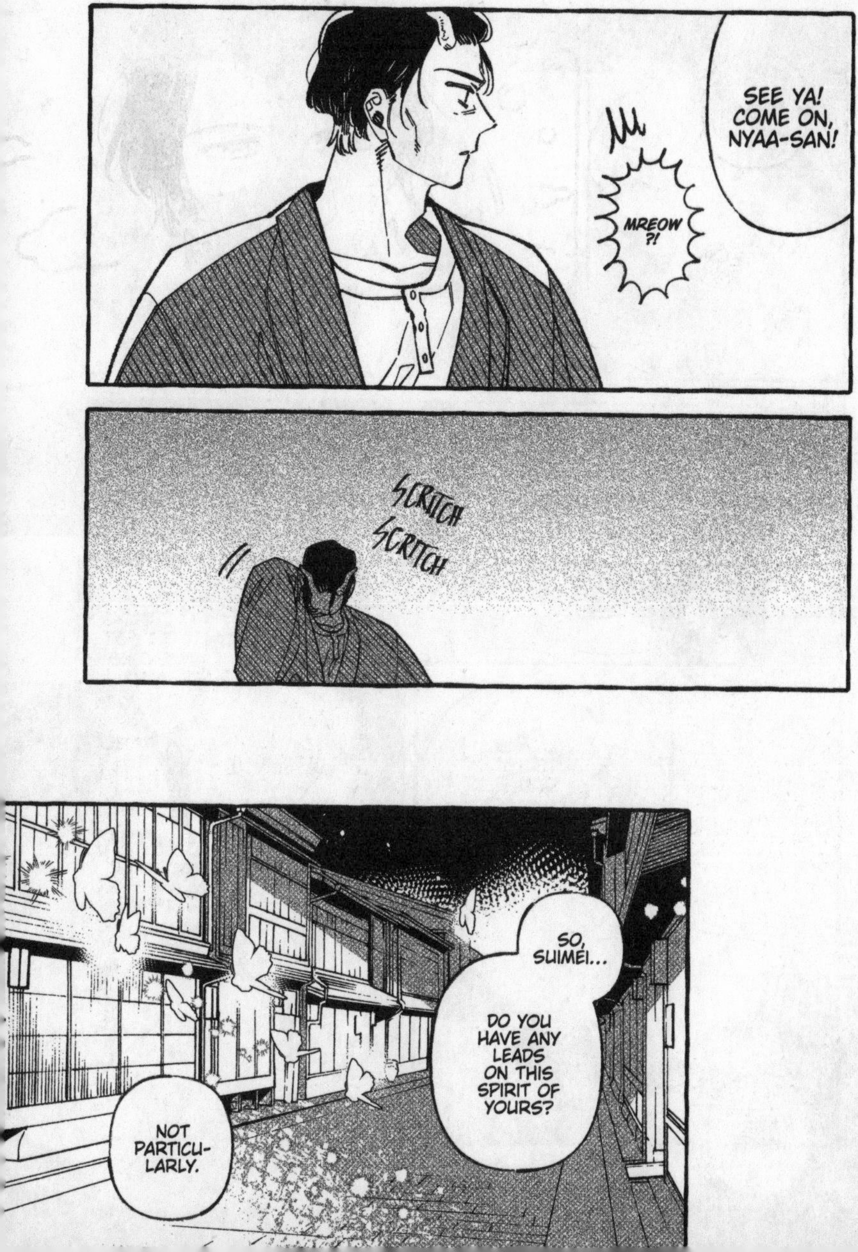
SEE YA! COME ON, NYAA-SAN!
MREOW ?!
SCRITCH
SCRITCH
SO, SUIMEI...
DO YOU HAVE ANY LEADS ON THIS SPIRIT OF YOURS?
NOT PARTICULARLY.

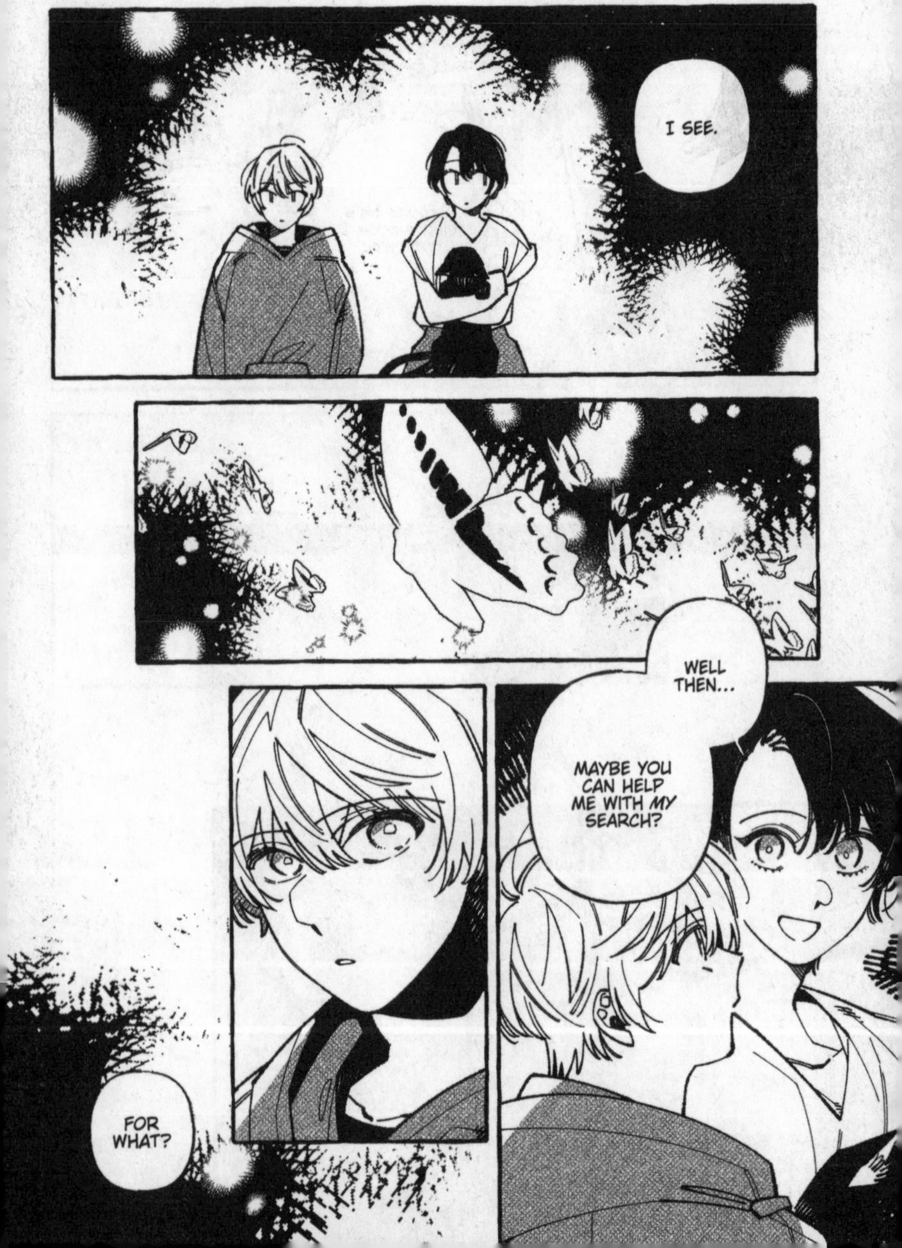
I SEE.
WELL THEN...
MAYBE YOU CAN HELP ME WITH *MY* SEARCH?
FOR WHAT?

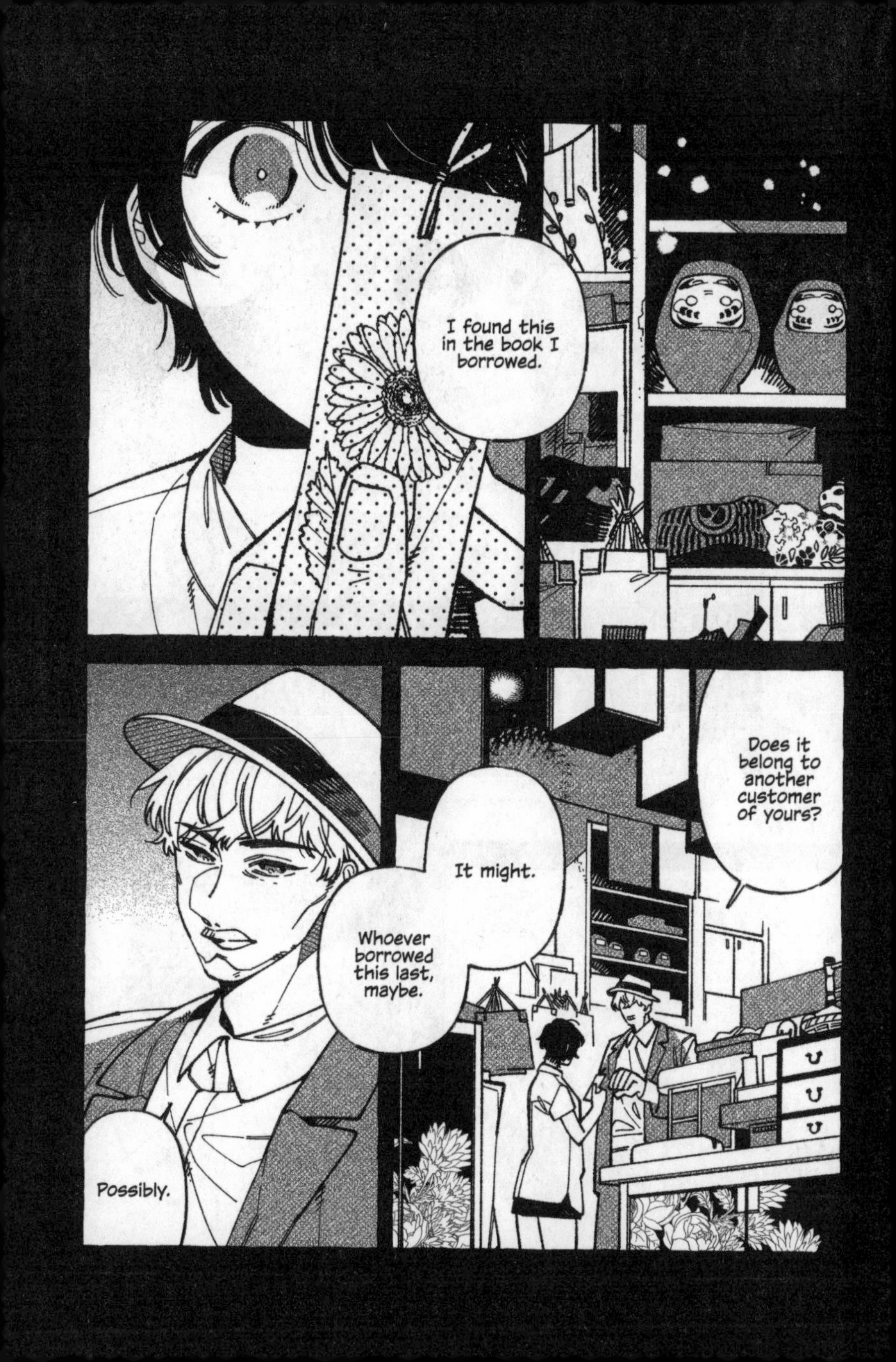
I found this in the book I borrowed.
Does it belong to another customer of yours?
It might.
Whoever borrowed this last, maybe.
Possibly.

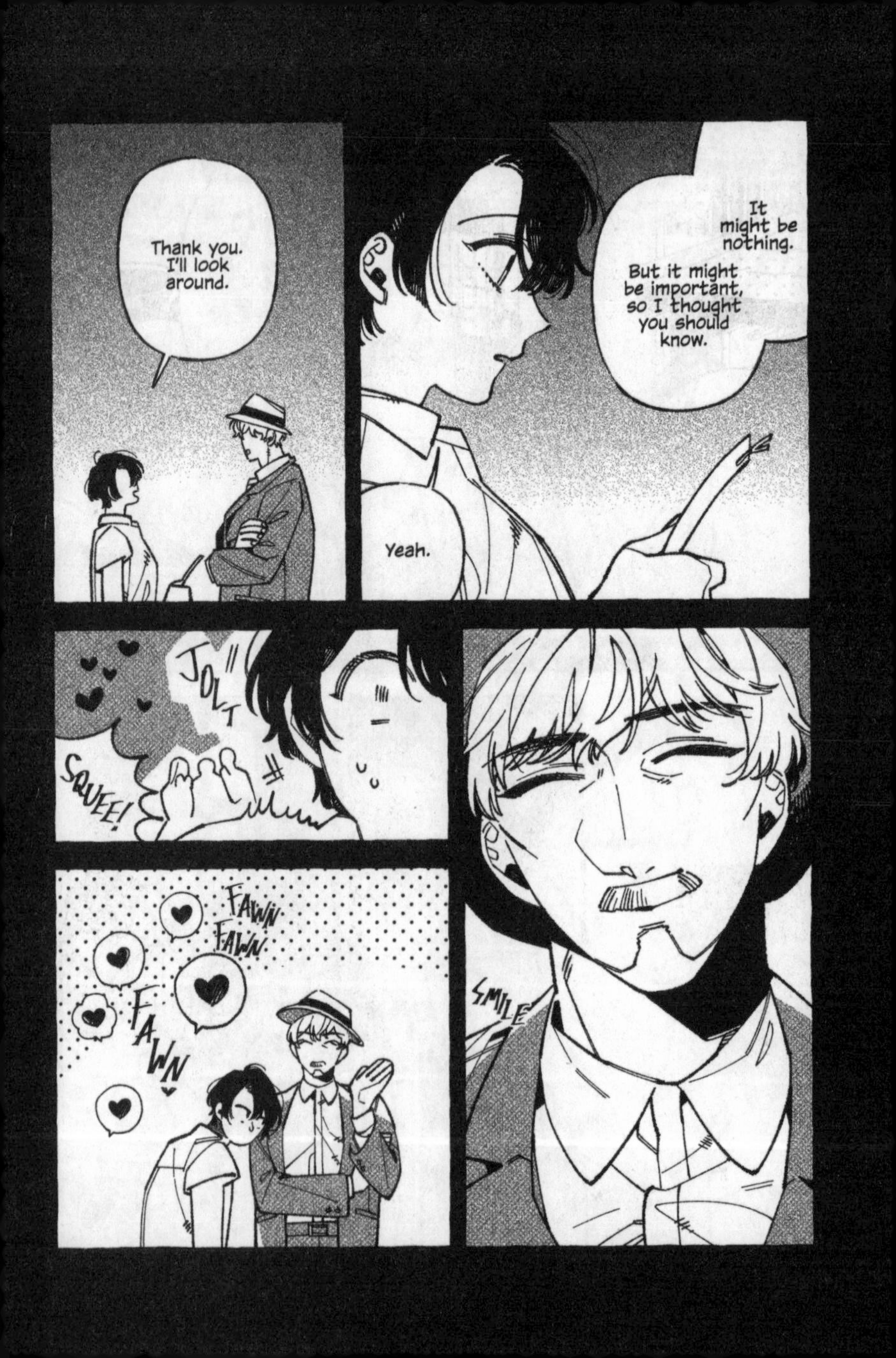
It might be nothing.
But it might be important, so I thought you should know.
Yeah.
Thank you. I'll look around.
SMILE
JOLT
SQUEE!
FAWN FAWN
FAWN

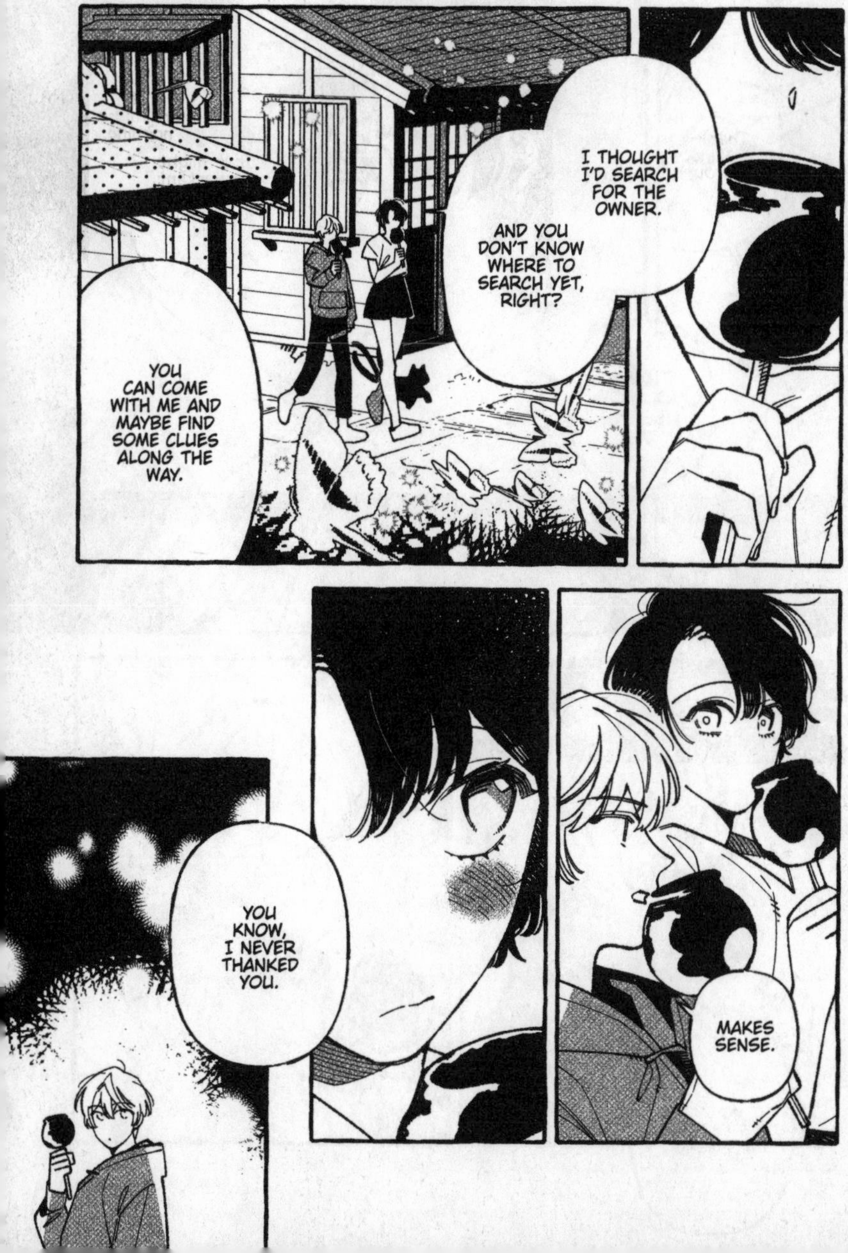
I THOUGHT I'D SEARCH FOR THE OWNER.
AND YOU DON'T KNOW WHERE TO SEARCH YET, RIGHT?
YOU CAN COME WITH ME AND MAYBE FIND SOME CLUES ALONG THE WAY.
MAKES SENSE.
YOU KNOW, I NEVER THANKED YOU.

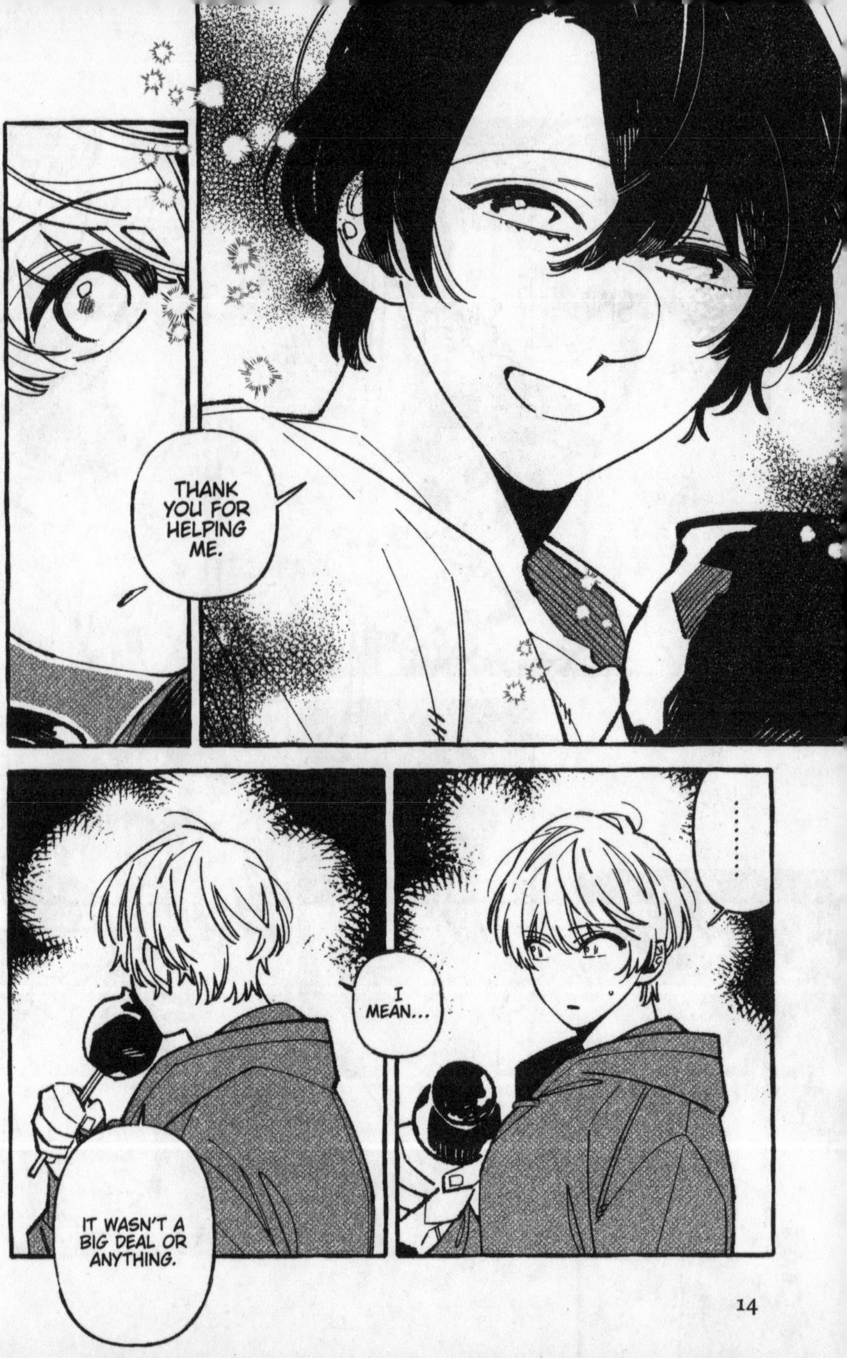
THANK YOU FOR HELPING ME.
……
I MEAN…
IT WASN'T A BIG DEAL OR ANYTHING.

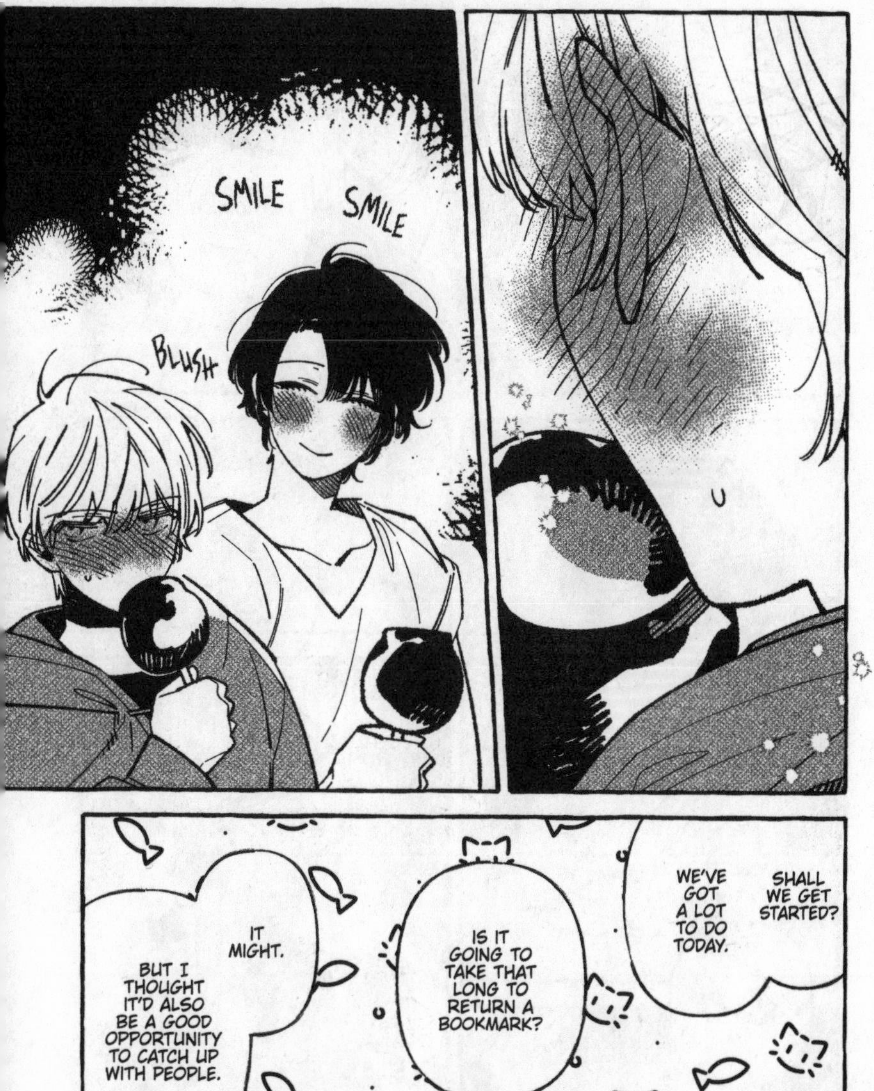
SMILE SMILE
BLUSH
SHALL WE GET STARTED?
WE'VE GOT A LOT TO DO TODAY.
IS IT GOING TO TAKE THAT LONG TO RETURN A BOOKMARK?
IT MIGHT.
BUT I THOUGHT IT'D ALSO BE A GOOD OPPORTUNITY TO CATCH UP WITH PEOPLE.

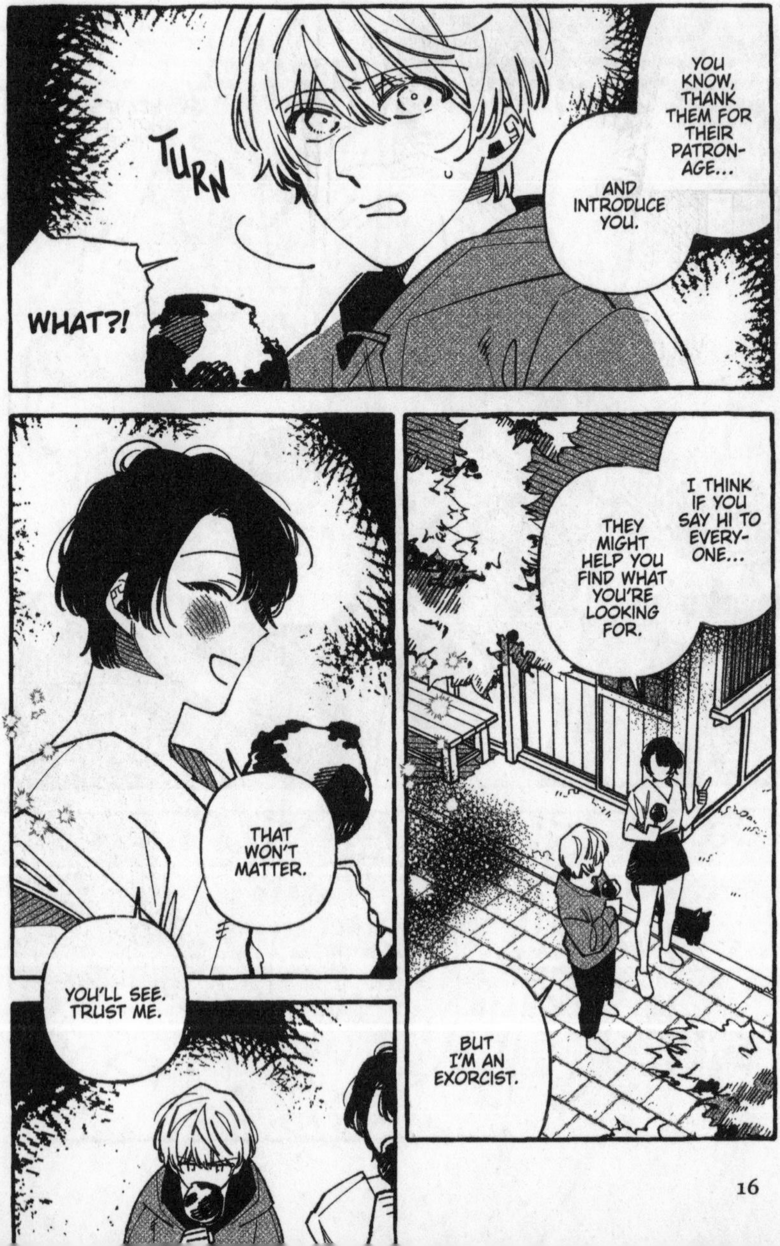
YOU KNOW, THANK THEM FOR THEIR PATRON-AGE...
AND INTRODUCE YOU.
TURN
WHAT?!
I THINK IF YOU SAY HI TO EVERY-ONE...
THEY MIGHT HELP YOU FIND WHAT YOU'RE LOOKING FOR.
BUT I'M AN EXORCIST.
THAT WON'T MATTER.
YOU'LL SEE. TRUST ME.

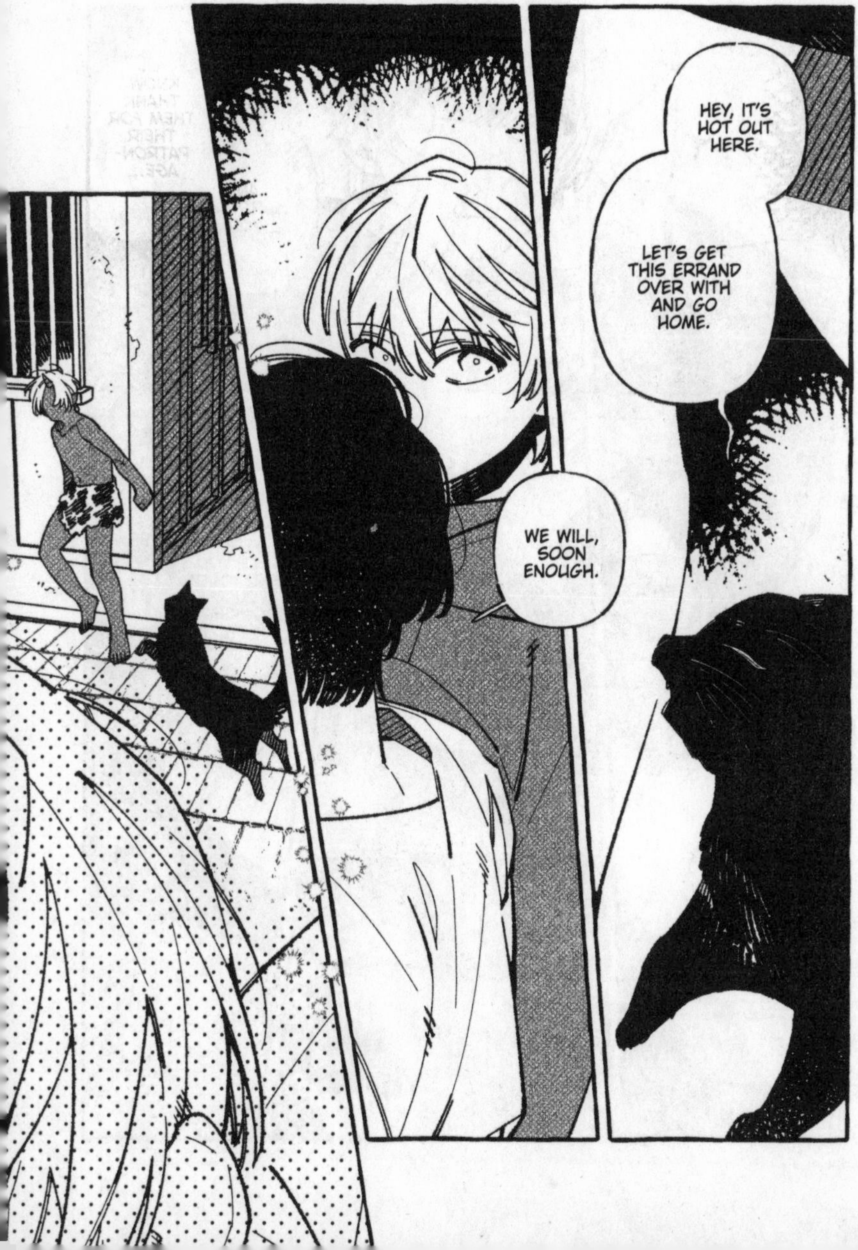
HEY, IT'S HOT OUT HERE.
LET'S GET THIS ERRAND OVER WITH AND GO HOME.
WE WILL, SOON ENOUGH.

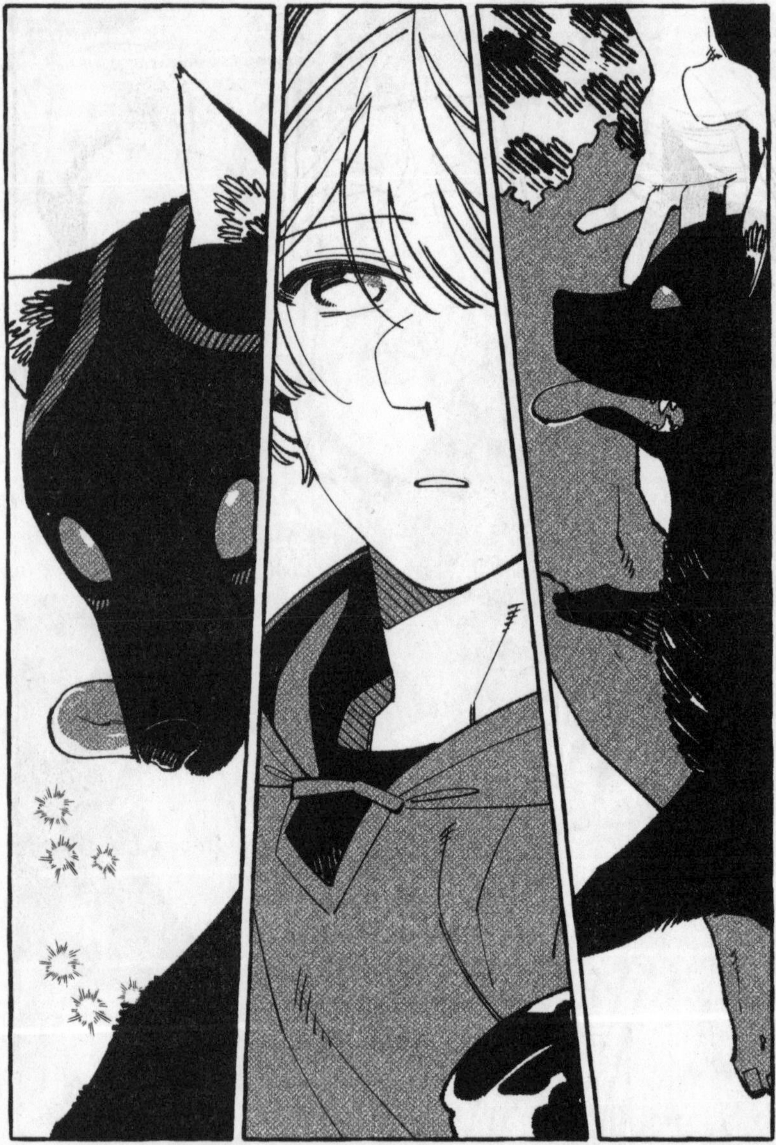

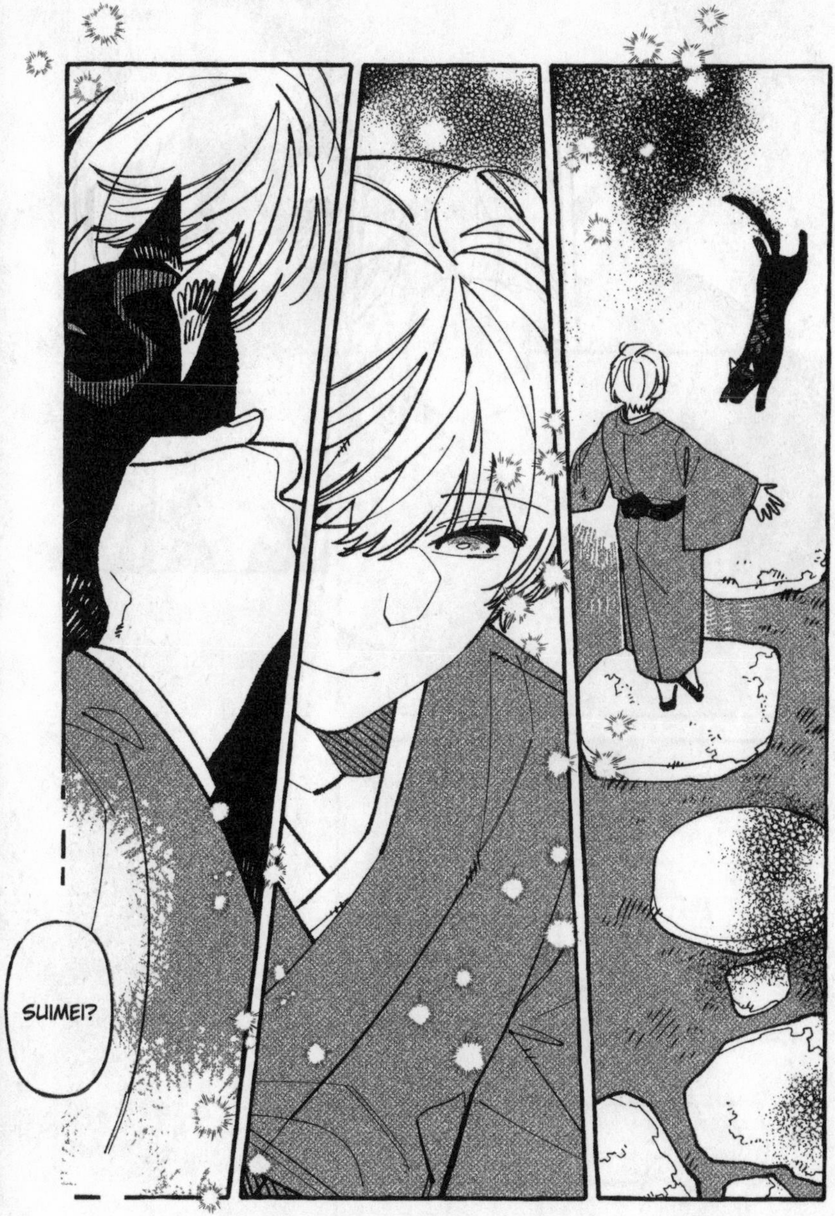
SUIMEI?

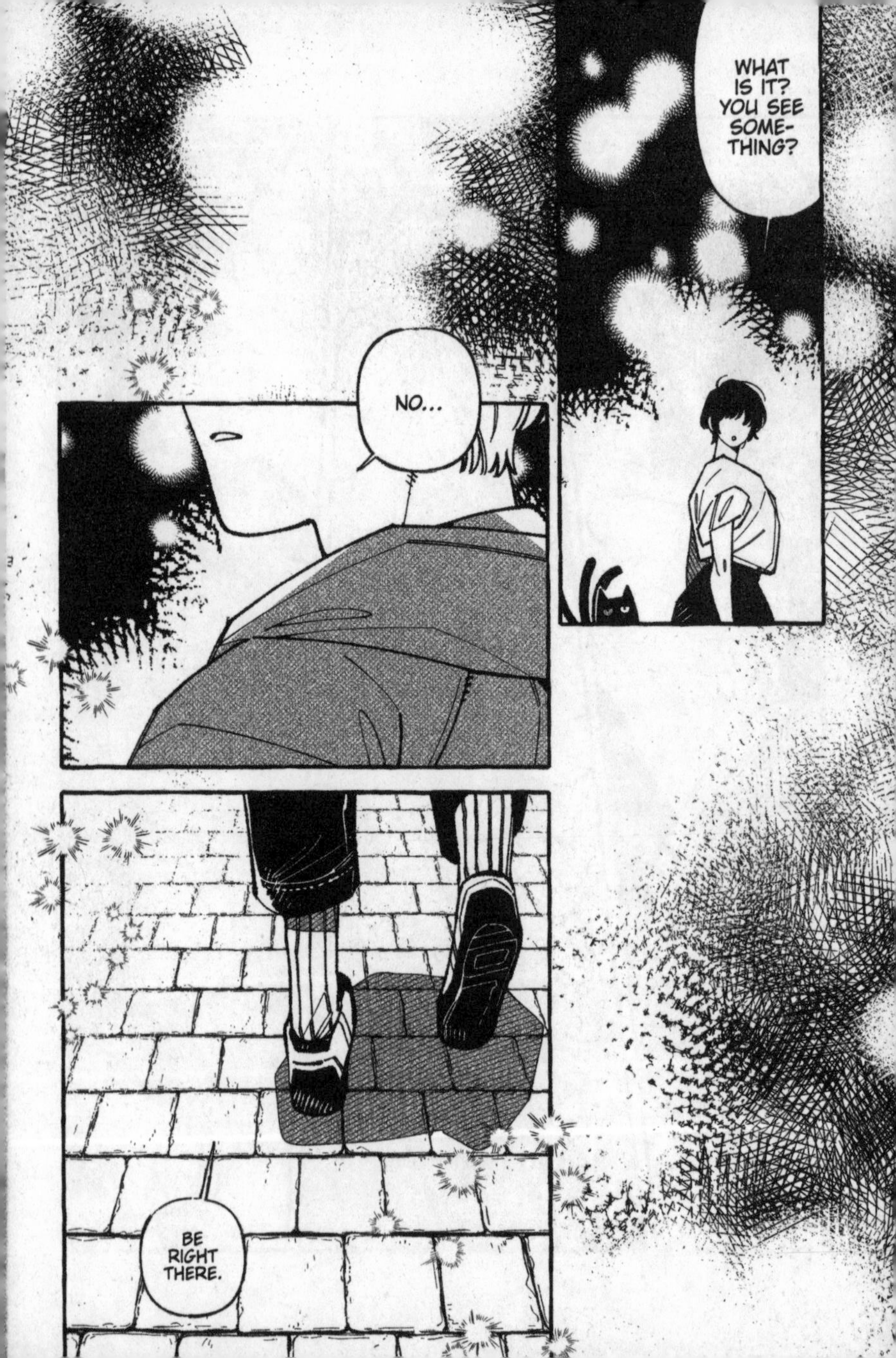
WHAT IS IT? YOU SEE SOME-THING?
NO...
BE RIGHT THERE.

THE HAUNTED BOOKSTORE

Gateway to a Parallel Universe

THE HAUNTED BOOKSTORE

Gateway to a Parallel Universe

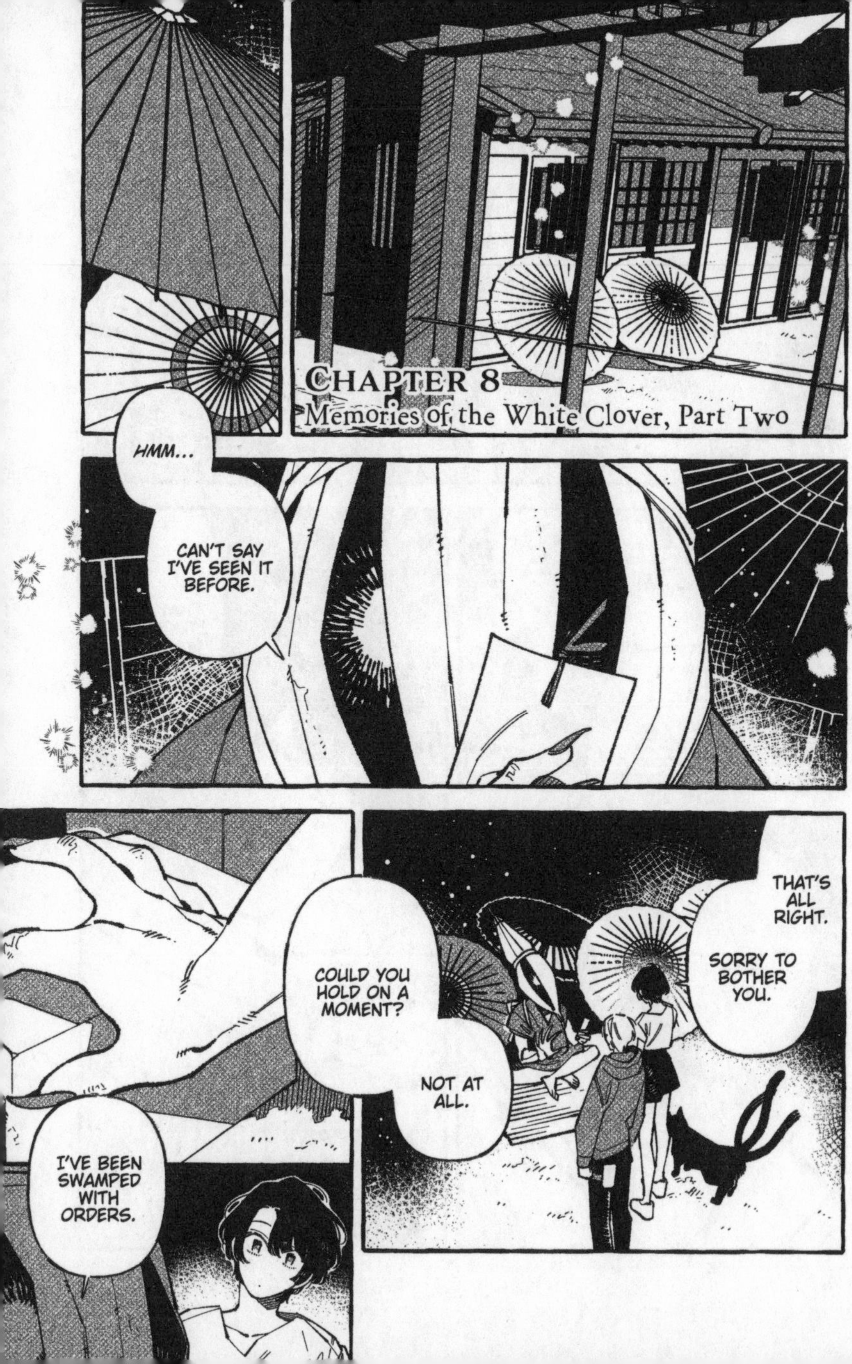
CHAPTER 8
Memories of the White Clover, Part Two
HMM...
CAN'T SAY I'VE SEEN IT BEFORE.
THAT'S ALL RIGHT.
SORRY TO BOTHER YOU.
COULD YOU HOLD ON A MOMENT?
NOT AT ALL.
I'VE BEEN SWAMPED WITH ORDERS.

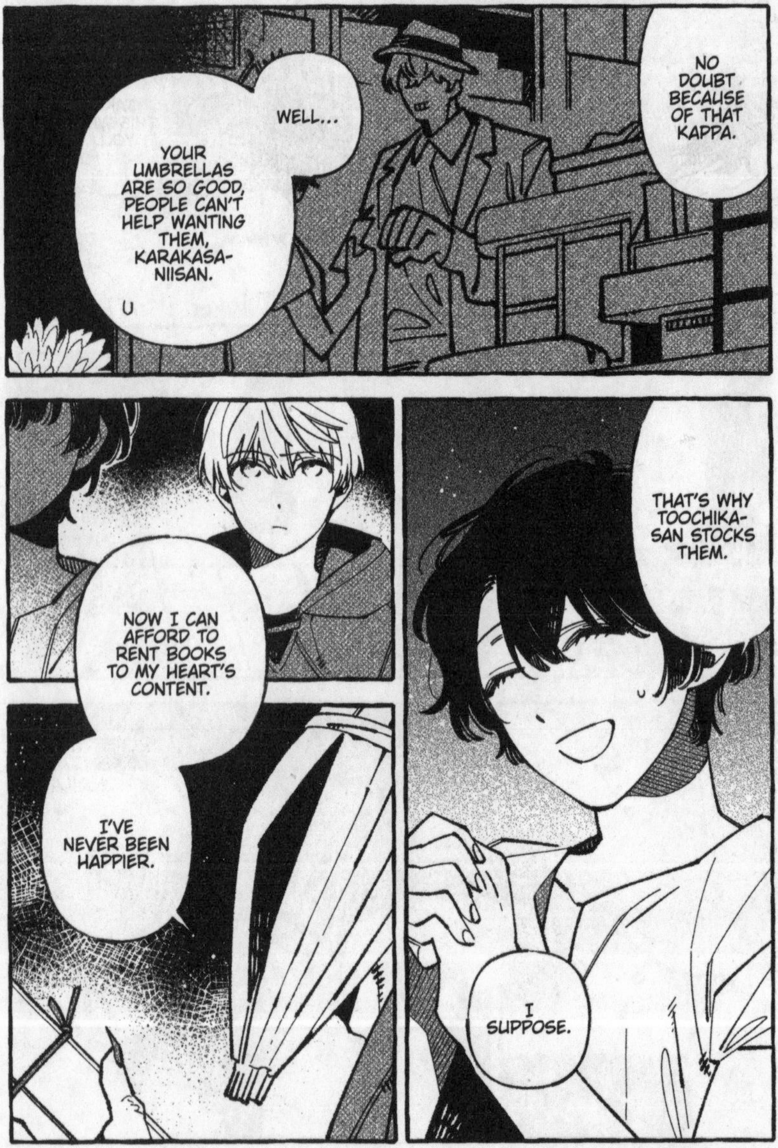
NO DOUBT BECAUSE OF THAT KAPPA.
WELL...
YOUR UMBRELLAS ARE SO GOOD, PEOPLE CAN'T HELP WANTING THEM, KARAKASA-NIISAN.
THAT'S WHY TOOCHIKA-SAN STOCKS THEM.
I SUPPOSE.
NOW I CAN AFFORD TO RENT BOOKS TO MY HEART'S CONTENT.
I'VE NEVER BEEN HAPPIER.

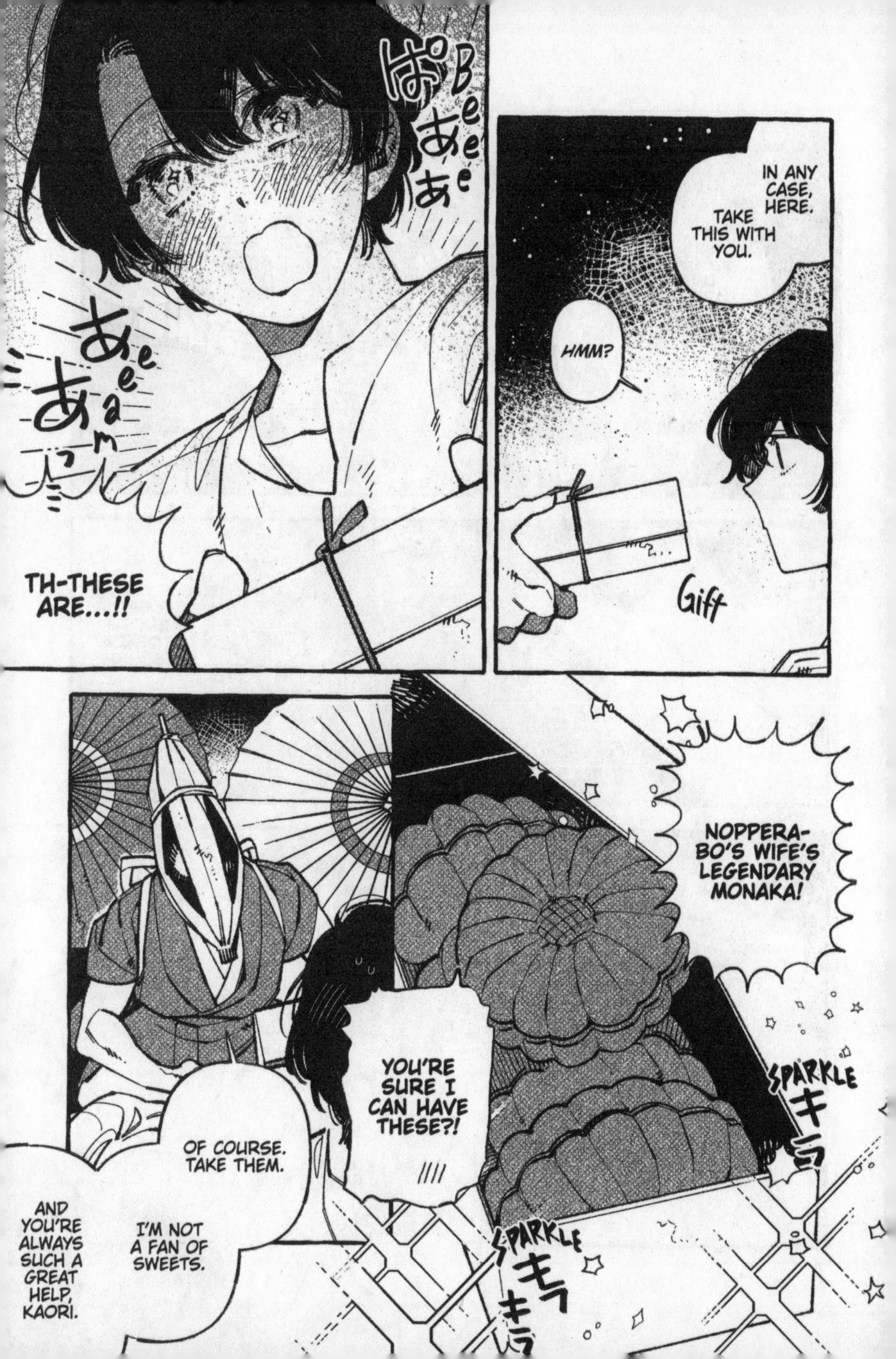
IN ANY CASE, HERE.
TAKE THIS WITH YOU.
HMM?
Gift
ぱああ
Beee
TH-THESE ARE...!!
NOPPERA-BO'S WIFE'S LEGENDARY MONAKA!
SPARKLE
キラ
SPARKLE
キラキラ
YOU'RE SURE I CAN HAVE THESE?!
OF COURSE. TAKE THEM.
I'M NOT A FAN OF SWEETS.
AND YOU'RE ALWAYS SUCH A GREAT HELP, KAORI.

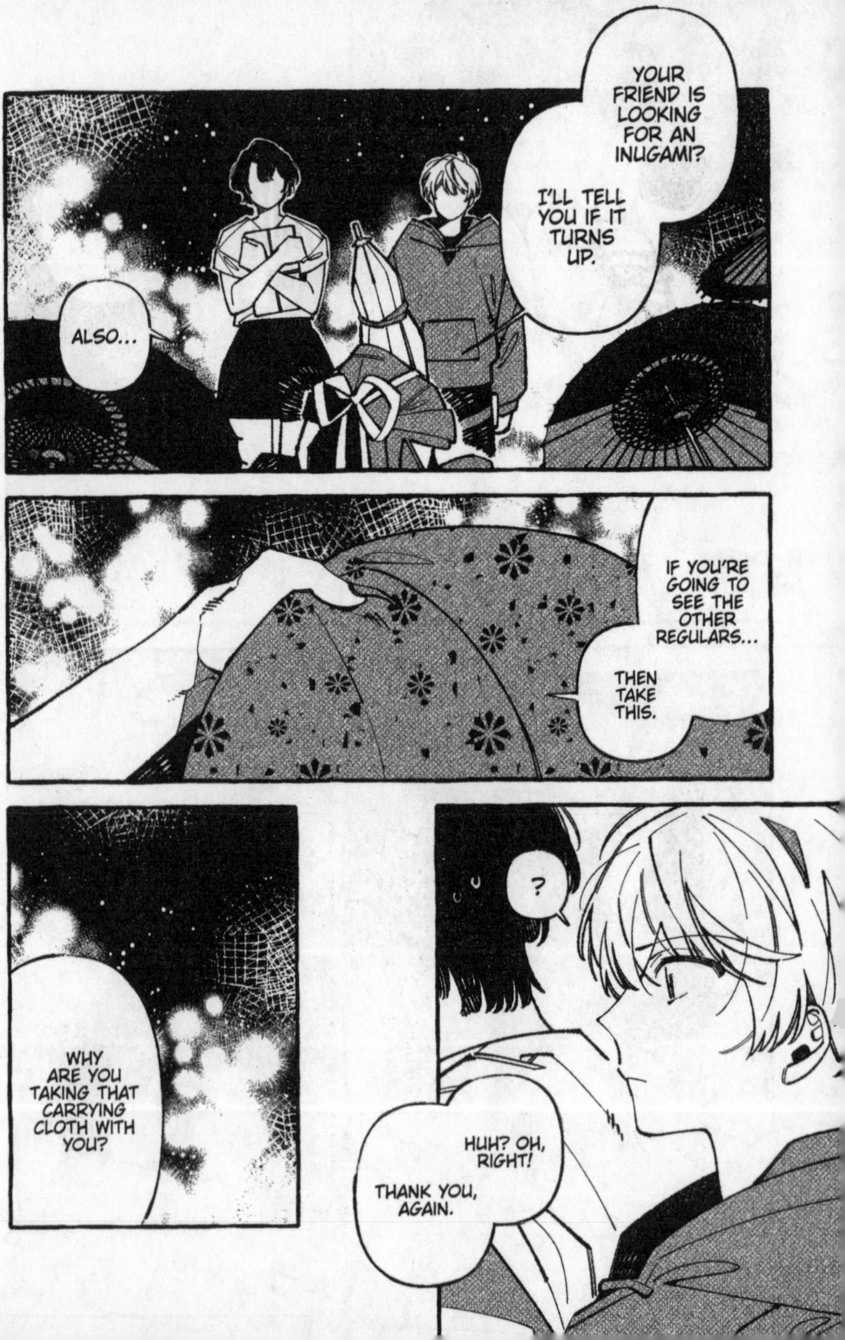
YOUR FRIEND IS LOOKING FOR AN INUGAMI?
I'LL TELL YOU IF IT TURNS UP.
ALSO...
IF YOU'RE GOING TO SEE THE OTHER REGULARS...
THEN TAKE THIS.
?
HUH? OH, RIGHT!
THANK YOU, AGAIN.
WHY ARE YOU TAKING THAT CARRYING CLOTH WITH YOU?

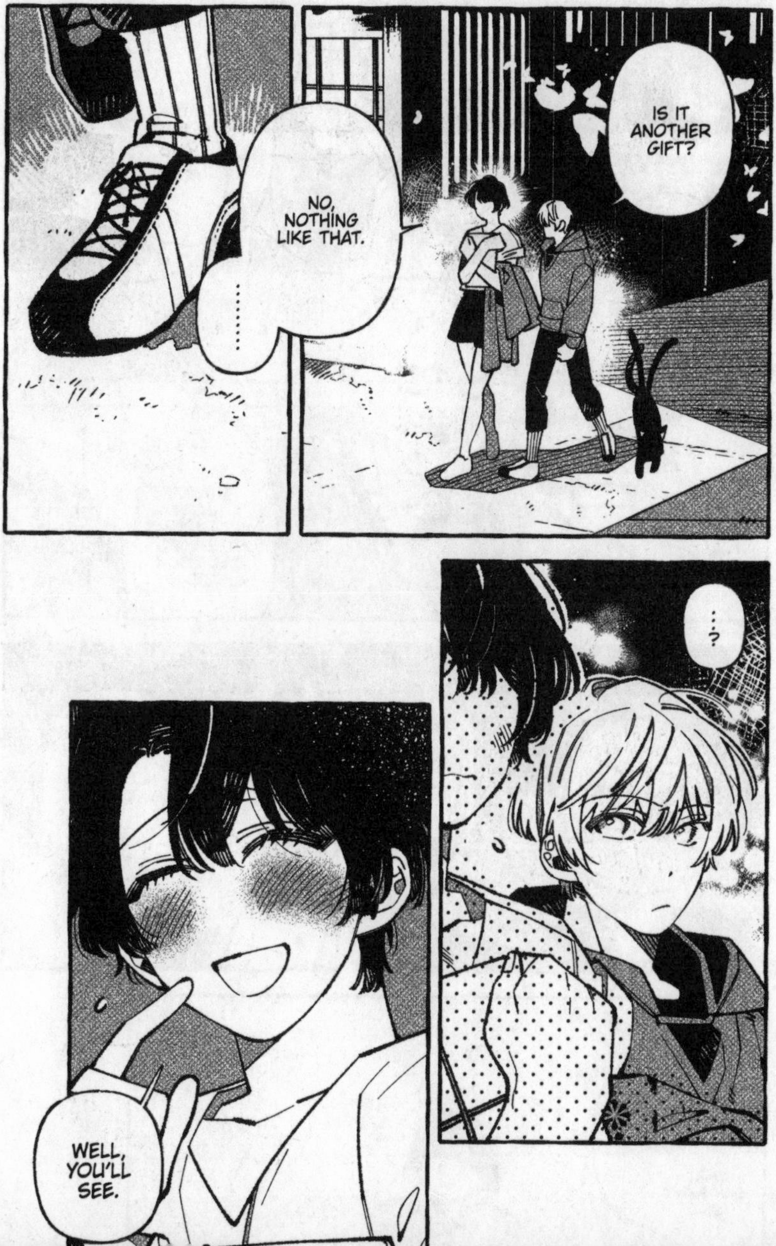
IS IT ANOTHER GIFT?
NO, NOTHING LIKE THAT.
......
...
...?
WELL, YOU'LL SEE.

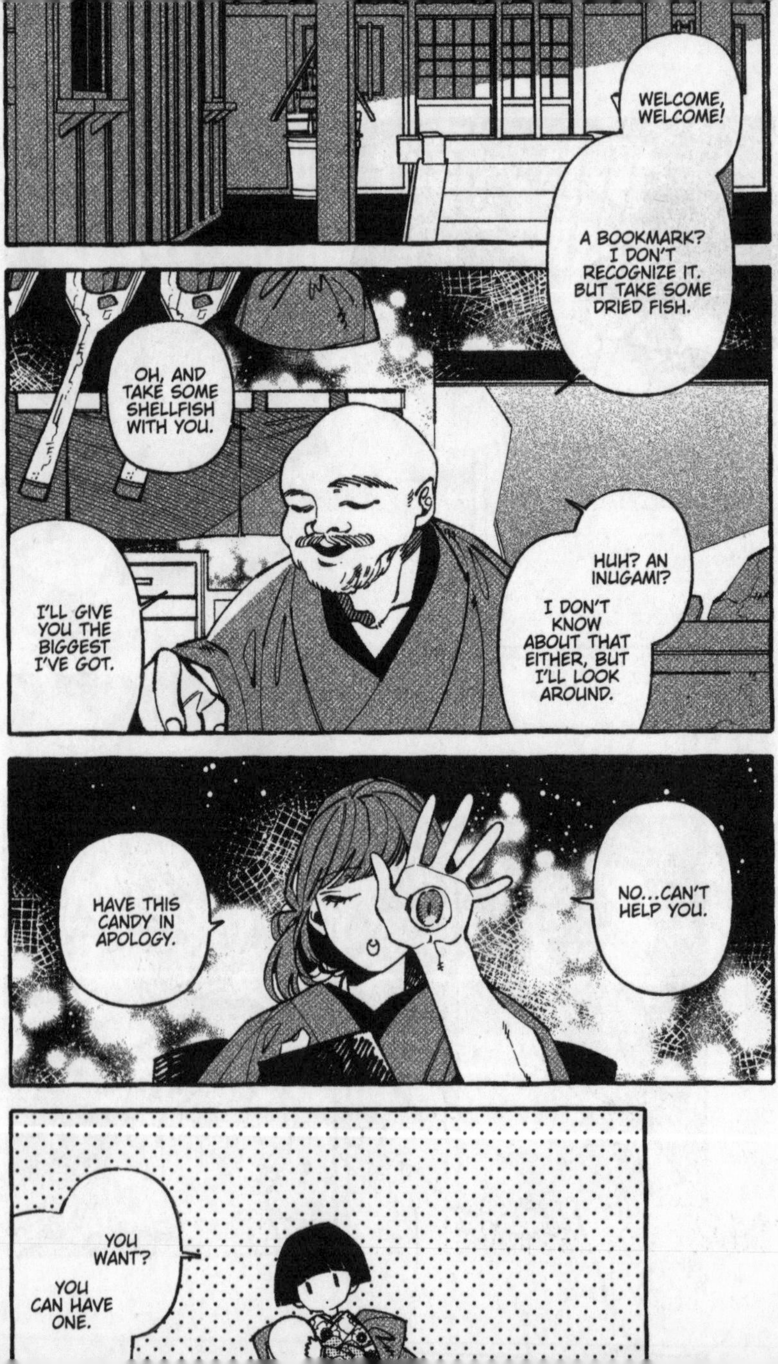
WELCOME, WELCOME!
A BOOKMARK? I DON'T RECOGNIZE IT. BUT TAKE SOME DRIED FISH.
OH, AND TAKE SOME SHELLFISH WITH YOU.
HUH? AN INUGAMI? I DON'T KNOW ABOUT THAT EITHER, BUT I'LL LOOK AROUND.
I'LL GIVE YOU THE BIGGEST I'VE GOT.
NO...CAN'T HELP YOU.
HAVE THIS CANDY IN APOLOGY.
YOU WANT? YOU CAN HAVE ONE.

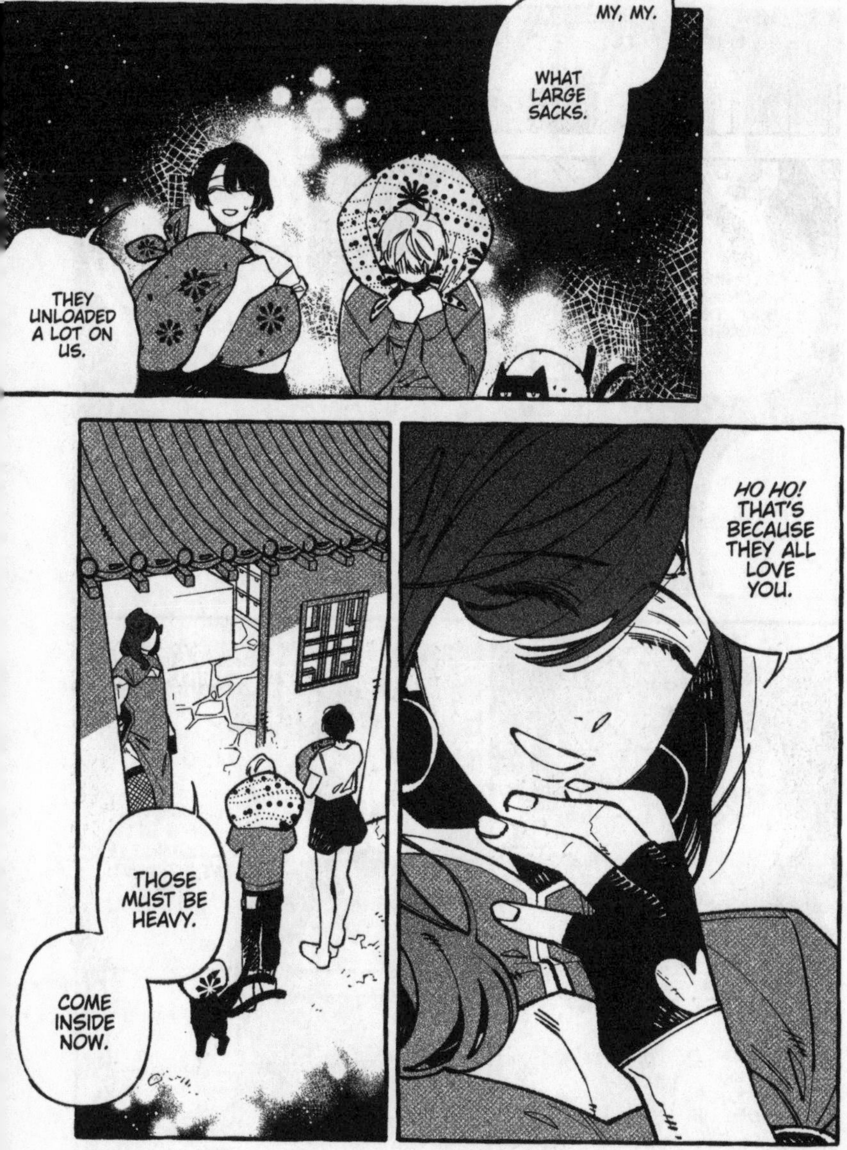
MY, MY.
WHAT LARGE SACKS.
THEY UNLOADED A LOT ON US.
HO HO! THAT'S BECAUSE THEY ALL LOVE YOU.
THOSE MUST BE HEAVY.
COME INSIDE NOW.

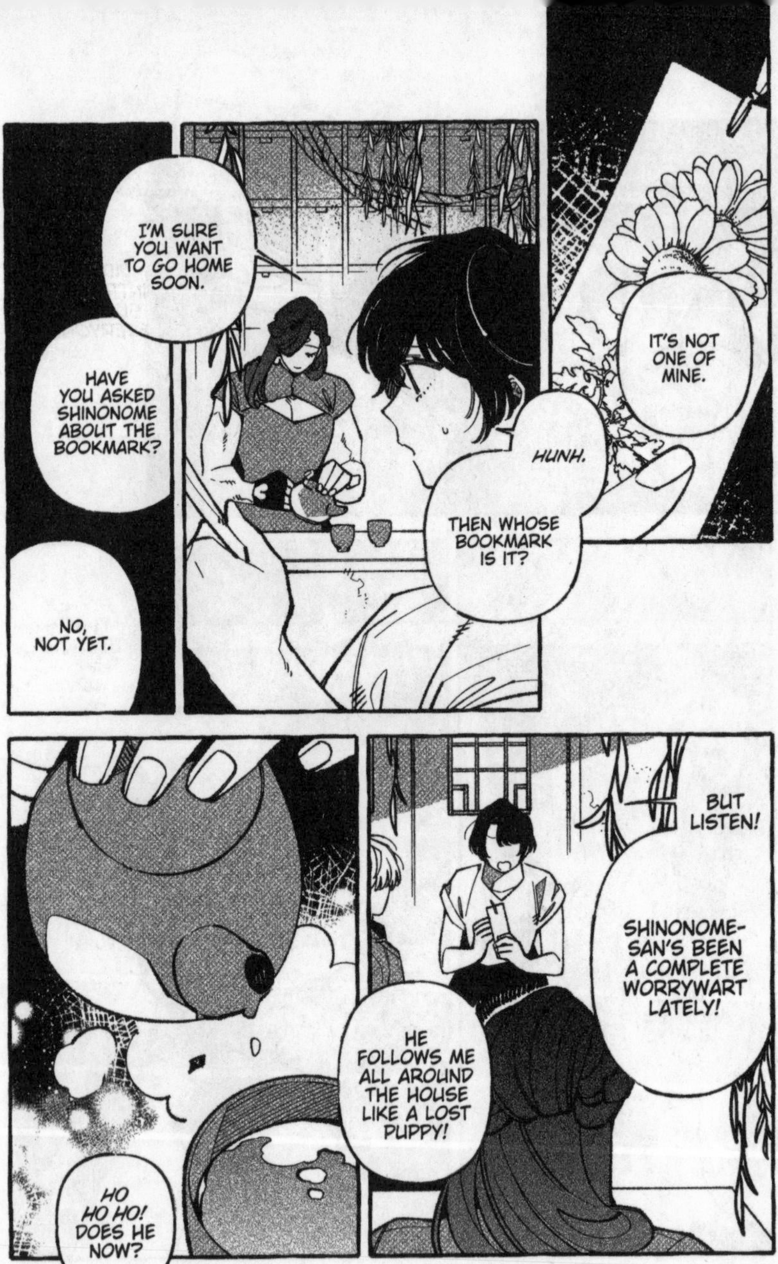
IT'S NOT ONE OF MINE.
HUNH.
THEN WHOSE BOOKMARK IS IT?
I'M SURE YOU WANT TO GO HOME SOON.
HAVE YOU ASKED SHINONOME ABOUT THE BOOKMARK?
NO, NOT YET.
BUT LISTEN!
SHINONOME-SAN'S BEEN A COMPLETE WORRYWART LATELY!
HE FOLLOWS ME ALL AROUND THE HOUSE LIKE A LOST PUPPY!
HO HO HO! DOES HE NOW?

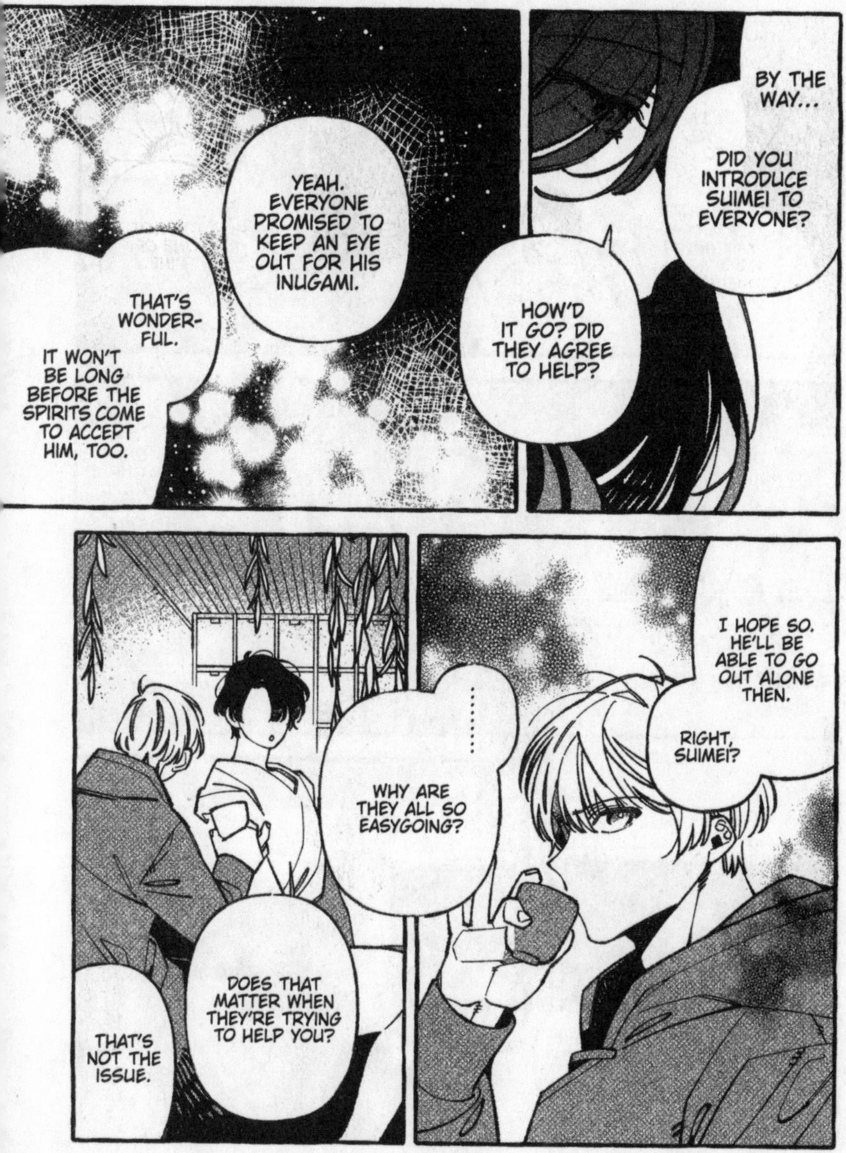
BY THE WAY...
DID YOU INTRODUCE SUIMEI TO EVERYONE?
HOW'D IT GO? DID THEY AGREE TO HELP?
YEAH. EVERYONE PROMISED TO KEEP AN EYE OUT FOR HIS INUGAMI.
THAT'S WONDER-FUL.
IT WON'T BE LONG BEFORE THE SPIRITS COME TO ACCEPT HIM, TOO.
I HOPE SO. HE'LL BE ABLE TO GO OUT ALONE THEN.
RIGHT, SUIMEI?
......
WHY ARE THEY ALL SO EASYGOING?
DOES THAT MATTER WHEN THEY'RE TRYING TO HELP YOU?
THAT'S NOT THE ISSUE.

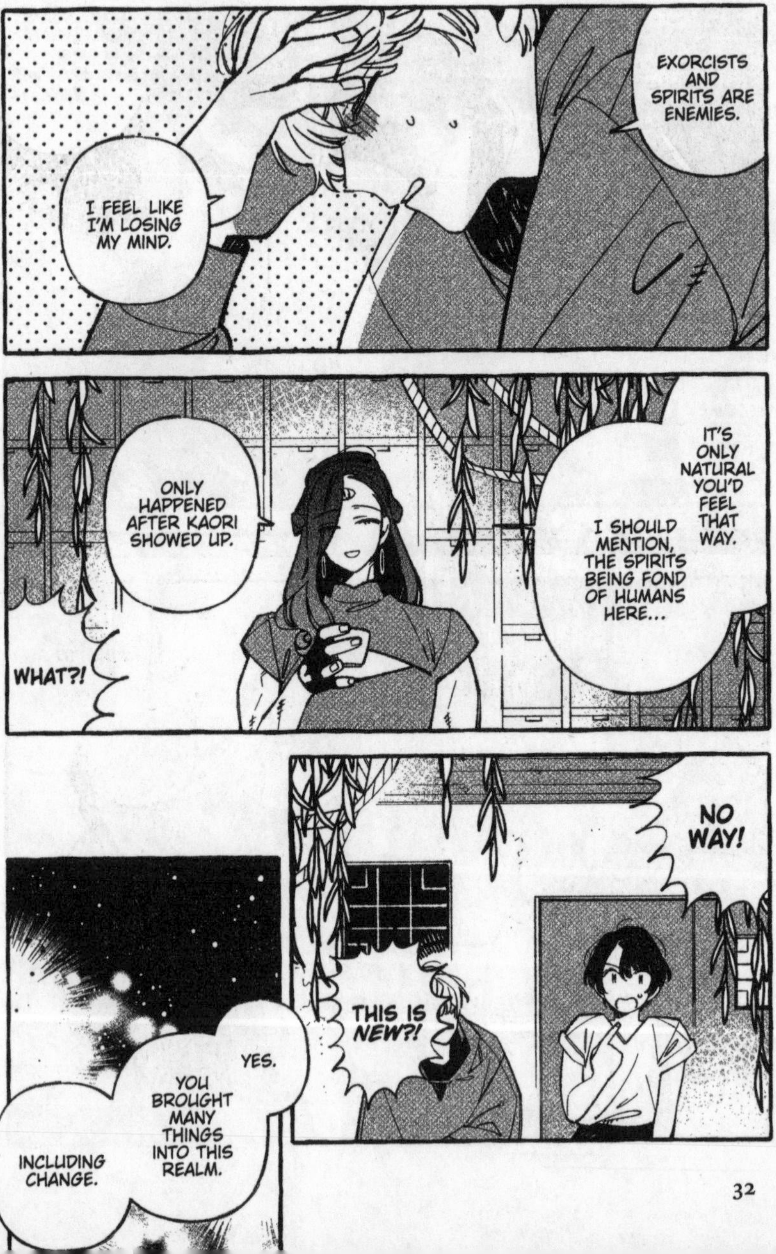
EXORCISTS AND SPIRITS ARE ENEMIES.
I FEEL LIKE I'M LOSING MY MIND.
IT'S ONLY NATURAL YOU'D FEEL THAT WAY.
I SHOULD MENTION, THE SPIRITS BEING FOND OF HUMANS HERE...
ONLY HAPPENED AFTER KAORI SHOWED UP.
WHAT?!
NO WAY!
THIS IS *NEW?!*
YES.
YOU BROUGHT MANY THINGS INTO THIS REALM.
INCLUDING CHANGE.

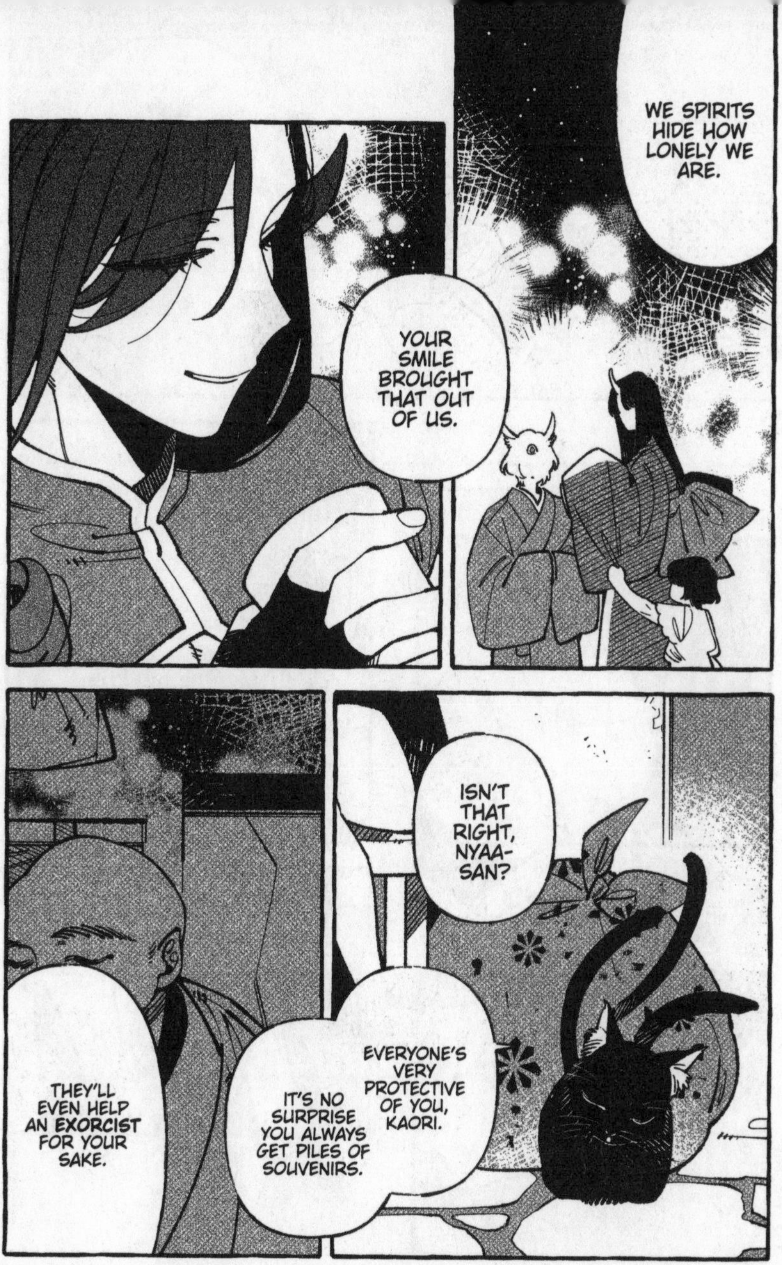
WE SPIRITS HIDE HOW LONELY WE ARE.
YOUR SMILE BROUGHT THAT OUT OF US.
ISN'T THAT RIGHT, NYAA-SAN?
EVERYONE'S VERY PROTECTIVE OF YOU, KAORI.
IT'S NO SURPRISE YOU ALWAYS GET PILES OF SOUVENIRS.
THEY'LL EVEN HELP AN **EXORCIST** FOR YOUR SAKE.

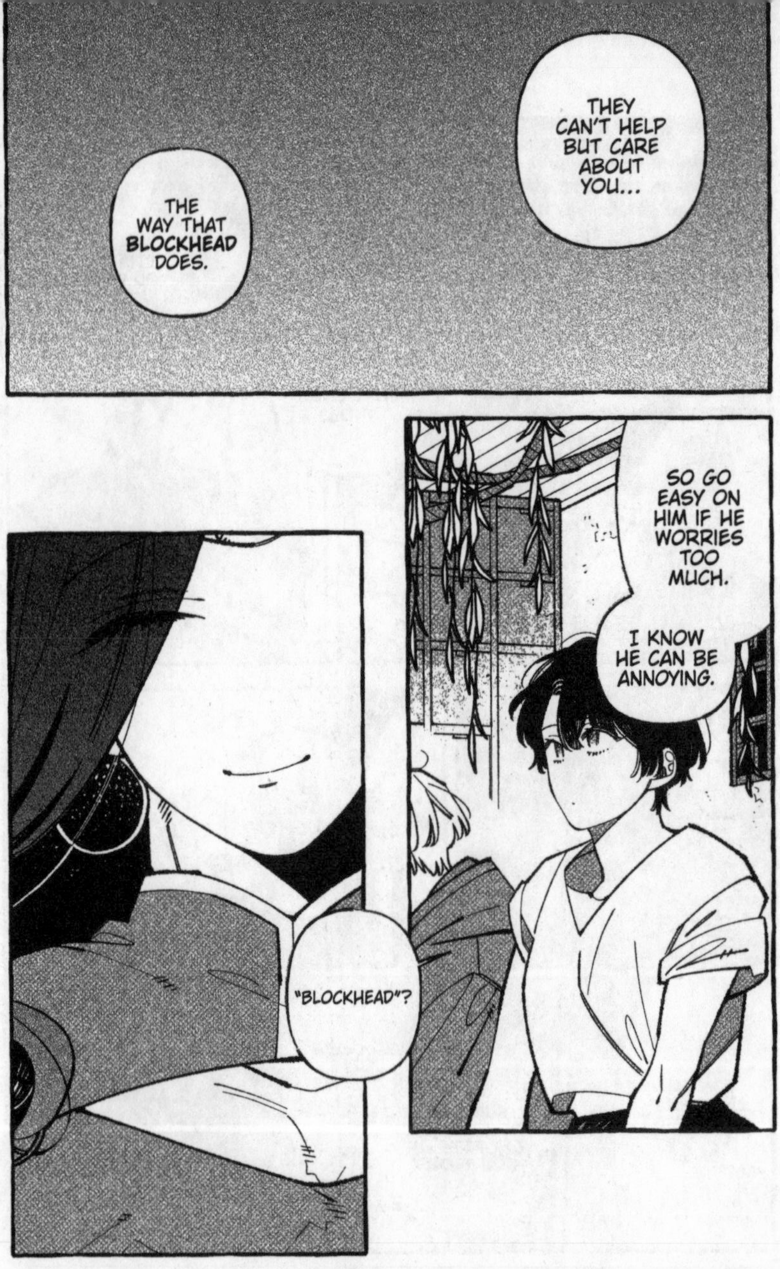
THEY CAN'T HELP BUT CARE ABOUT YOU...
THE WAY THAT BLOCKHEAD DOES.
SO GO EASY ON HIM IF HE WORRIES TOO MUCH.
I KNOW HE CAN BE ANNOYING.
"BLOCKHEAD"?

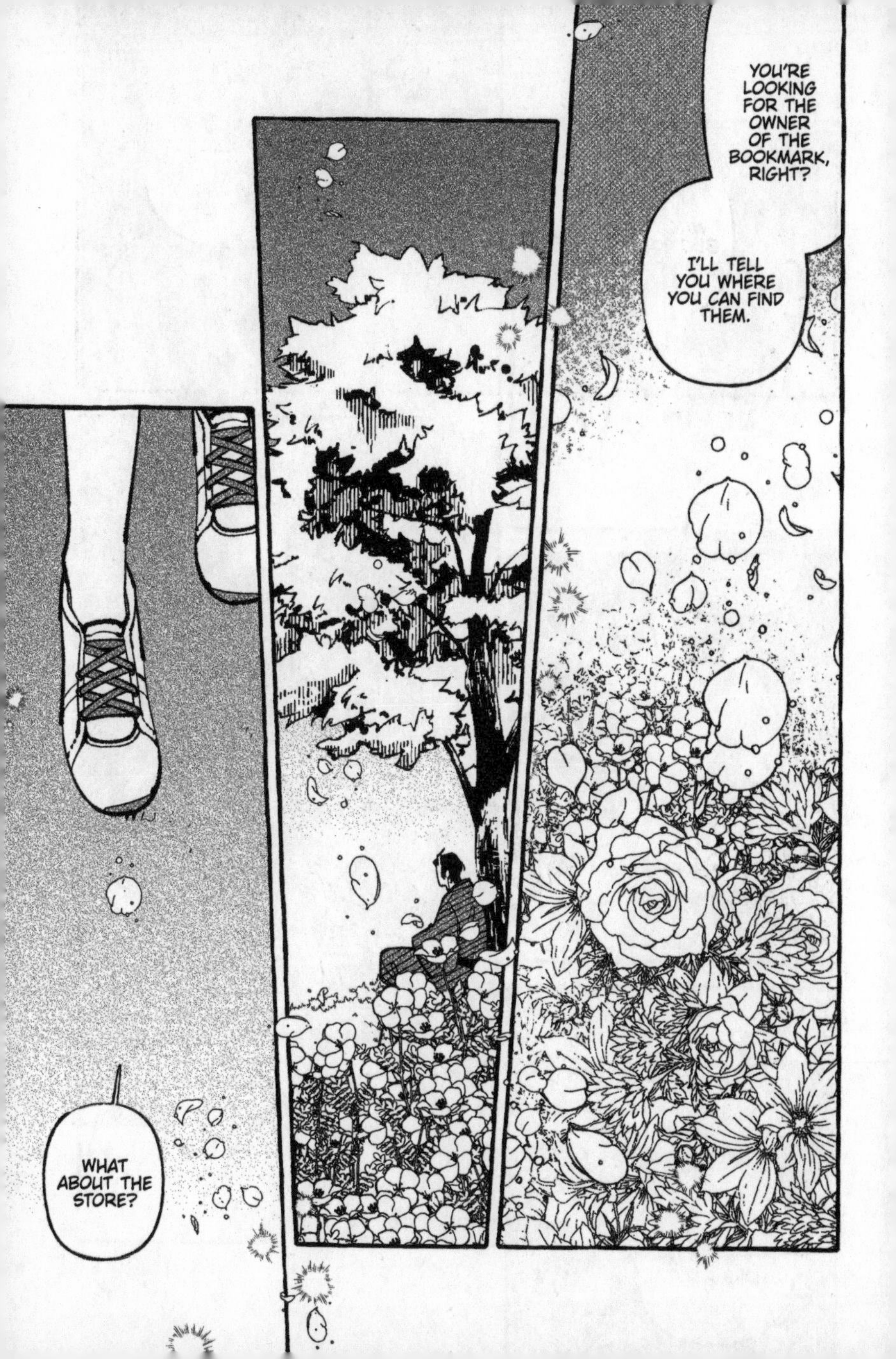
YOU'RE LOOKING FOR THE OWNER OF THE BOOKMARK, RIGHT?
I'LL TELL YOU WHERE YOU CAN FIND THEM.
WHAT ABOUT THE STORE?

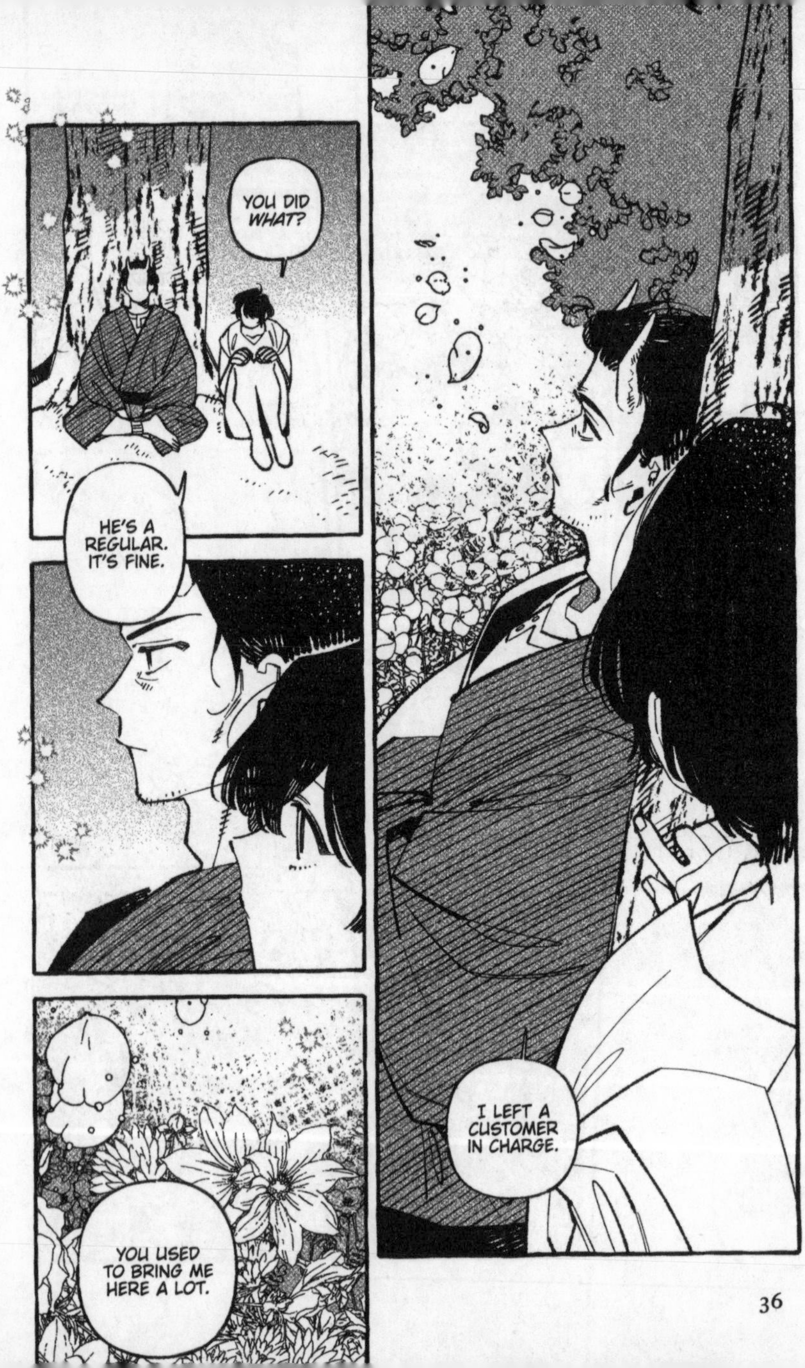
I LEFT A CUSTOMER IN CHARGE.
YOU DID WHAT?
HE'S A REGULAR. IT'S FINE.
YOU USED TO BRING ME HERE A LOT.

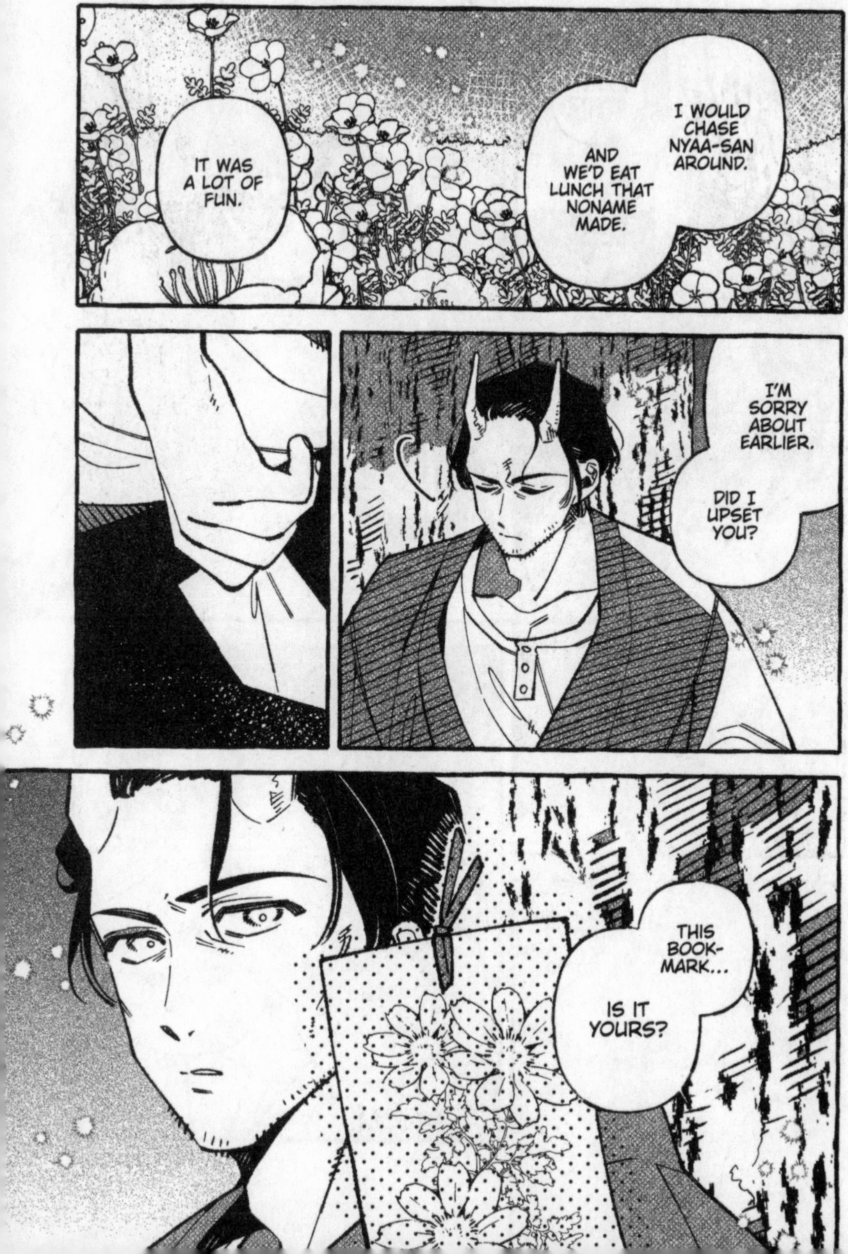
I WOULD CHASE NYAA-SAN AROUND.
AND WE'D EAT LUNCH THAT NONAME MADE.
IT WAS A LOT OF FUN.
I'M SORRY ABOUT EARLIER.
DID I UPSET YOU?
THIS BOOK-MARK...
IS IT YOURS?

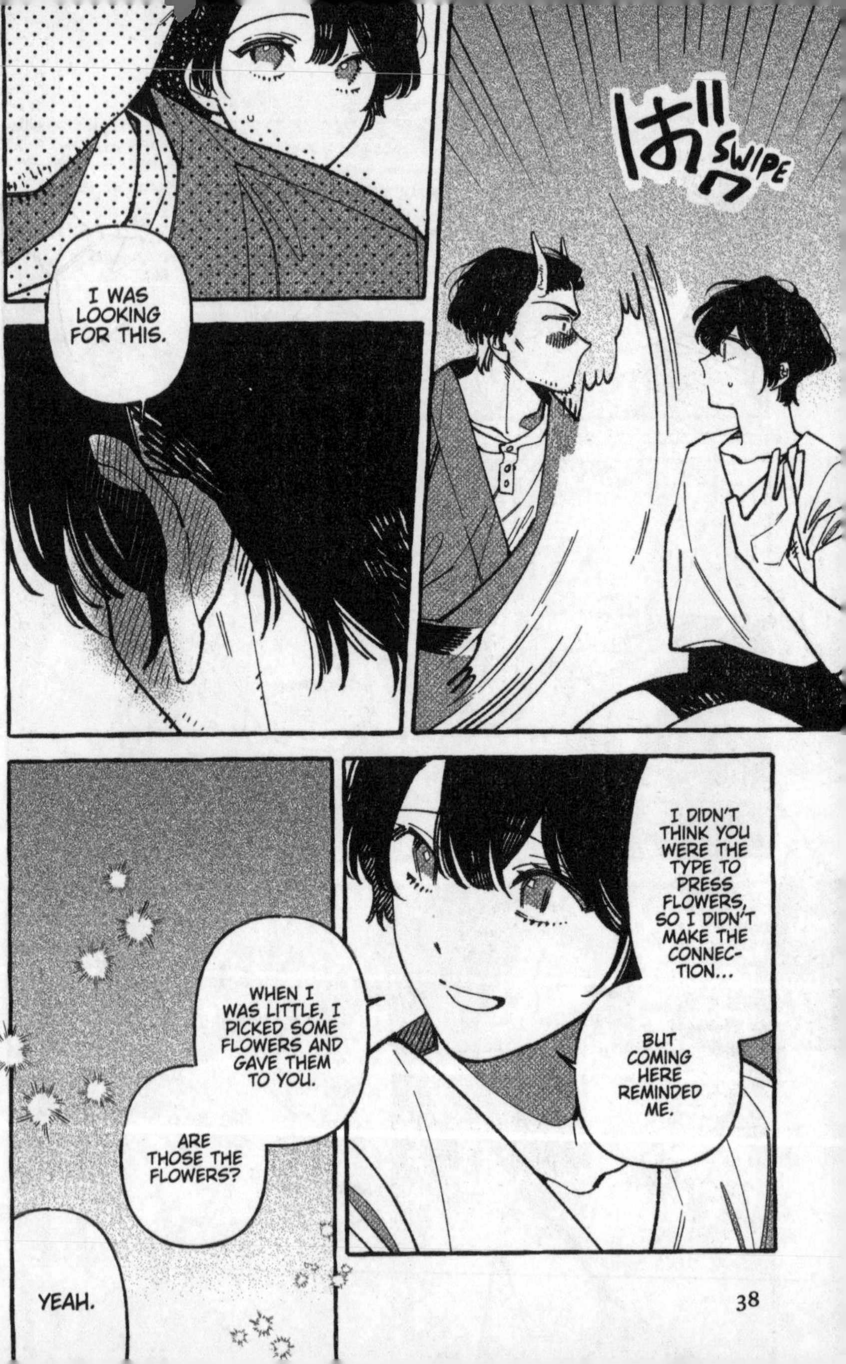
SWIPE
I WAS LOOKING FOR THIS.
I DIDN'T THINK YOU WERE THE TYPE TO PRESS FLOWERS, SO I DIDN'T MAKE THE CONNEC-TION...
BUT COMING HERE REMINDED ME.
WHEN I WAS LITTLE, I PICKED SOME FLOWERS AND GAVE THEM TO YOU.
ARE THOSE THE FLOWERS?
YEAH.

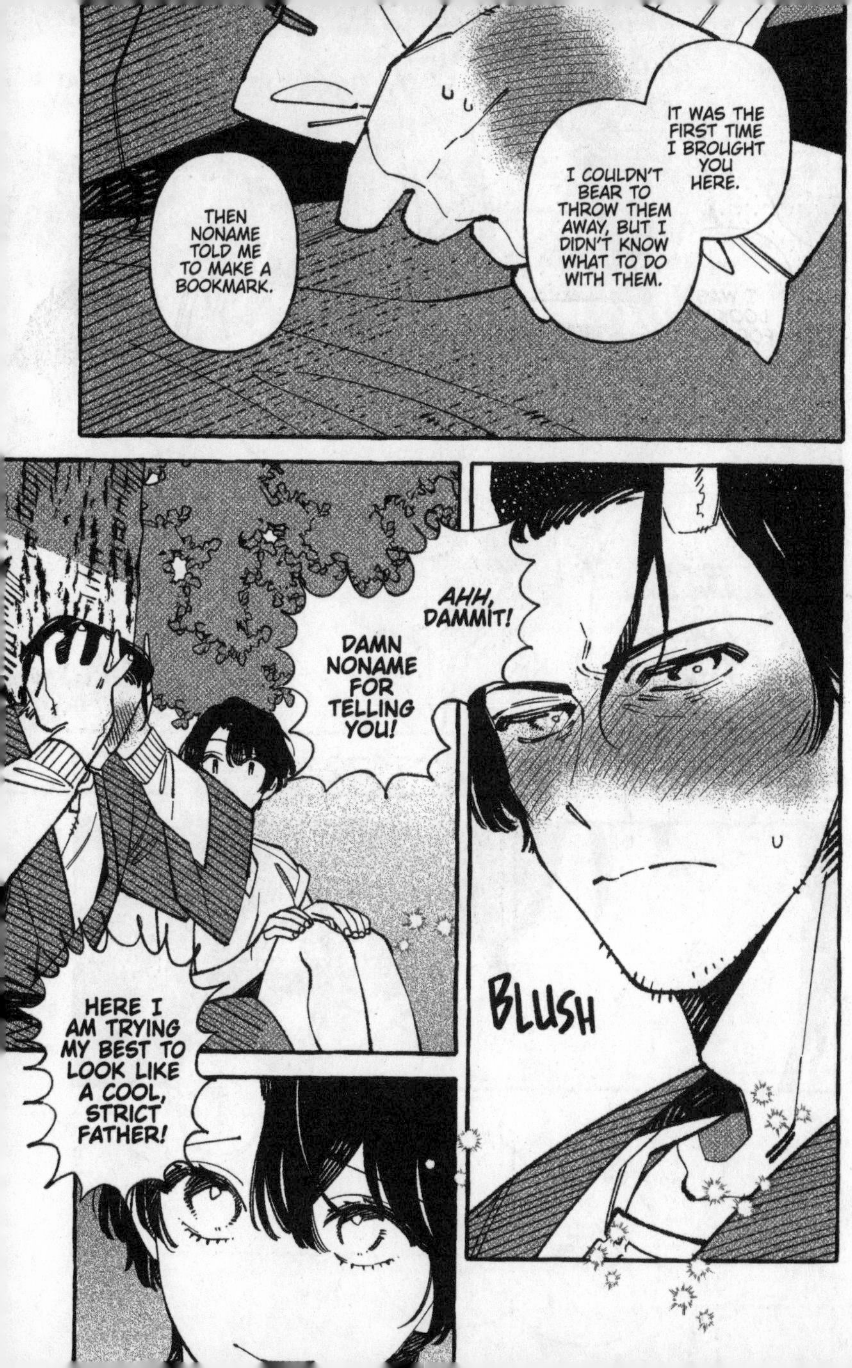
IT WAS THE FIRST TIME I BROUGHT YOU HERE.
I COULDN'T BEAR TO THROW THEM AWAY, BUT I DIDN'T KNOW WHAT TO DO WITH THEM.
THEN NONAME TOLD ME TO MAKE A BOOKMARK.
AHH, DAMMIT!
BLUSH
DAMN NONAME FOR TELLING YOU!
HERE I AM TRYING MY BEST TO LOOK LIKE A COOL, STRICT FATHER!

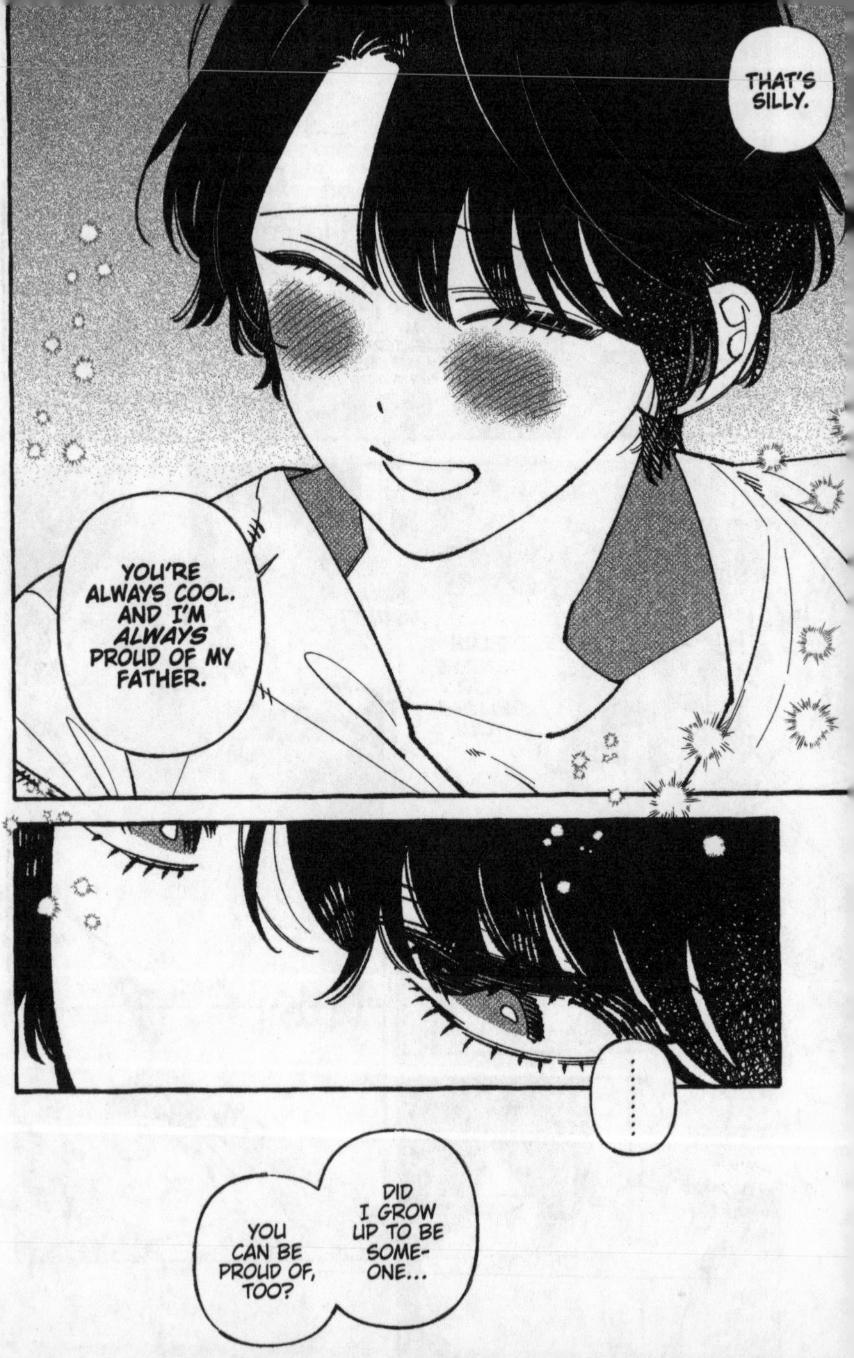
THAT'S SILLY.
YOU'RE ALWAYS COOL. AND I'M *ALWAYS* PROUD OF MY FATHER.
......
DID I GROW UP TO BE SOME-ONE... YOU CAN BE PROUD OF, TOO?

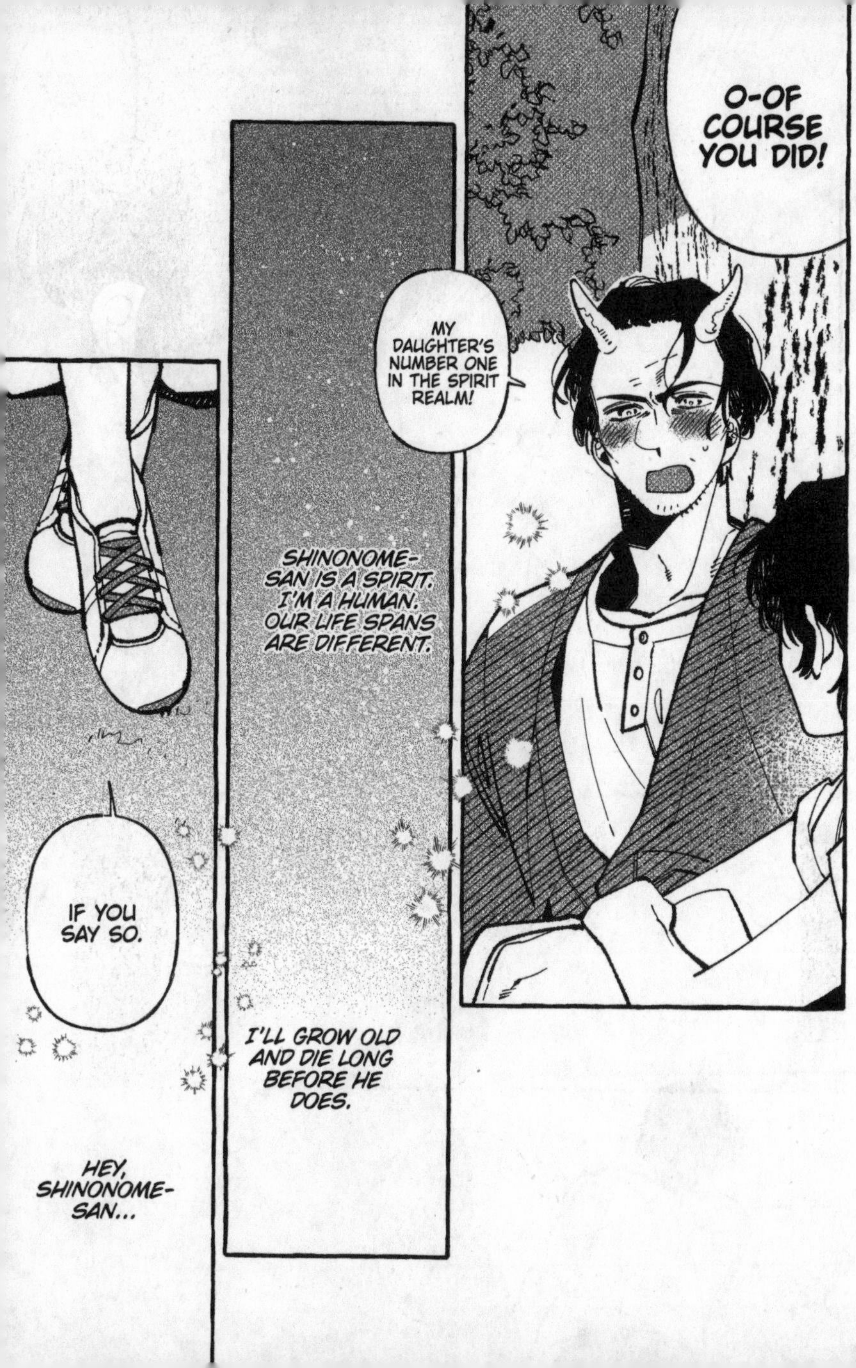

O-OF COURSE YOU DID!
MY DAUGHTER'S NUMBER ONE IN THE SPIRIT REALM!
SHINONOME-SAN IS A SPIRIT. I'M A HUMAN. OUR LIFE SPANS ARE DIFFERENT.
I'LL GROW OLD AND DIE LONG BEFORE HE DOES.
IF YOU SAY SO.
HEY, SHINONOME-SAN...

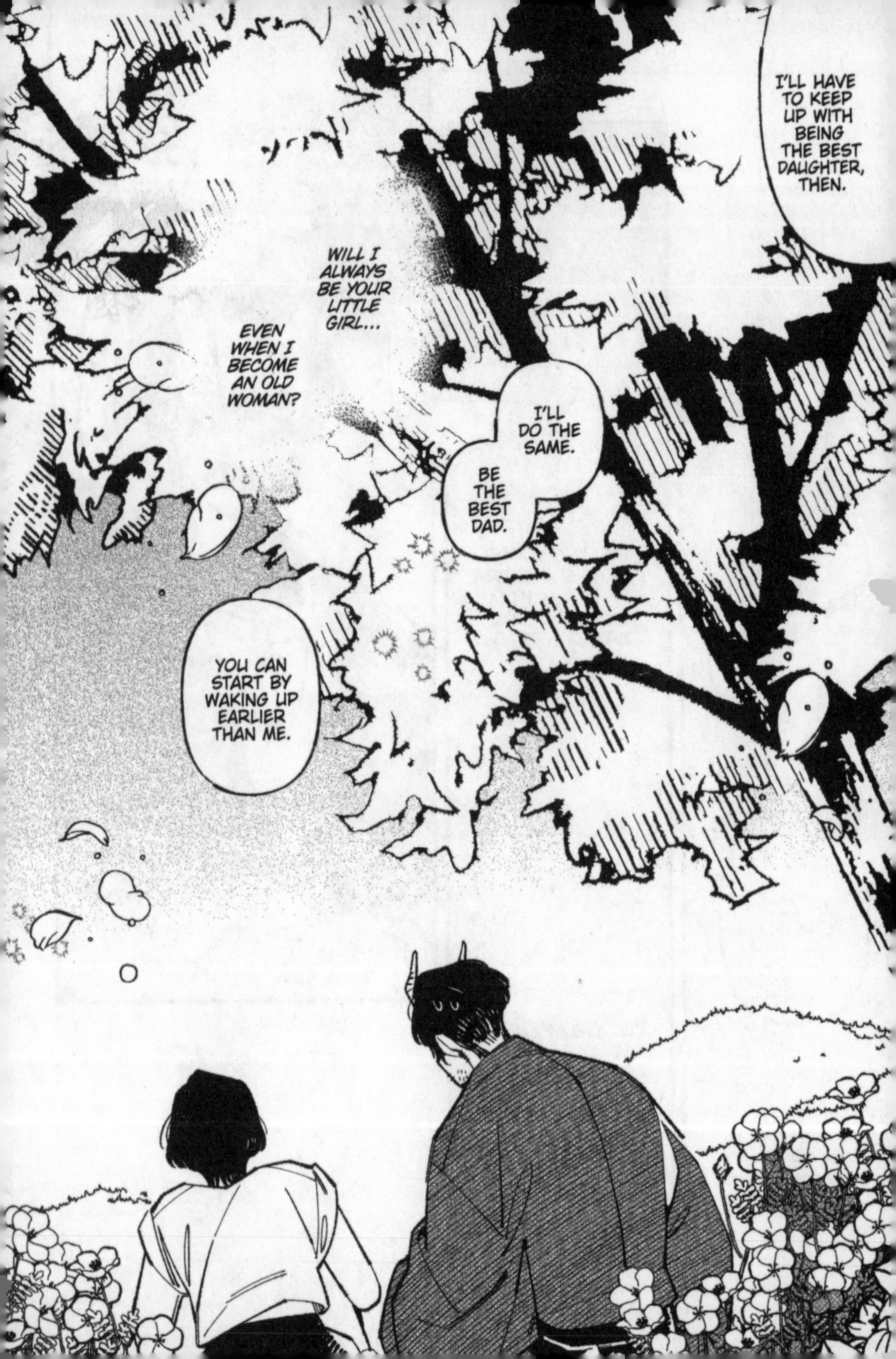
I'LL HAVE TO KEEP UP WITH BEING THE BEST DAUGHTER, THEN.
WILL I ALWAYS BE YOUR LITTLE GIRL...
EVEN WHEN I BECOME AN OLD WOMAN?
I'LL DO THE SAME.
BE THE BEST DAD.
YOU CAN START BY WAKING UP EARLIER THAN ME.

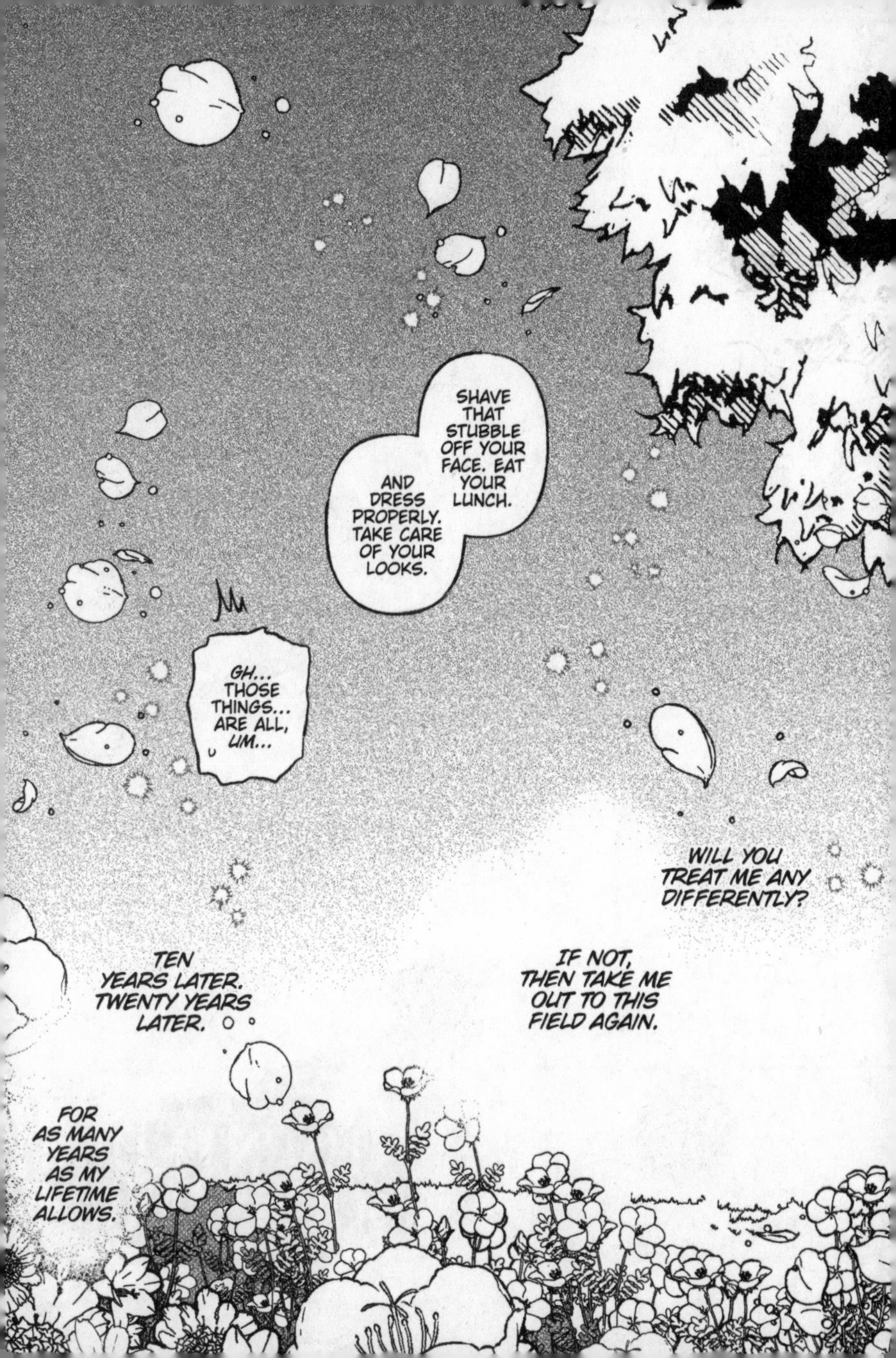

SHAVE THAT STUBBLE OFF YOUR FACE. EAT YOUR LUNCH.
AND DRESS PROPERLY. TAKE CARE OF YOUR LOOKS.
GH... THOSE THINGS... ARE ALL, UM...
WILL YOU TREAT ME ANY DIFFERENTLY?
IF NOT, THEN TAKE ME OUT TO THIS FIELD AGAIN.
TEN YEARS LATER. TWENTY YEARS LATER.
FOR AS MANY YEARS AS MY LIFETIME ALLOWS.

THE HAUNTED BOOKSTORE
Gateway to a Parallel Universe

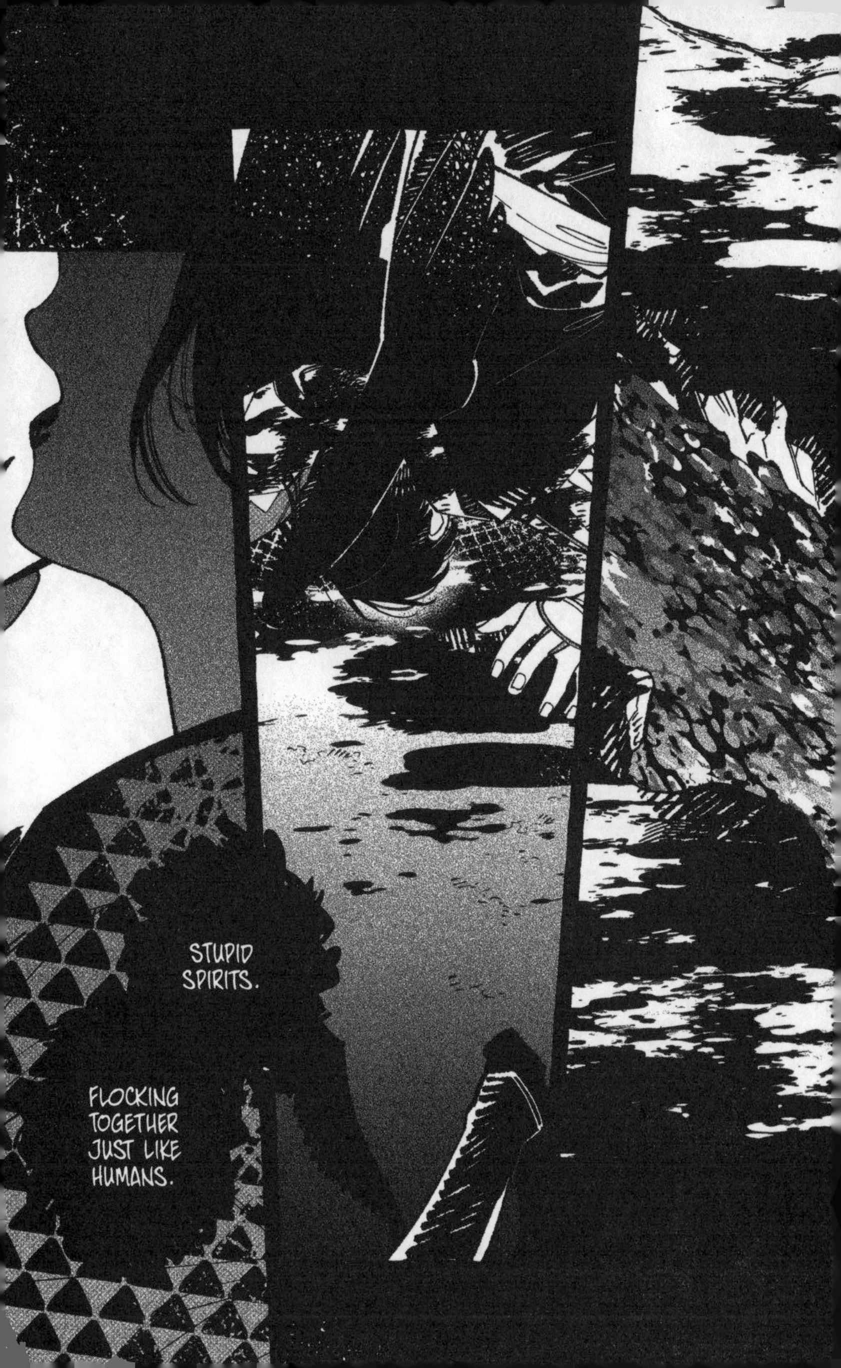
STUPID SPIRITS.
FLOCKING TOGETHER JUST LIKE HUMANS.

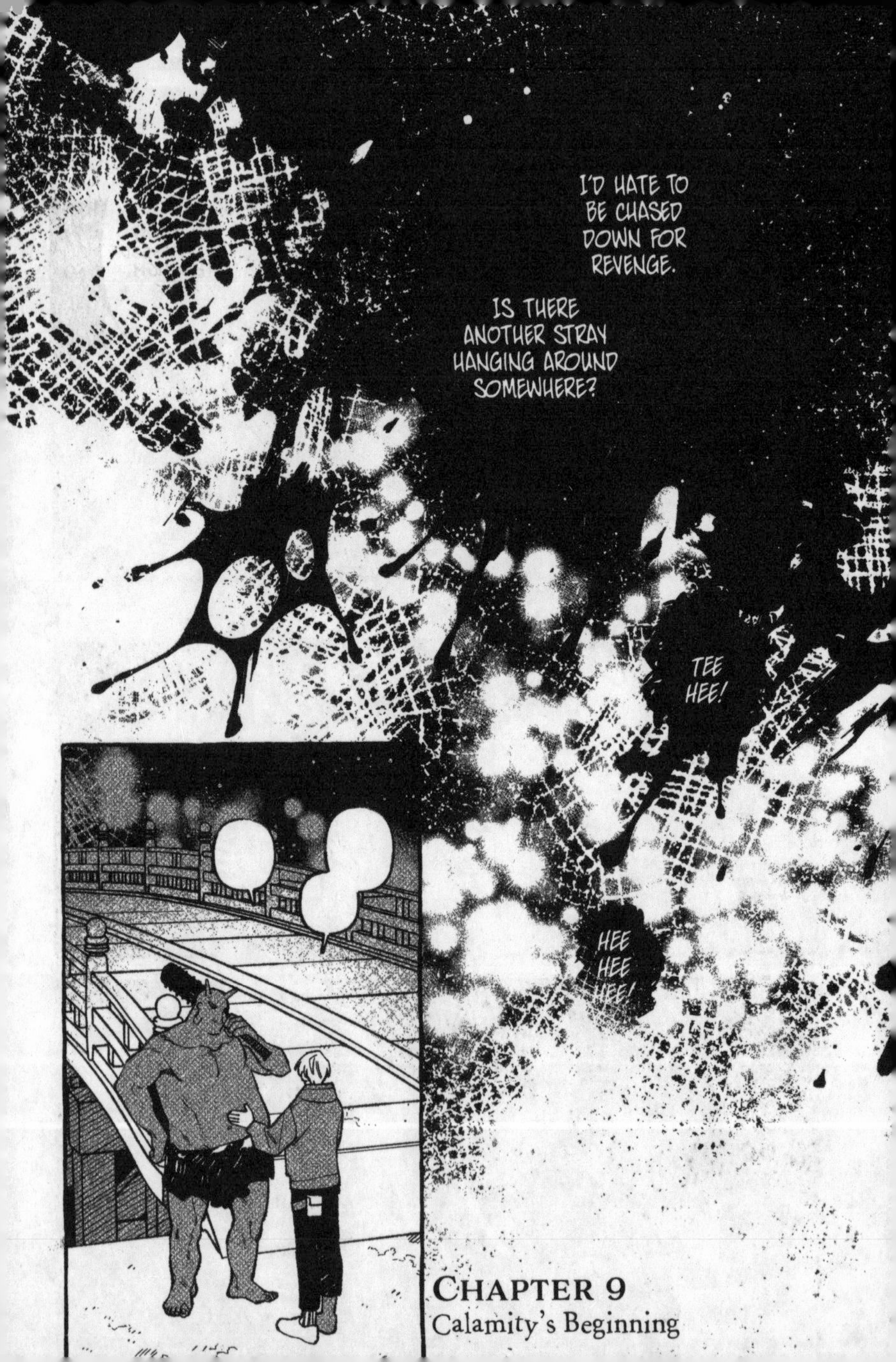
I'D HATE TO BE CHASED DOWN FOR REVENGE.
IS THERE ANOTHER STRAY HANGING AROUND SOMEWHERE?
TEE HEE!
HEE HEE HEE!

CHAPTER 9
Calamity's Beginning

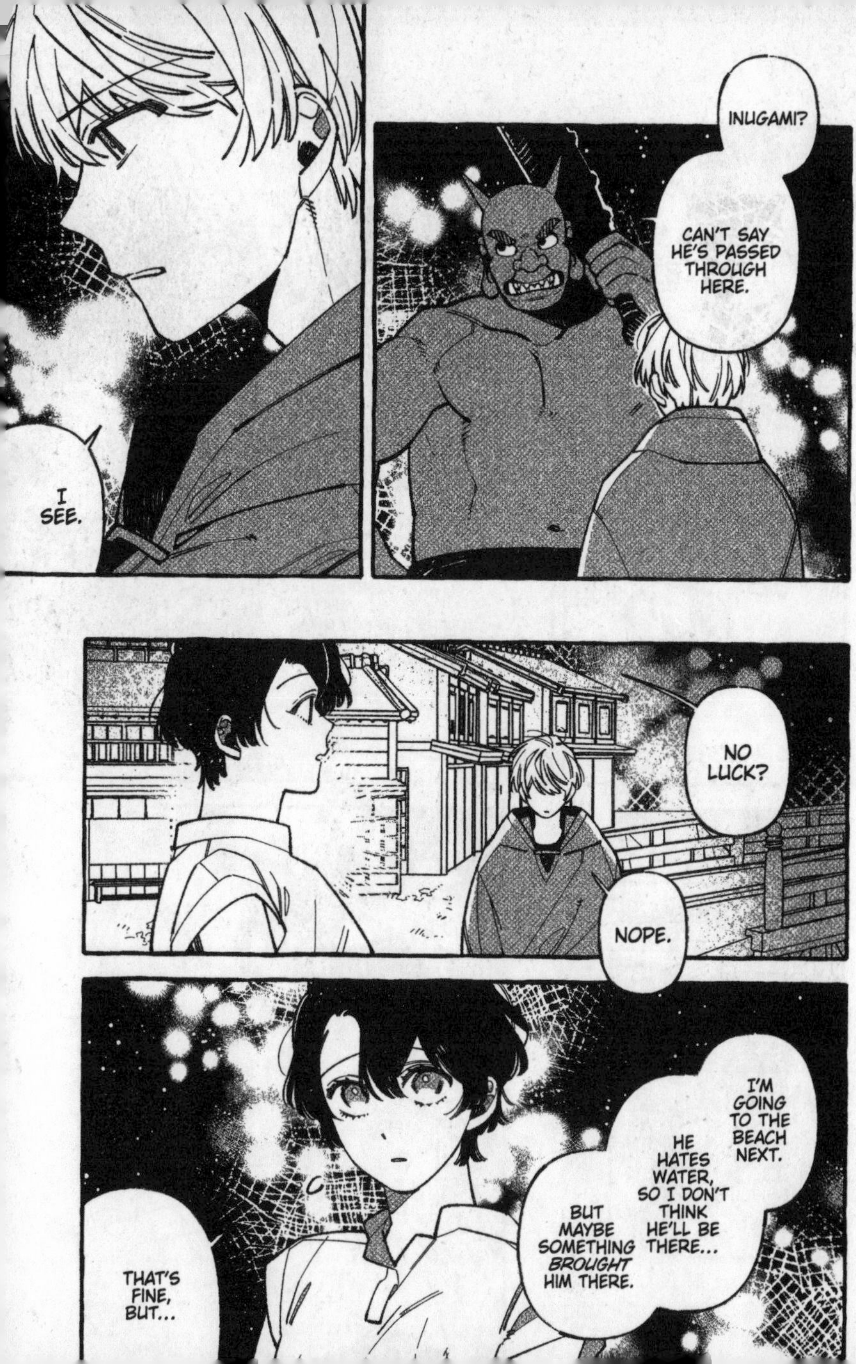
INUGAMI?
CAN'T SAY HE'S PASSED THROUGH HERE.
I SEE.
NO LUCK?
NOPE.
I'M GOING TO THE BEACH NEXT.
HE HATES WATER, SO I DON'T THINK HE'LL BE THERE...
BUT MAYBE SOMETHING *BROUGHT* HIM THERE.
THAT'S FINE, BUT...

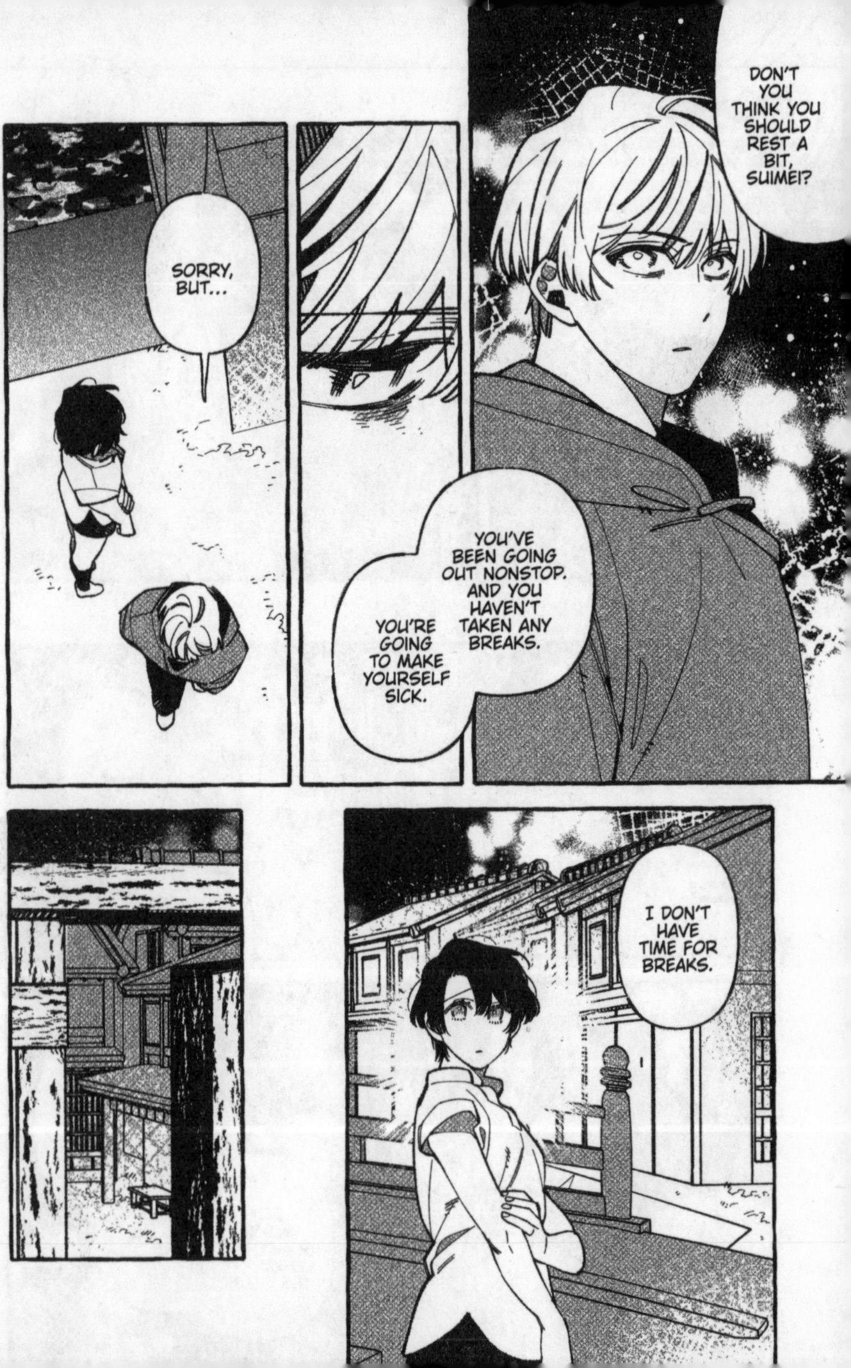
DON'T YOU THINK YOU SHOULD REST A BIT, SUIMEI?
YOU'VE BEEN GOING OUT NONSTOP. AND YOU HAVEN'T TAKEN ANY BREAKS.
YOU'RE GOING TO MAKE YOURSELF SICK.
SORRY, BUT...
I DON'T HAVE TIME FOR BREAKS.

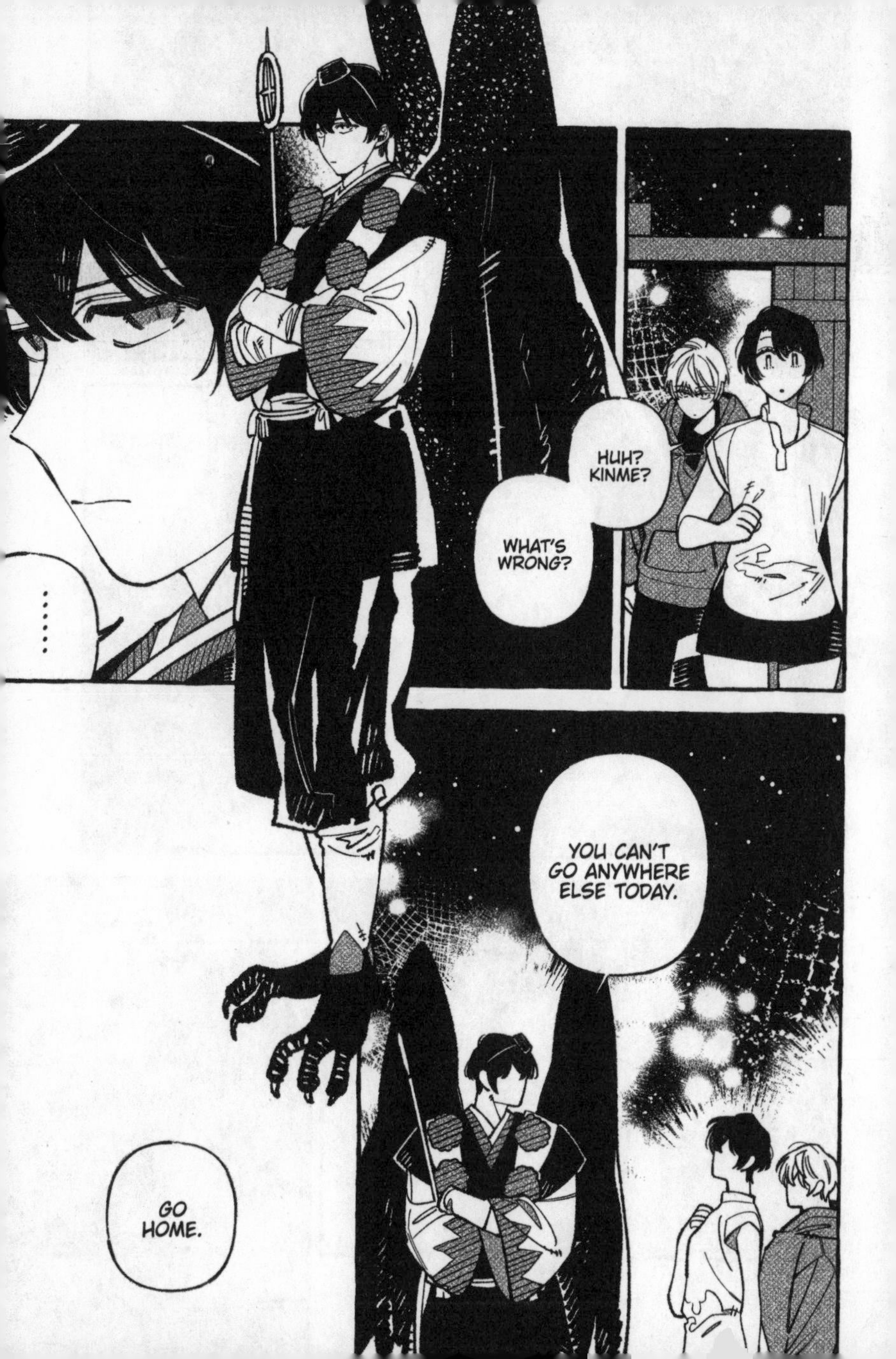
HUH? KINME?
WHAT'S WRONG?
......
YOU CAN'T GO ANYWHERE ELSE TODAY.
GO HOME.

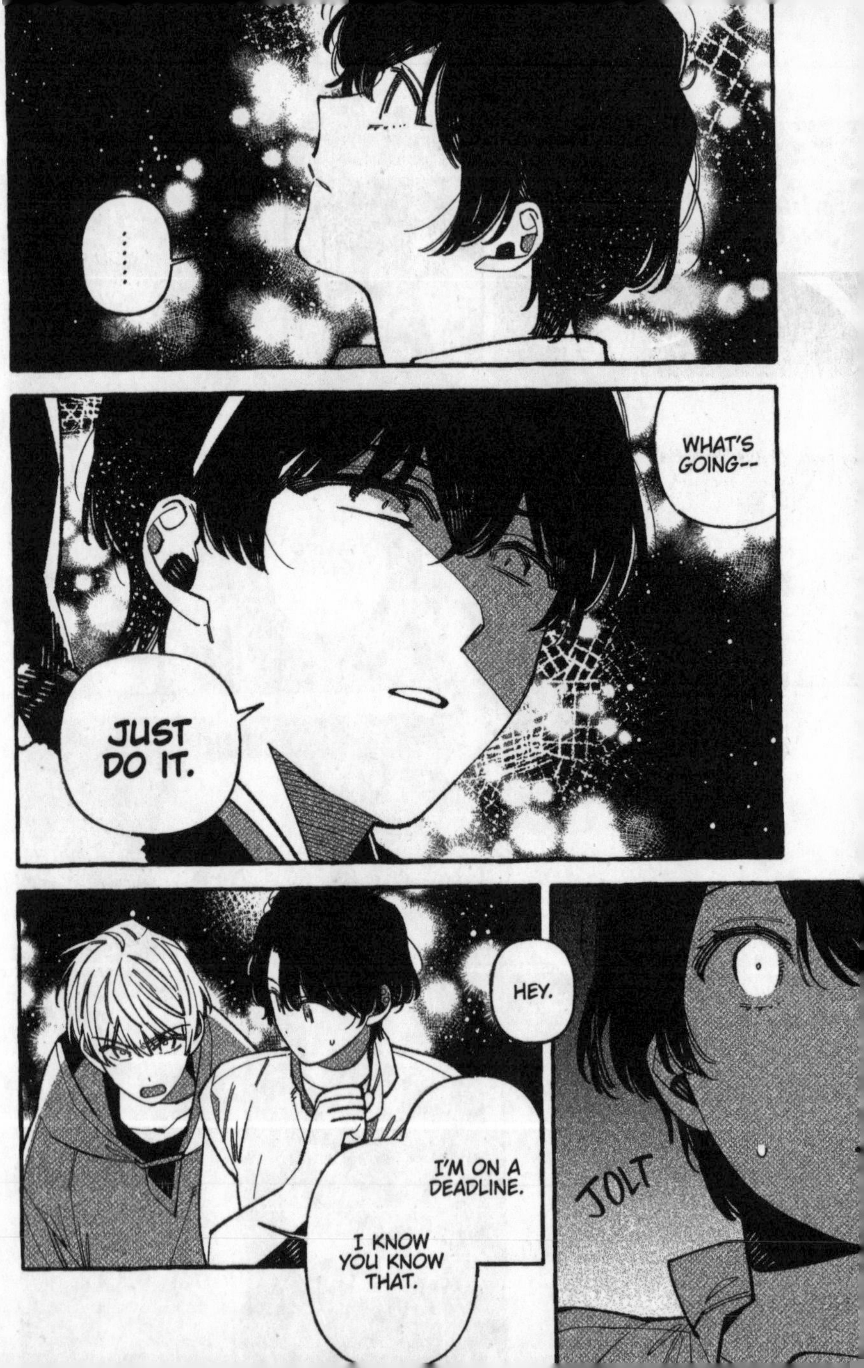
……
WHAT'S GOING--
JUST DO IT.
JOLT
HEY.
I'M ON A DEADLINE.
I KNOW YOU KNOW THAT.

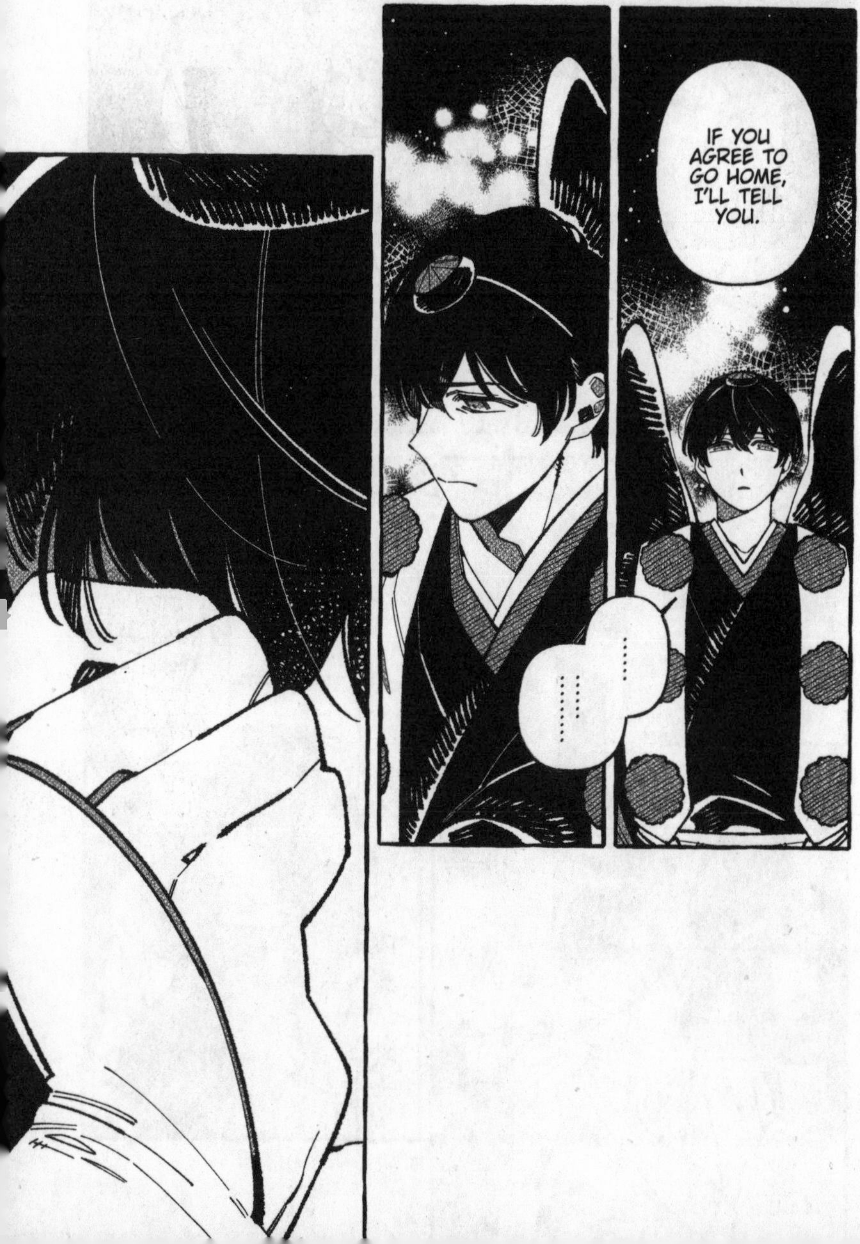
IF YOU AGREE TO GO HOME, I'LL TELL YOU.
......

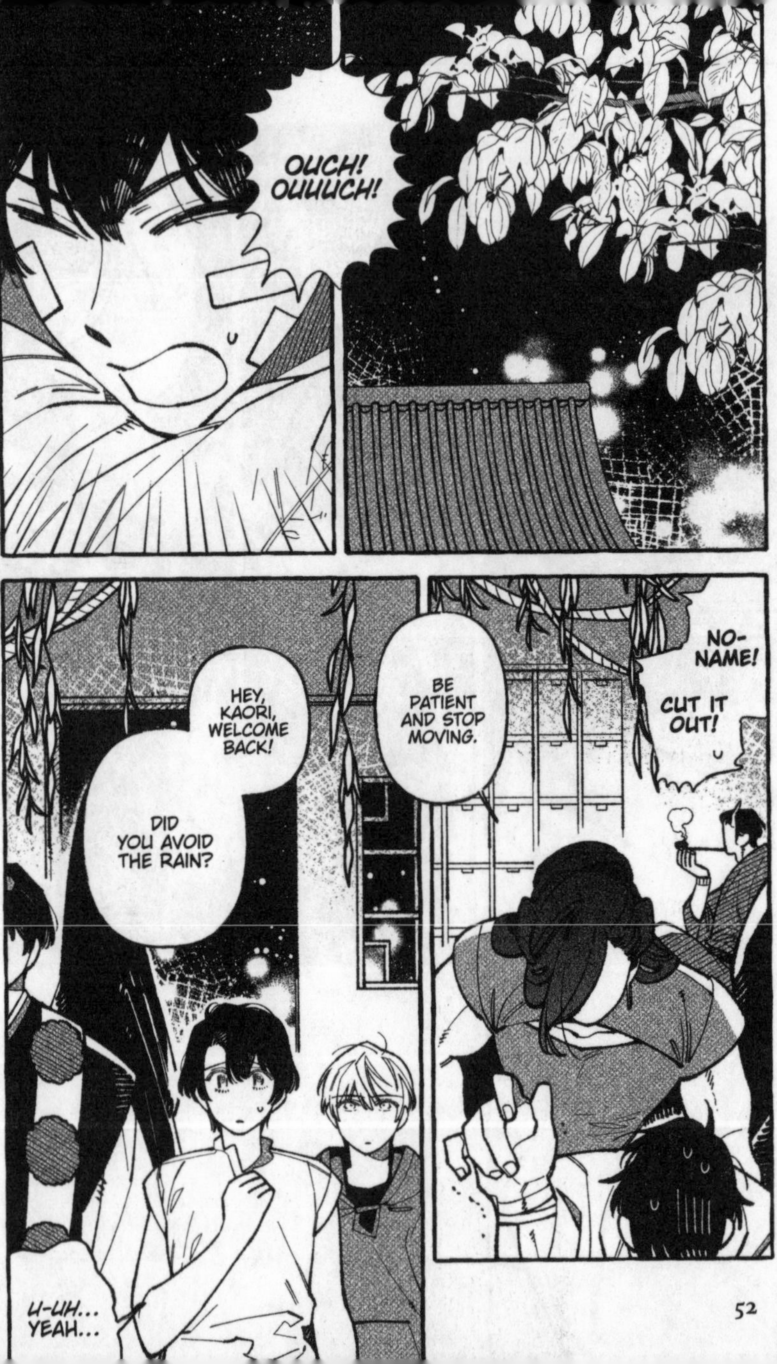
OUCH! OUUUCH!
NO-NAME! CUT IT OUT!
BE PATIENT AND STOP MOVING.
HEY, KAORI, WELCOME BACK!
DID YOU AVOID THE RAIN?
U-UH... YEAH...

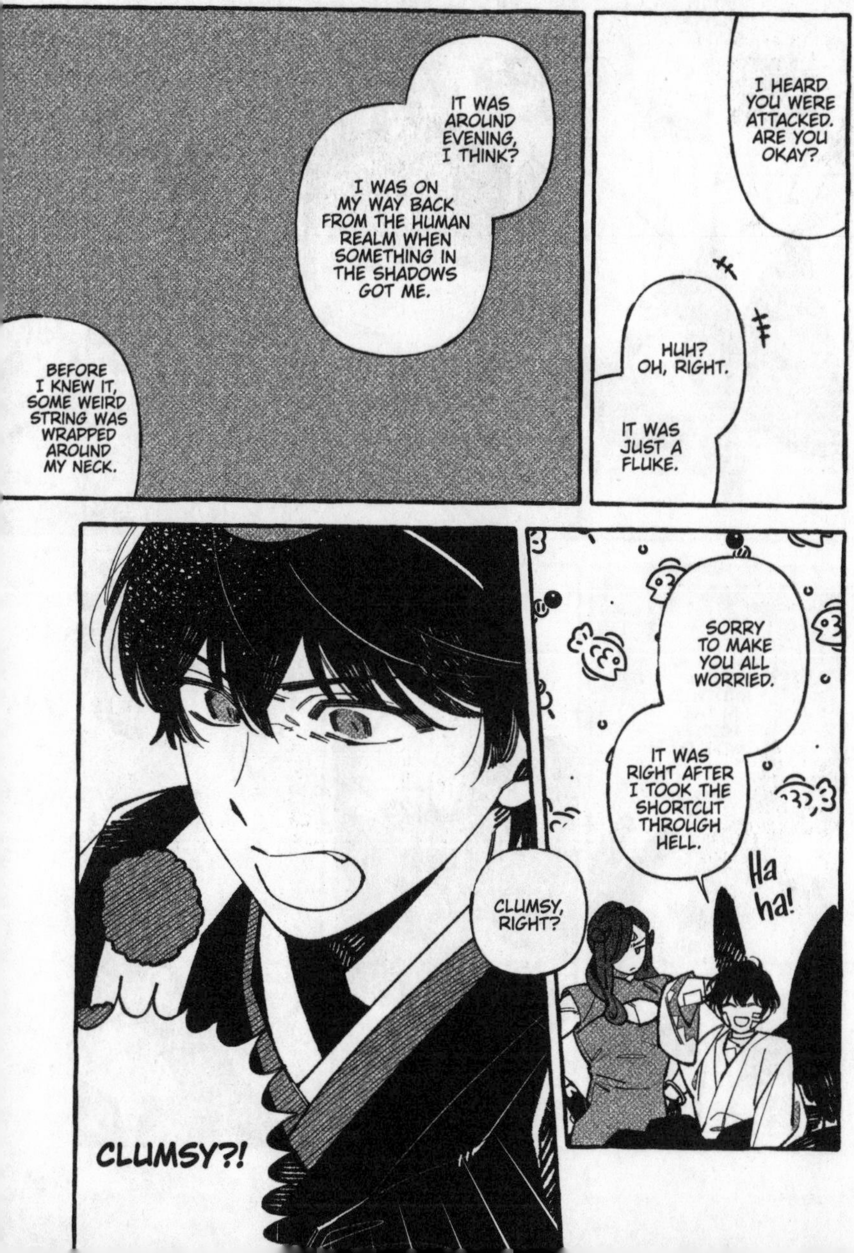
I HEARD YOU WERE ATTACKED. ARE YOU OKAY?
HUH? OH, RIGHT.
IT WAS JUST A FLUKE.
IT WAS AROUND EVENING, I THINK?
I WAS ON MY WAY BACK FROM THE HUMAN REALM WHEN SOMETHING IN THE SHADOWS GOT ME.
BEFORE I KNEW IT, SOME WEIRD STRING WAS WRAPPED AROUND MY NECK.
SORRY TO MAKE YOU ALL WORRIED.
IT WAS RIGHT AFTER I TOOK THE SHORTCUT THROUGH HELL.
Ha ha!
CLUMSY, RIGHT?
CLUMSY?!

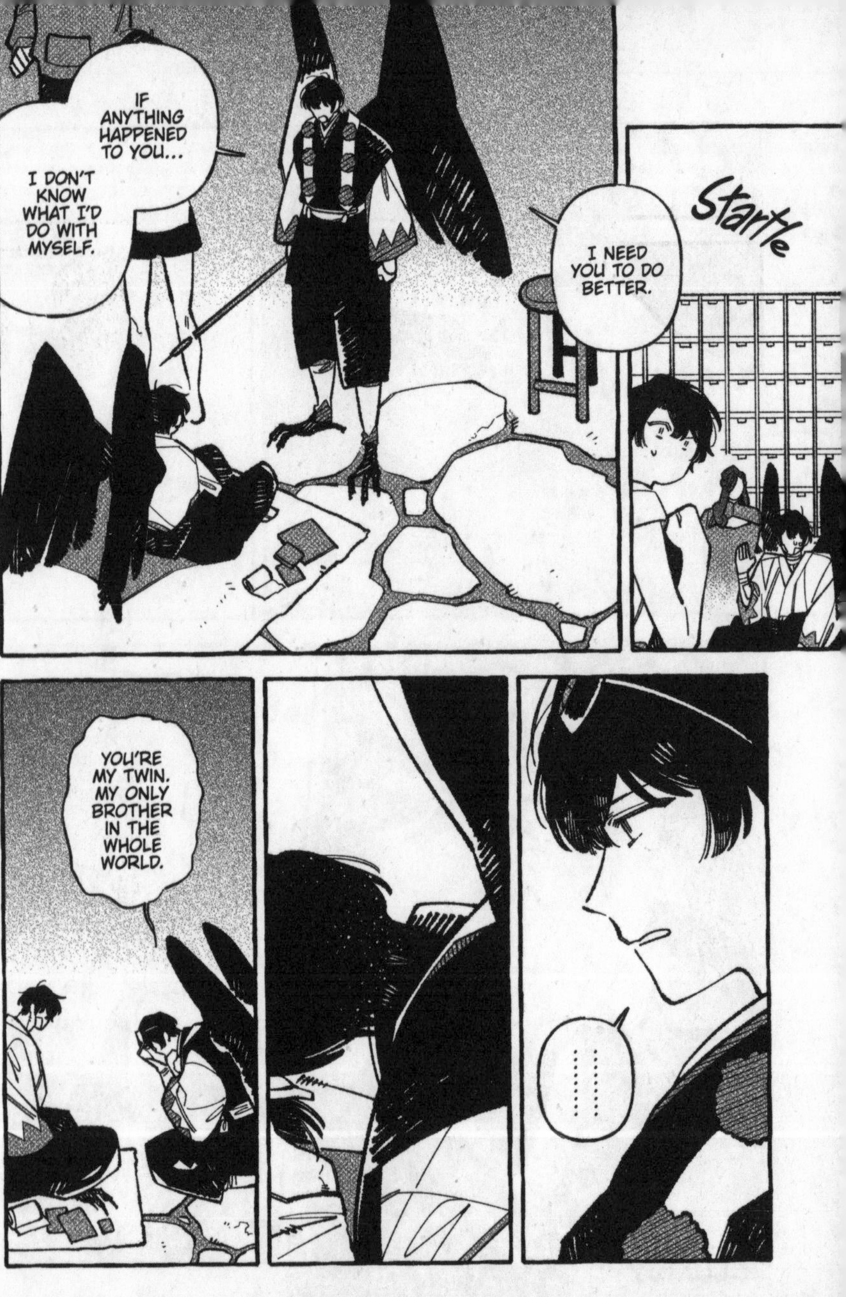
Startle
I NEED YOU TO DO BETTER.
IF ANYTHING HAPPENED TO YOU...
I DON'T KNOW WHAT I'D DO WITH MYSELF.
......
YOU'RE MY TWIN. MY ONLY BROTHER IN THE WHOLE WORLD.

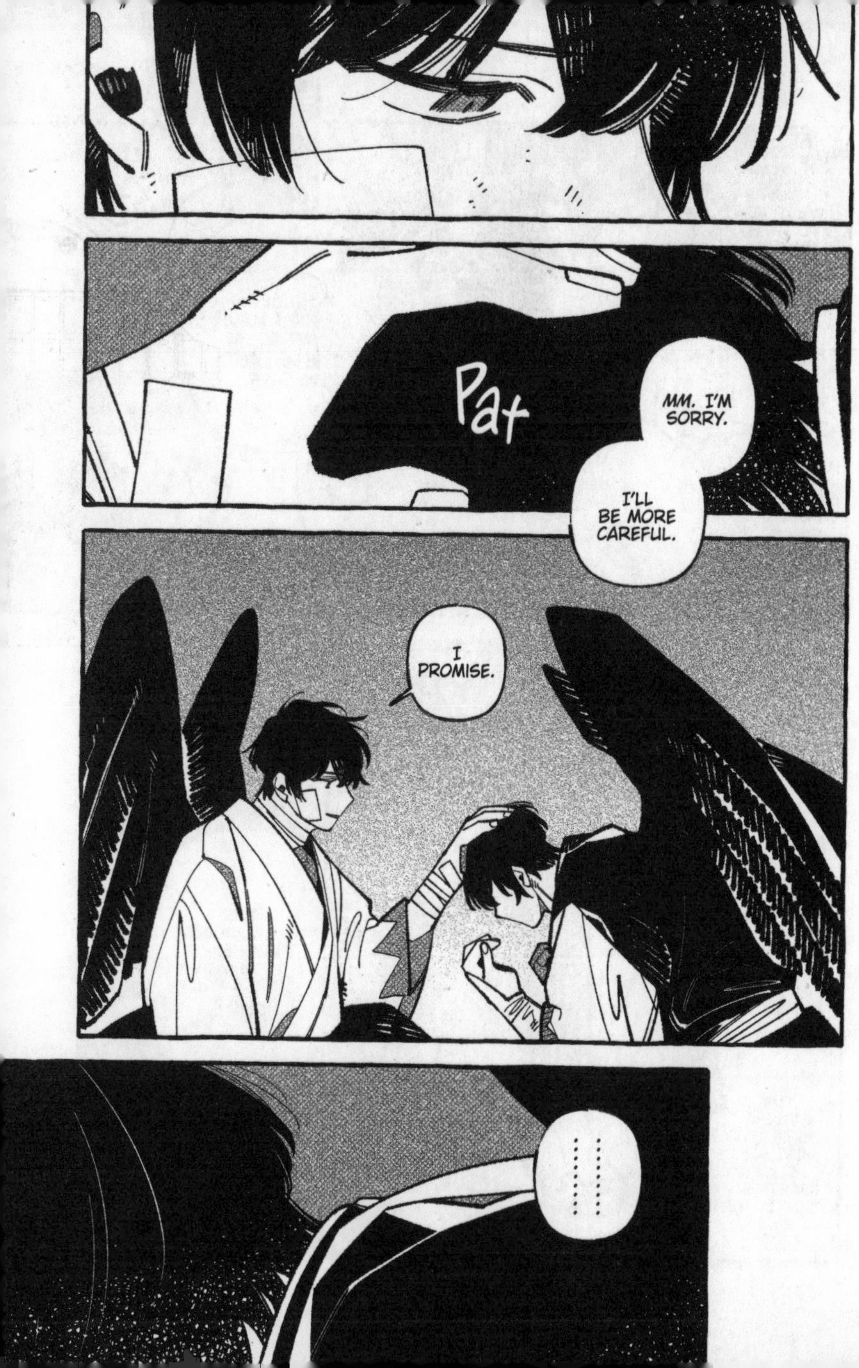
Pat
MM. I'M SORRY.
I'LL BE MORE CAREFUL.
I PROMISE.
......

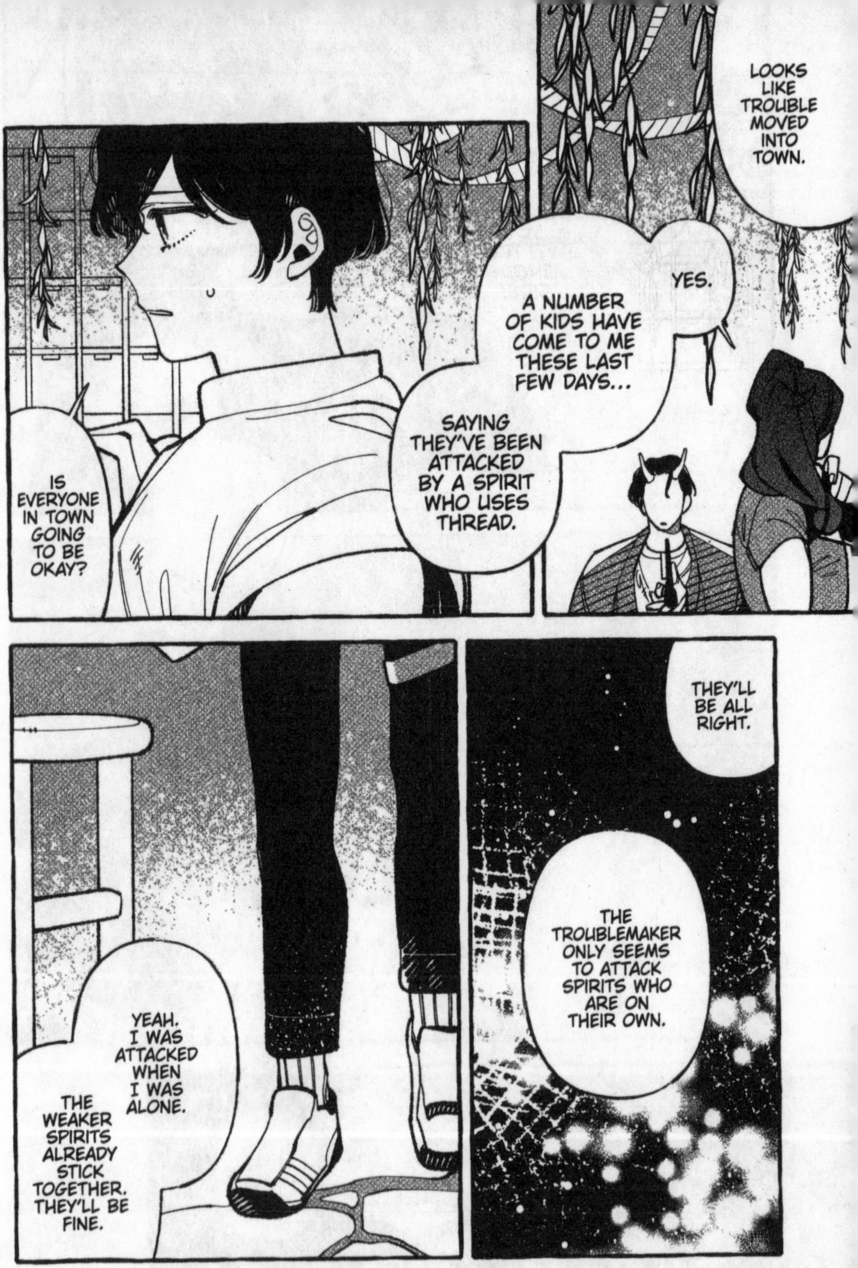

LOOKS LIKE TROUBLE MOVED INTO TOWN.
YES.
A NUMBER OF KIDS HAVE COME TO ME THESE LAST FEW DAYS...
SAYING THEY'VE BEEN ATTACKED BY A SPIRIT WHO USES THREAD.
IS EVERYONE IN TOWN GOING TO BE OKAY?
THEY'LL BE ALL RIGHT.
THE TROUBLEMAKER ONLY SEEMS TO ATTACK SPIRITS WHO ARE ON THEIR OWN.
YEAH. I WAS ATTACKED WHEN I WAS ALONE.
THE WEAKER SPIRITS ALREADY STICK TOGETHER. THEY'LL BE FINE.

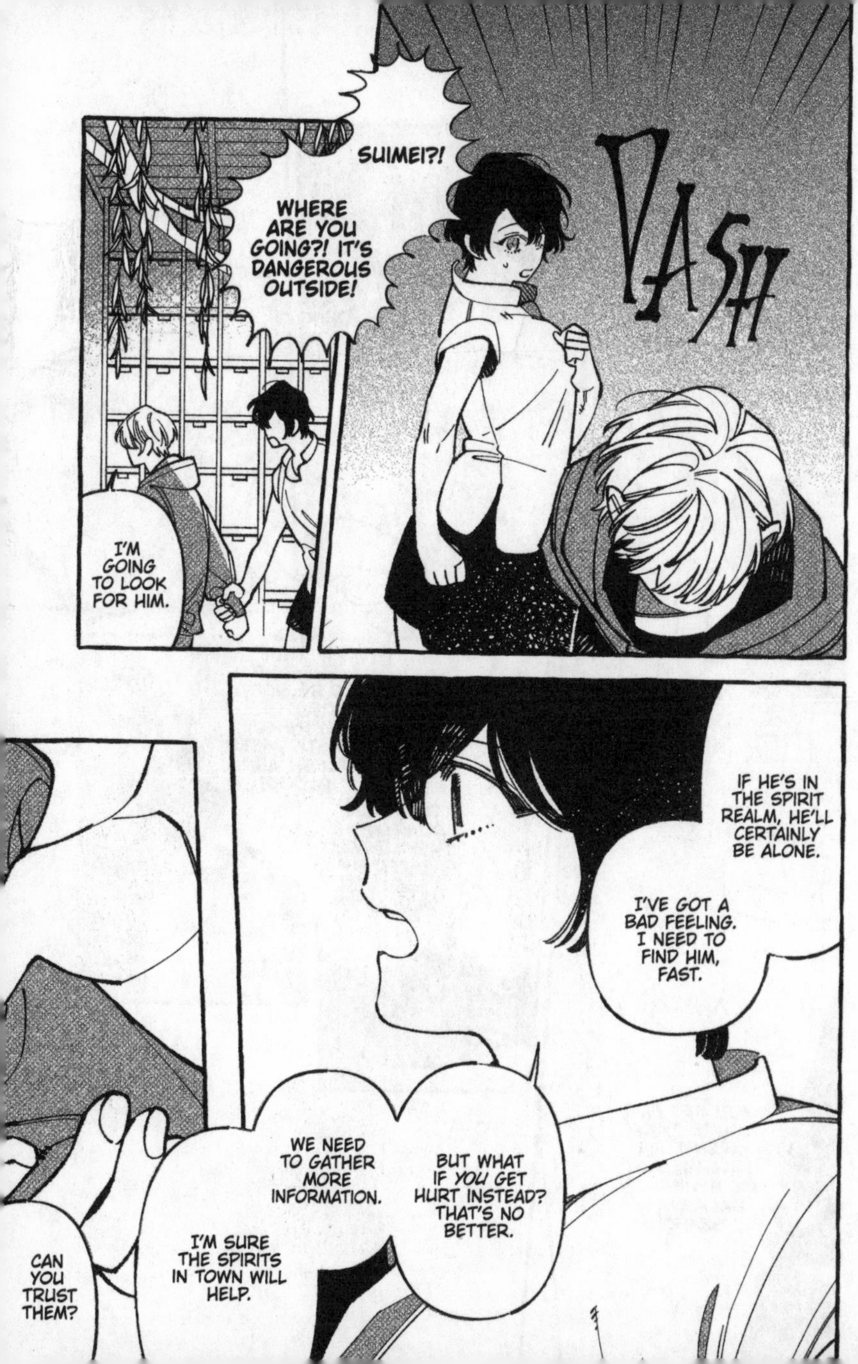
DASH
SUIMEI?!
WHERE ARE YOU GOING?! IT'S DANGEROUS OUTSIDE!
I'M GOING TO LOOK FOR HIM.
IF HE'S IN THE SPIRIT REALM, HE'LL CERTAINLY BE ALONE.
I'VE GOT A BAD FEELING. I NEED TO FIND HIM, FAST.
BUT WHAT IF *YOU* GET HURT INSTEAD? THAT'S NO BETTER.
WE NEED TO GATHER MORE INFORMATION.
I'M SURE THE SPIRITS IN TOWN WILL HELP.
CAN YOU TRUST THEM?

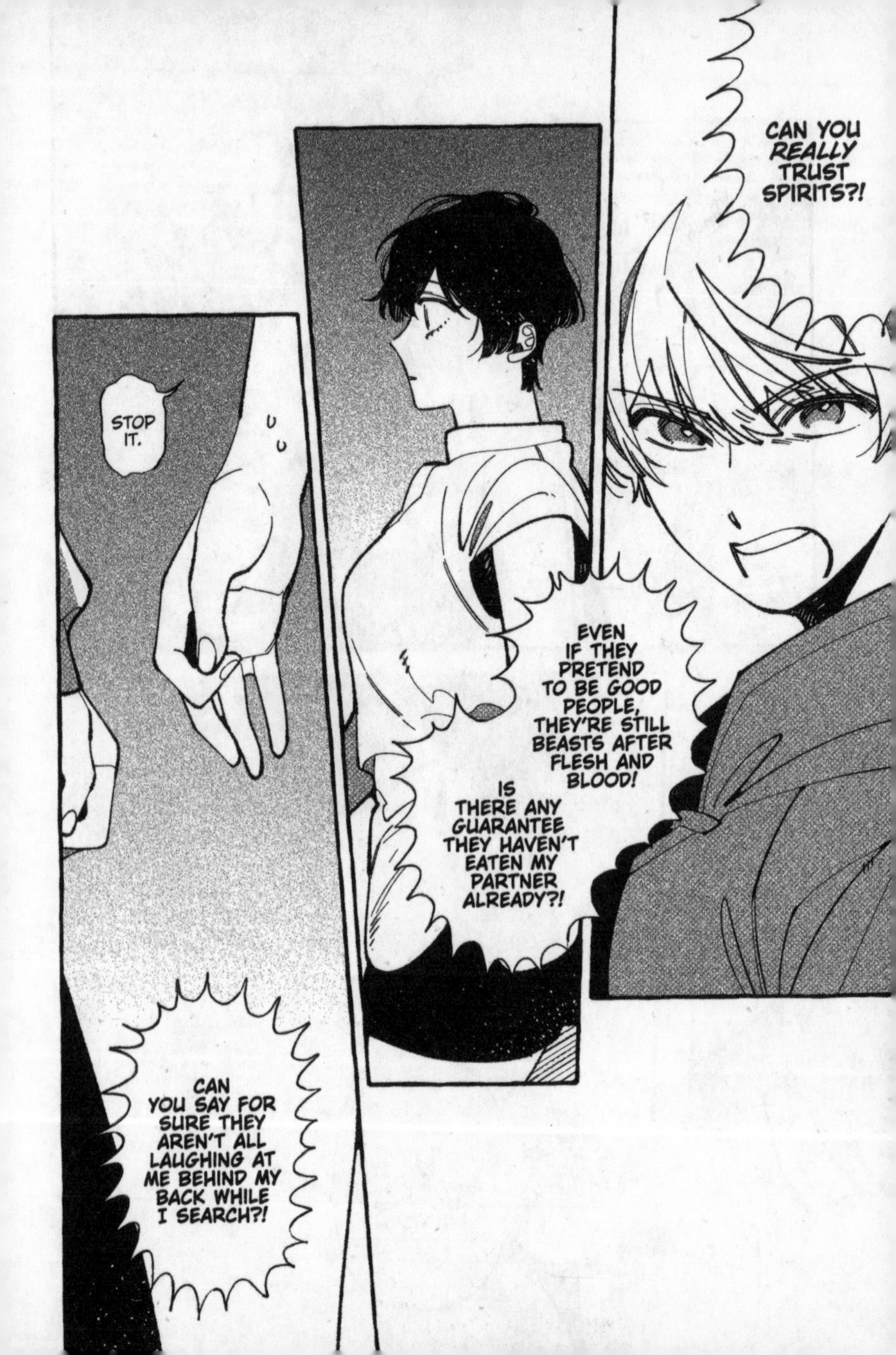
CAN YOU *REALLY* TRUST SPIRITS?!
EVEN IF THEY PRETEND TO BE GOOD PEOPLE, THEY'RE STILL BEASTS AFTER FLESH AND BLOOD!
IS THERE ANY GUARANTEE THEY HAVEN'T EATEN MY PARTNER ALREADY?!
STOP IT.
CAN YOU SAY FOR SURE THEY AREN'T ALL LAUGHING AT ME BEHIND MY BACK WHILE I SEARCH?!

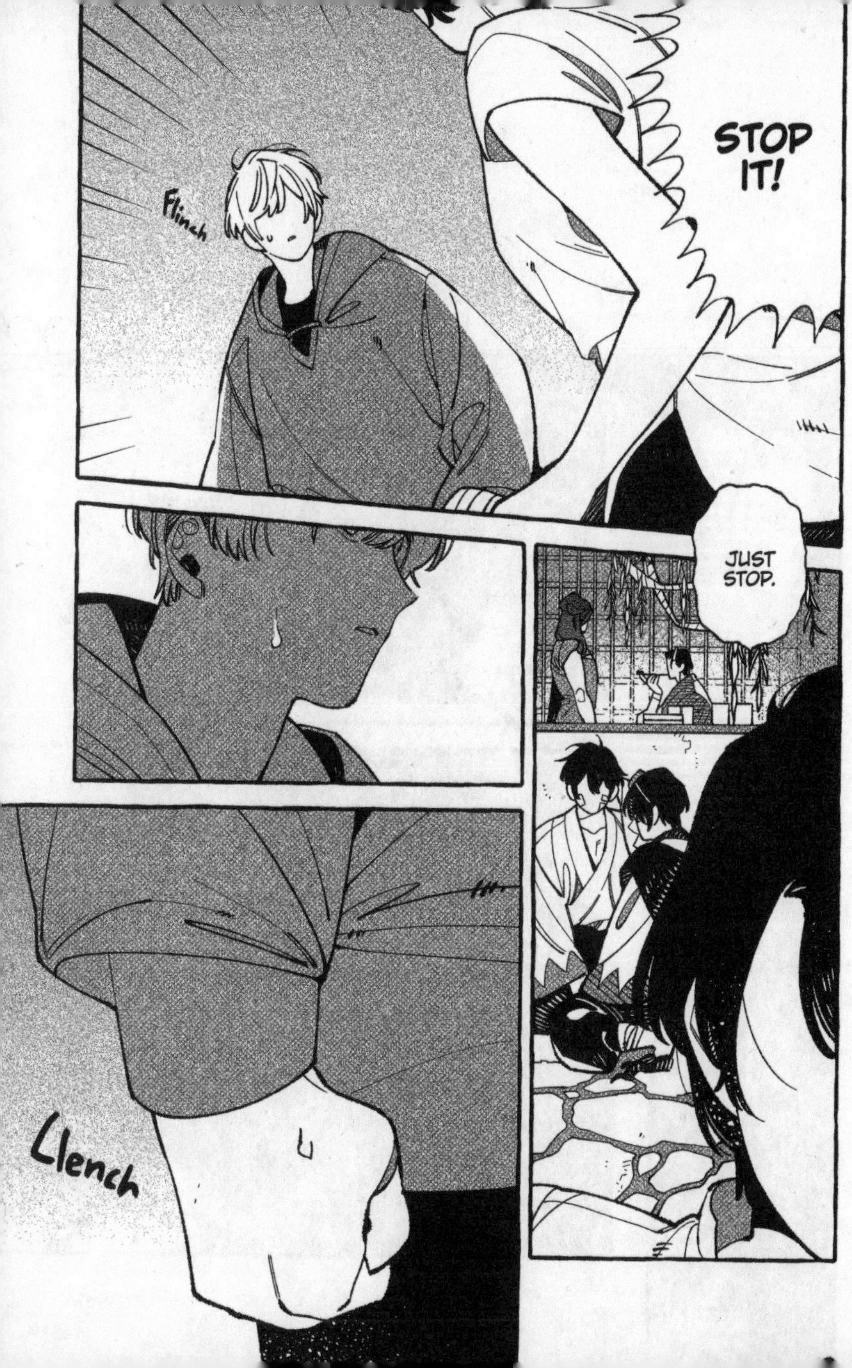
STOP IT!
Flinch
JUST STOP.
Clench

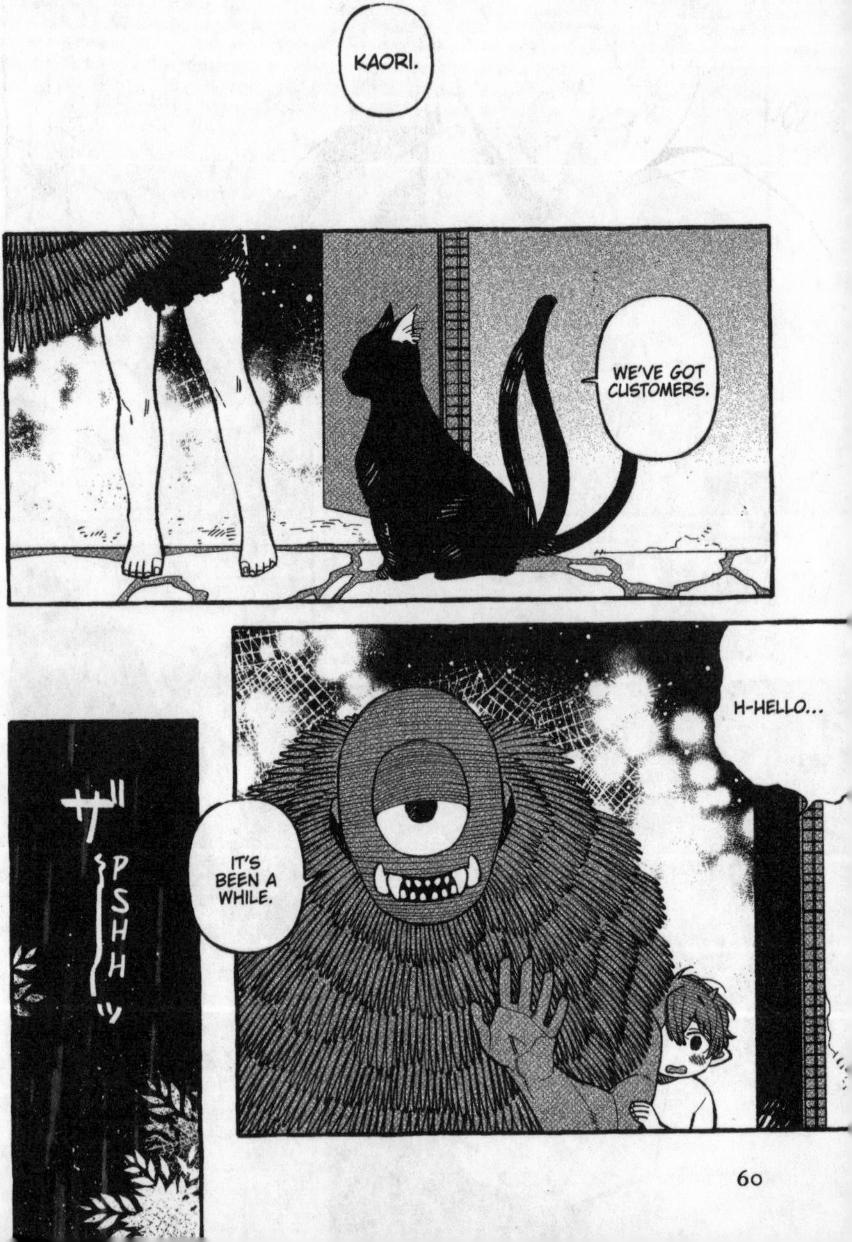
KAORI.
WE'VE GOT CUSTOMERS.
H-HELLO...
IT'S BEEN A WHILE.
ザッ
PSHH

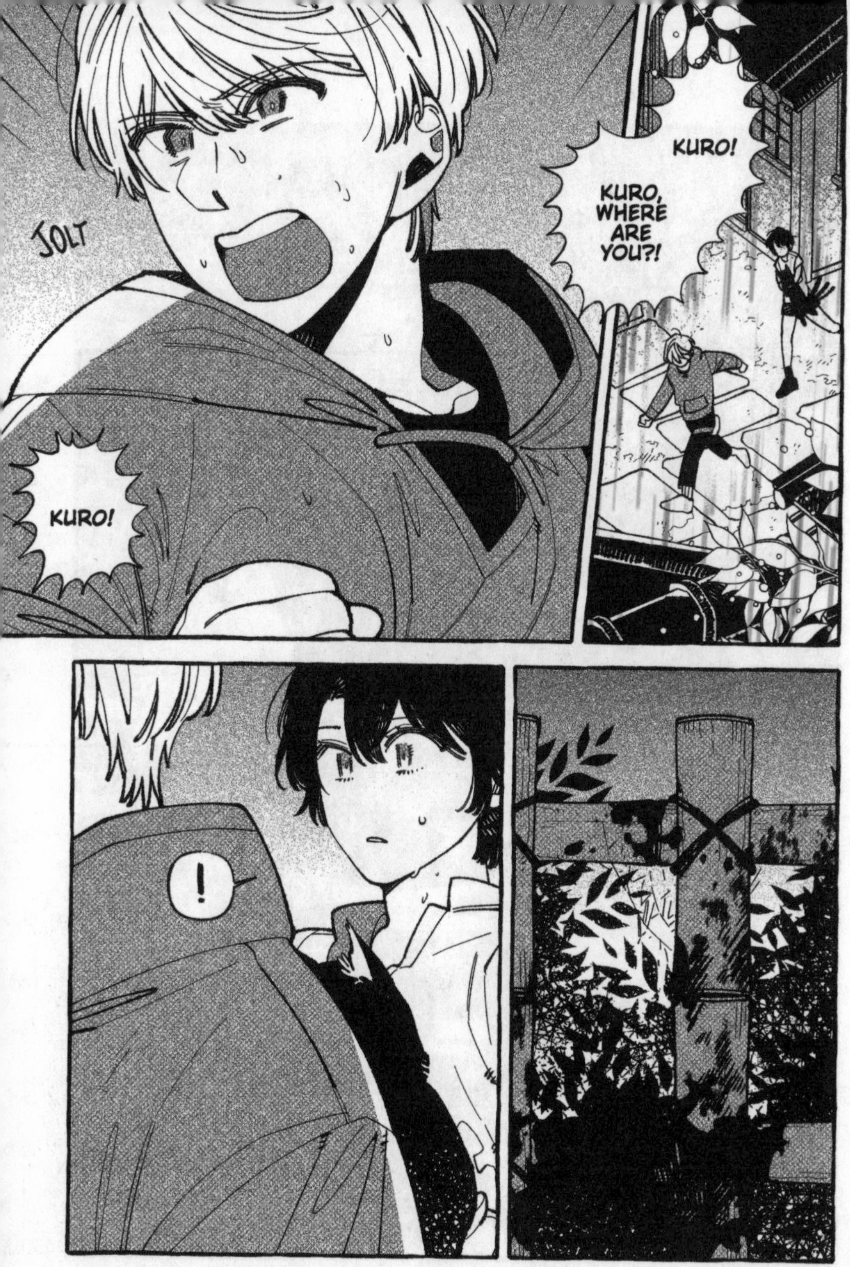
KURO!
KURO, WHERE ARE YOU?!
JOLT
KURO!
!

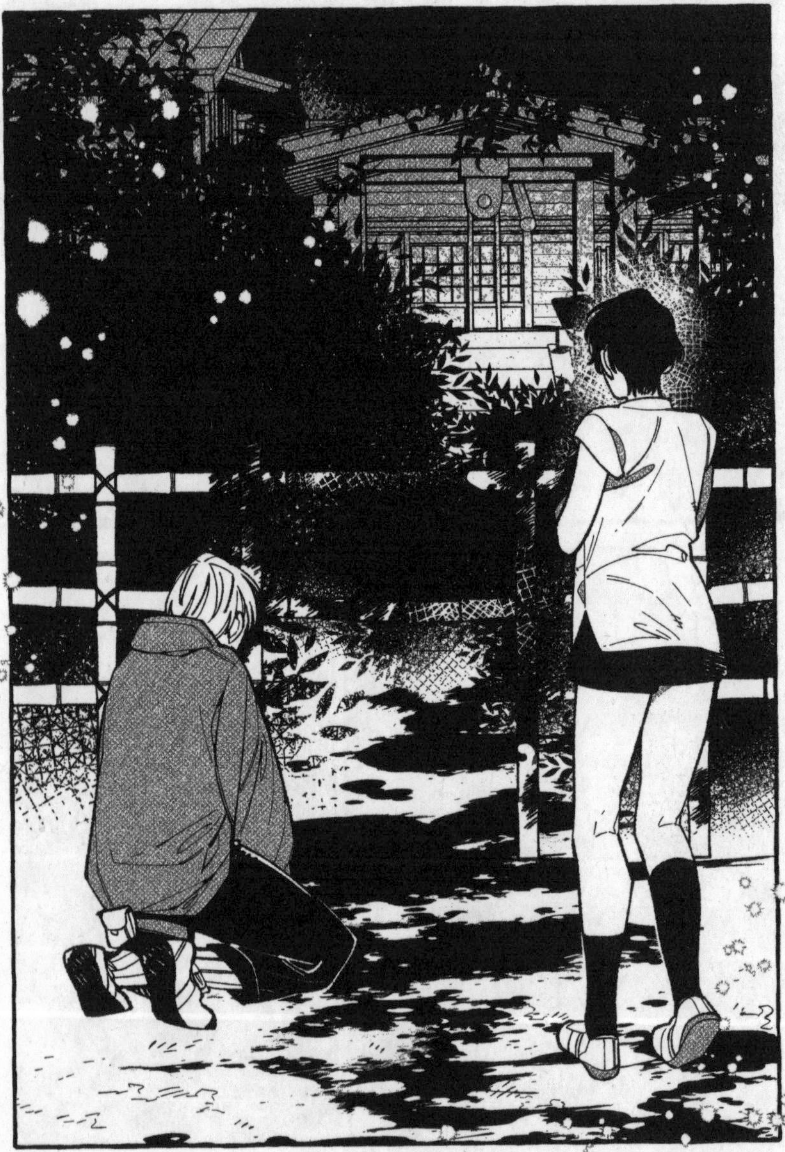

THE
HAUNTED
BOOKSTORE
Gateway to a
Parallel Universe

THE HAUNTED BOOKSTORE
Gateway to a Parallel Universe

CHAPTER 10
Reunion

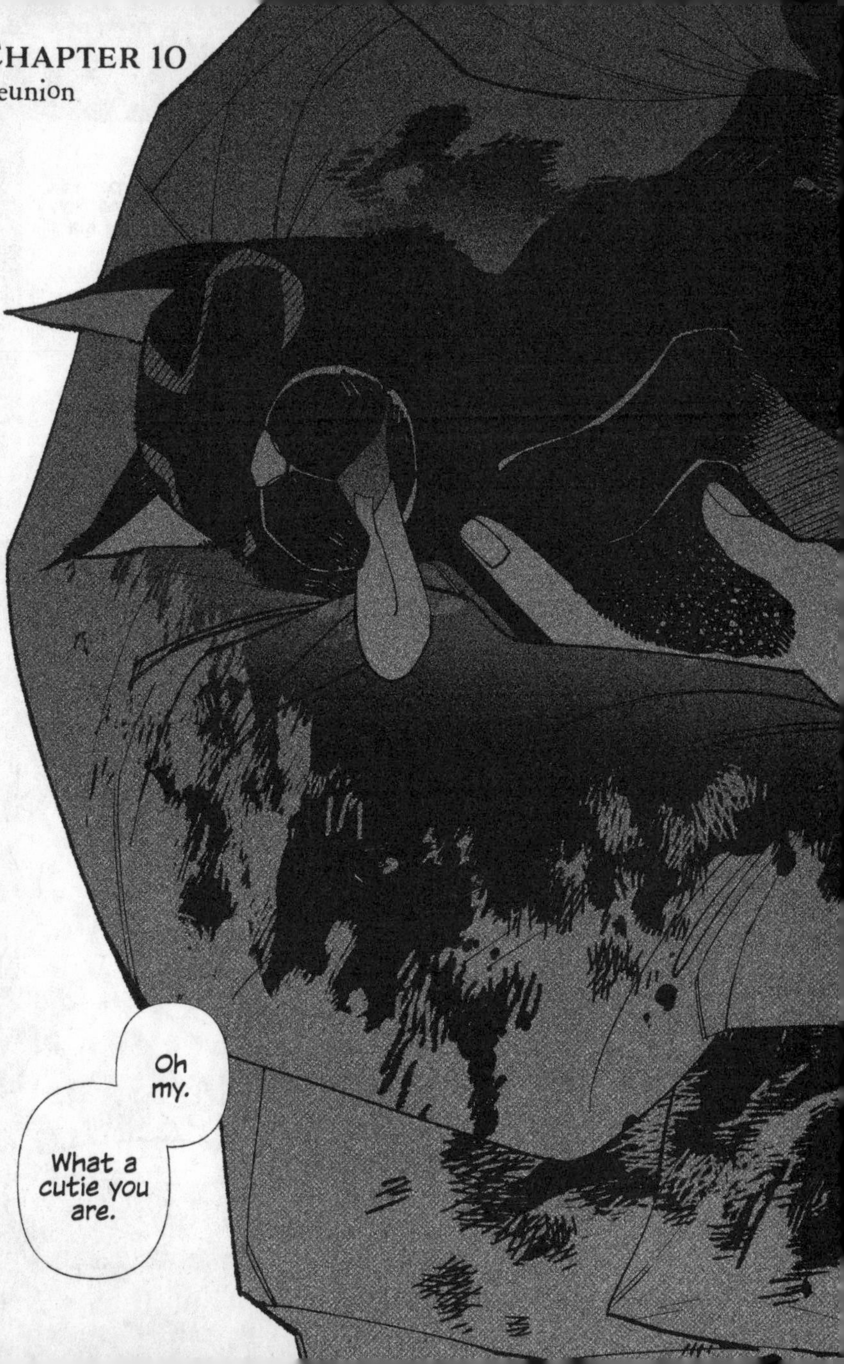
Oh my.
What a cutie you are.

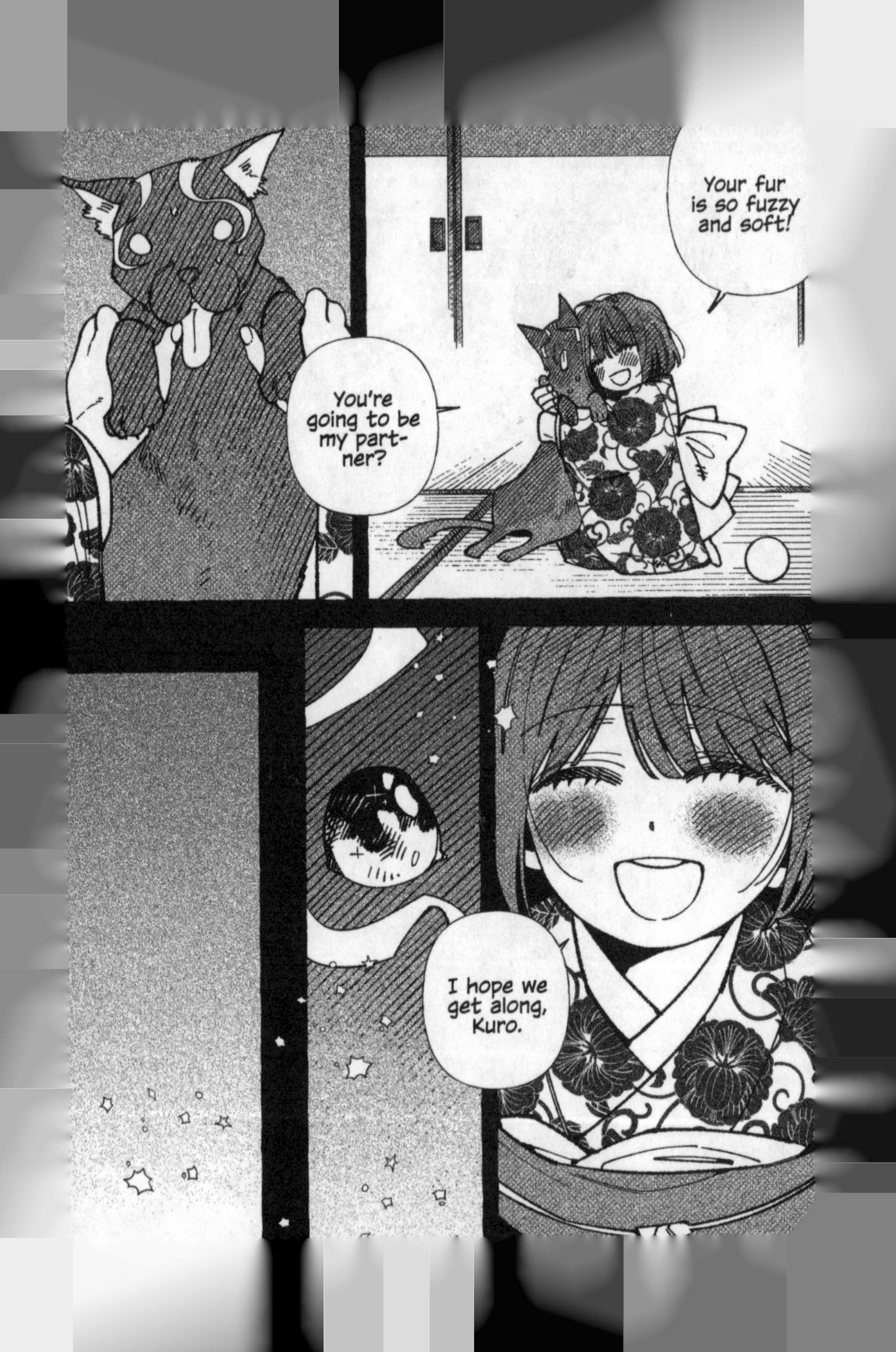
Your fur is so fuzzy and soft!
You're going to be my part-ner?
I hope we get along, Kuro.

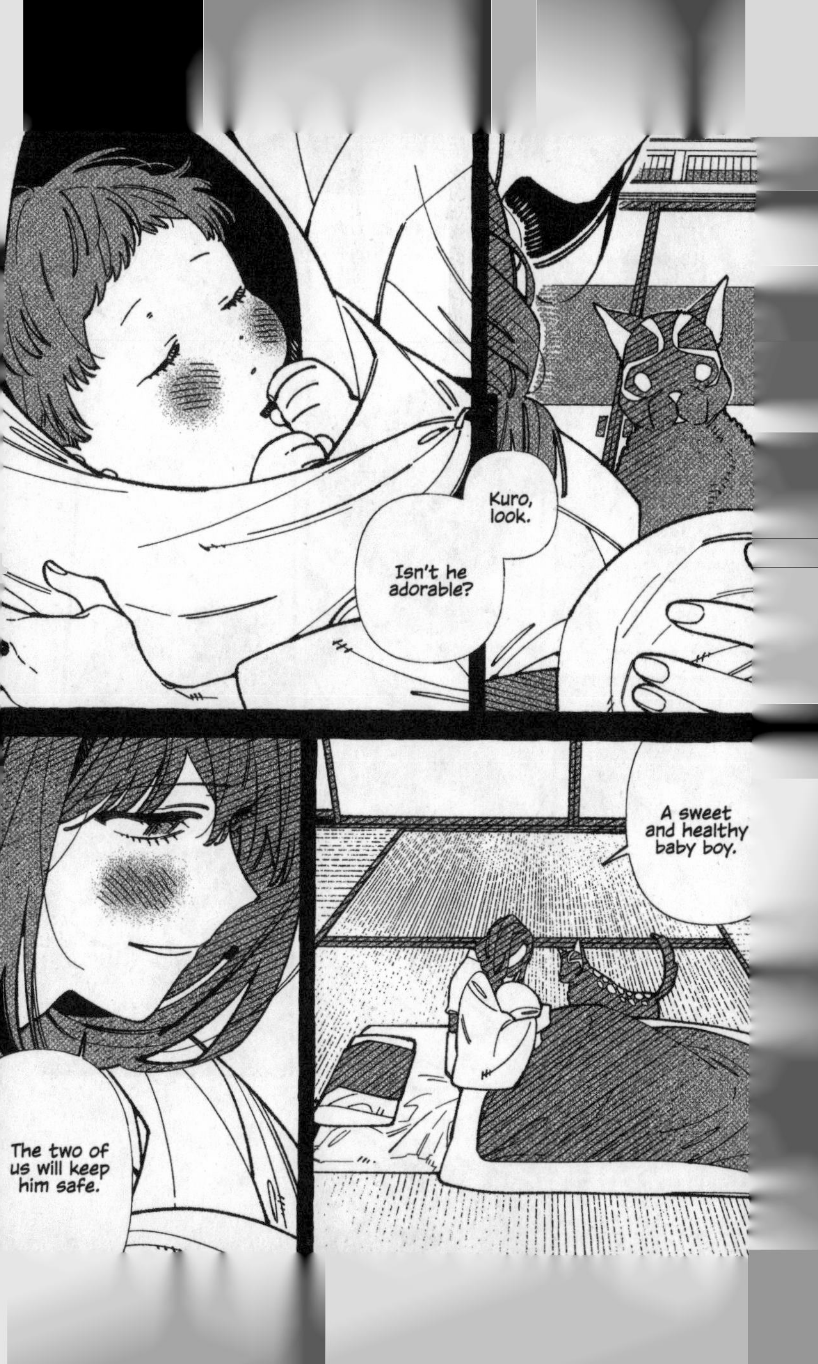
Kuro, look.
Isn't he adorable?
A sweet and healthy baby boy.
The two of us will keep him safe.

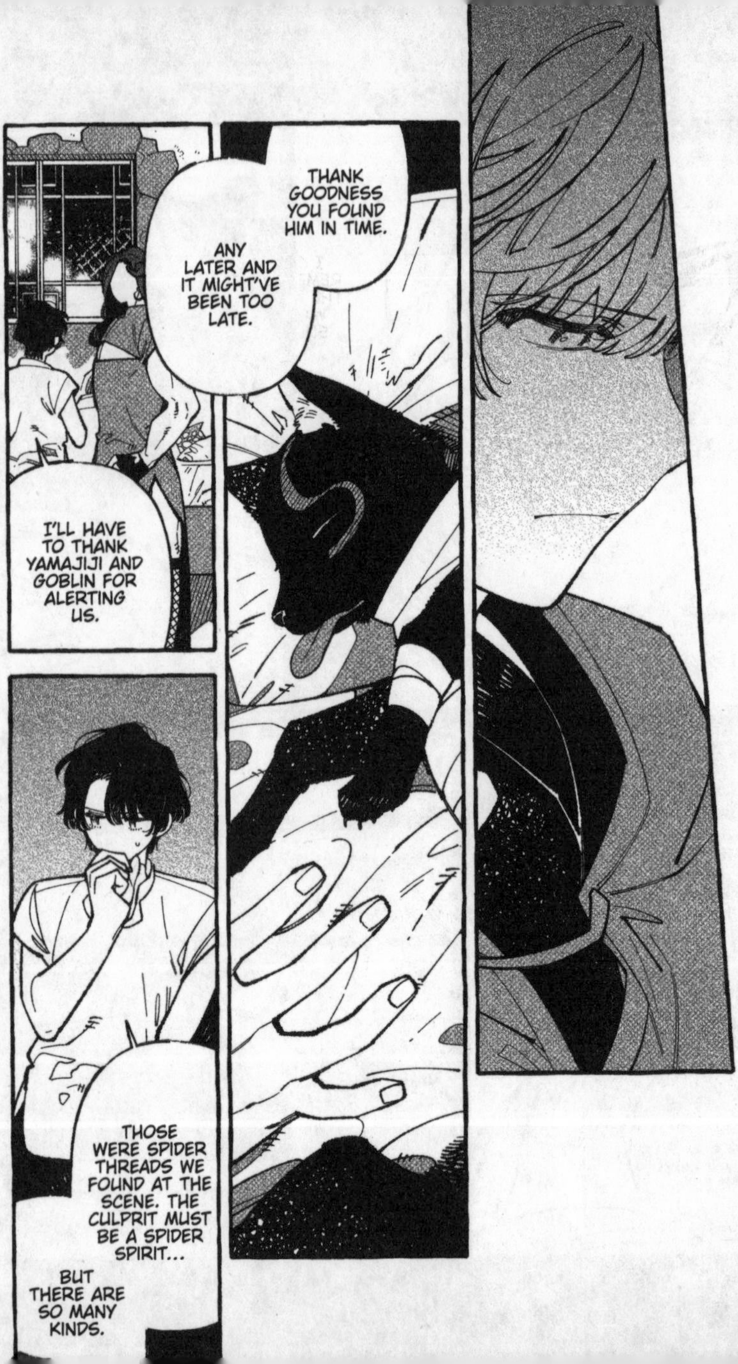
THANK GOODNESS YOU FOUND HIM IN TIME.
ANY LATER AND IT MIGHT'VE BEEN TOO LATE.
I'LL HAVE TO THANK YAMAJIJI AND GOBLIN FOR ALERTING US.
THOSE WERE SPIDER THREADS WE FOUND AT THE SCENE. THE CULPRIT MUST BE A SPIDER SPIRIT...
BUT THERE ARE SO MANY KINDS.

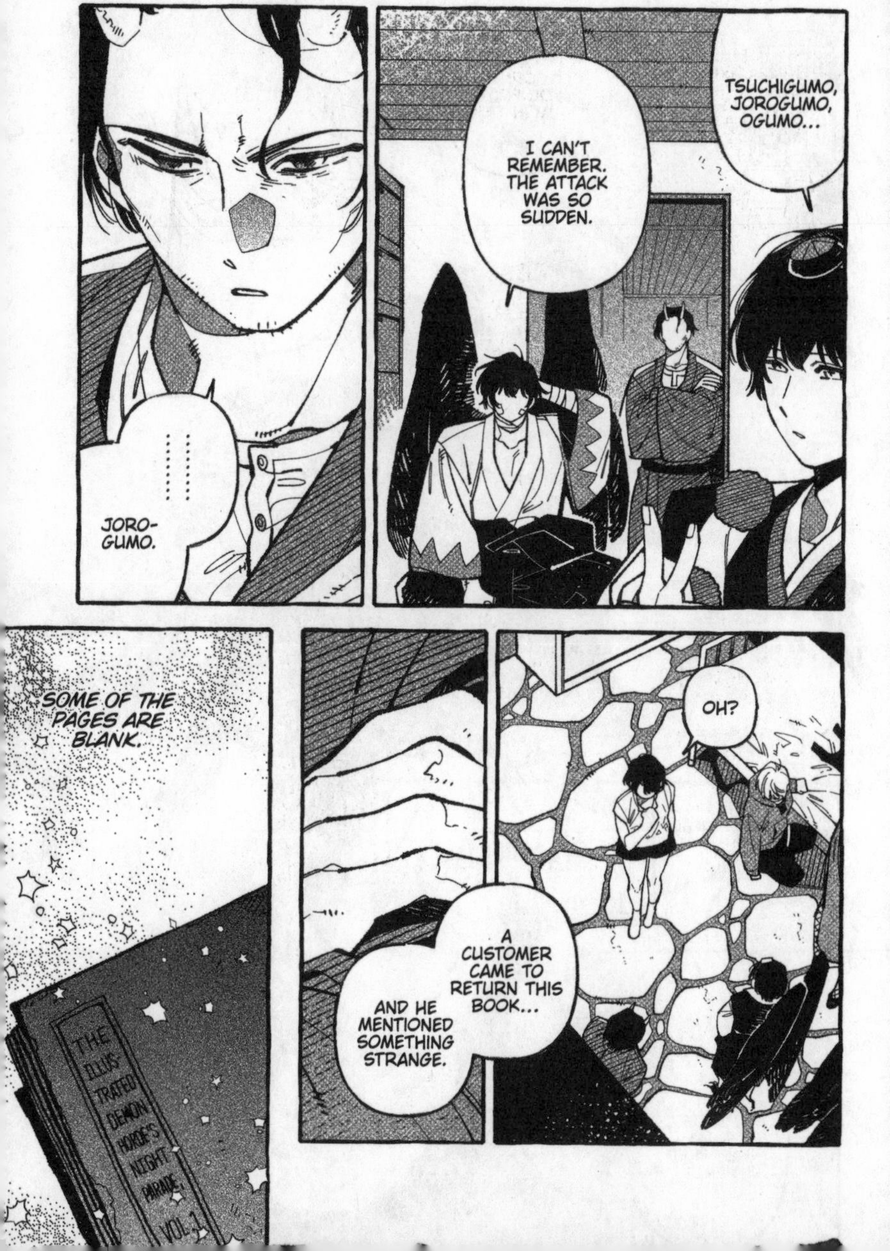
TSUCHIGUMO, JOROGUMO, OGUMO...
I CAN'T REMEMBER. THE ATTACK WAS SO SUDDEN.
......
JORO-GUMO.
OH?
A CUSTOMER CAME TO RETURN THIS BOOK...
AND HE MENTIONED SOMETHING STRANGE.
SOME OF THE PAGES ARE BLANK.
THE ILLUS-TRATED DEMON HORDE'S NIGHT PARADE, VOL.1

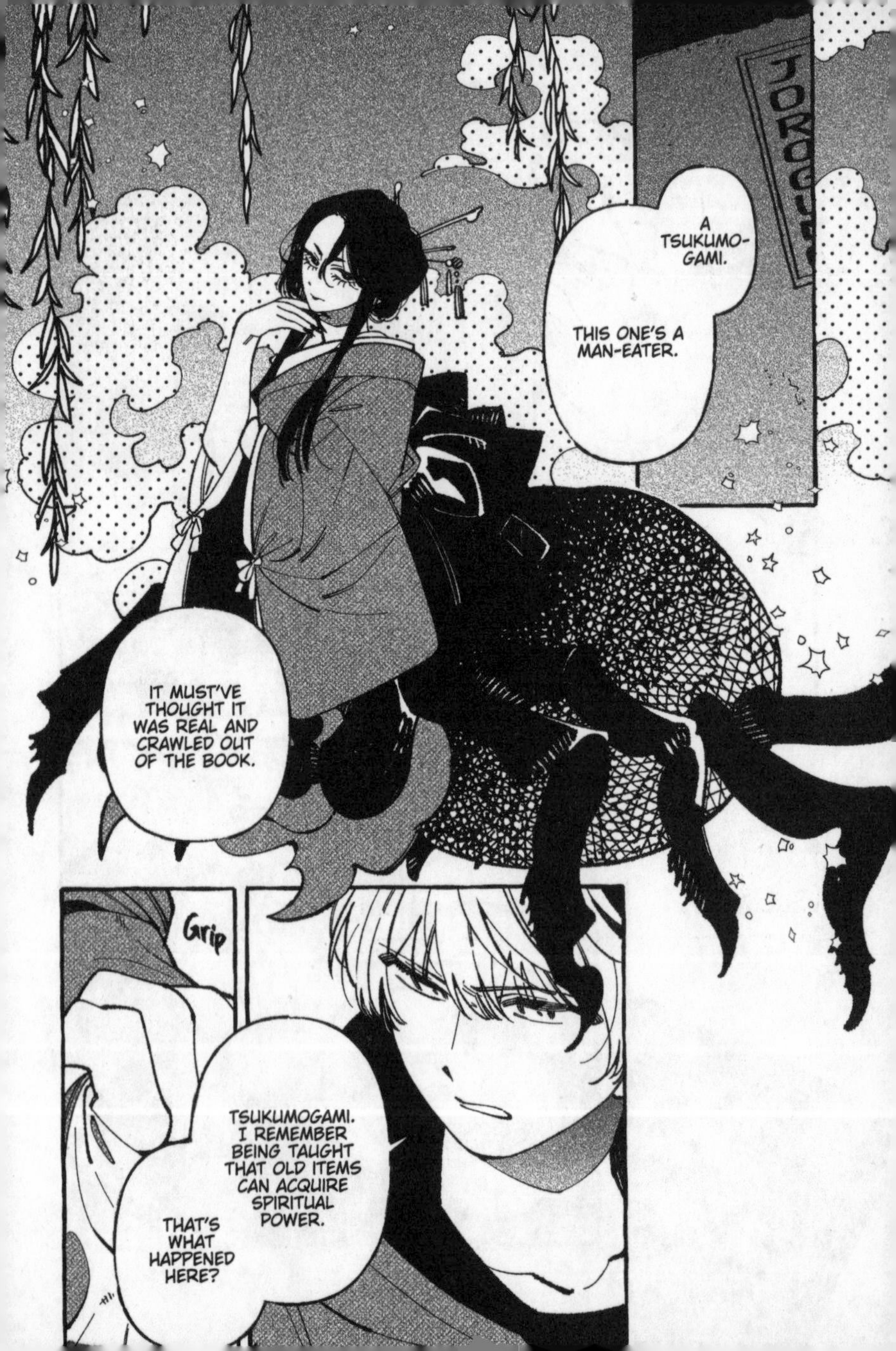
A TSUKUMO-GAMI.
THIS ONE'S A MAN-EATER.
IT MUST'VE THOUGHT IT WAS REAL AND CRAWLED OUT OF THE BOOK.
TSUKUMOGAMI. I REMEMBER BEING TAUGHT THAT OLD ITEMS CAN ACQUIRE SPIRITUAL POWER.
THAT'S WHAT HAPPENED HERE?
Grip

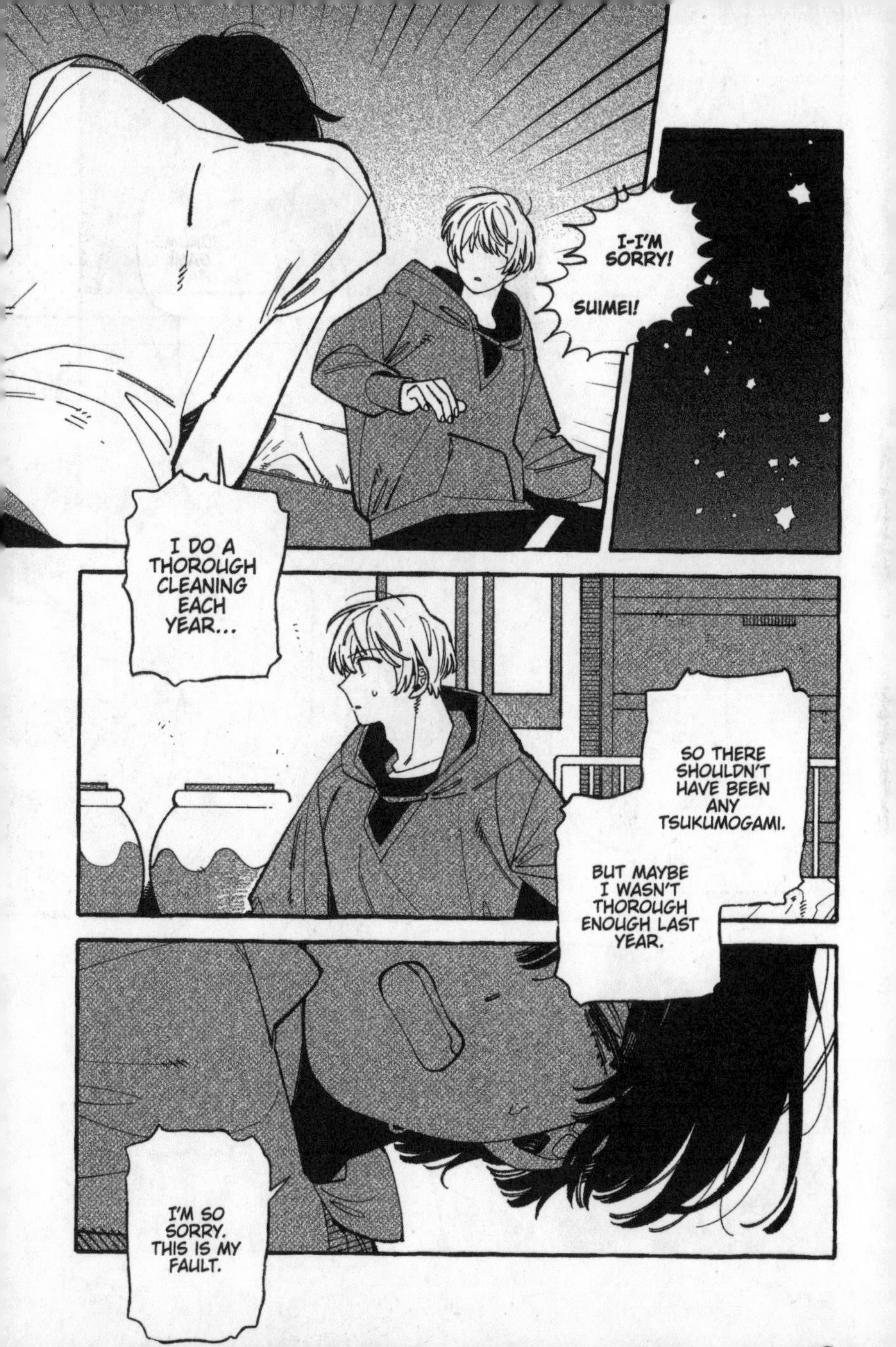
I-I'M SORRY!
SUIMEI!
I DO A THOROUGH CLEANING EACH YEAR...
SO THERE SHOULDN'T HAVE BEEN ANY TSUKUMOGAMI.
BUT MAYBE I WASN'T THOROUGH ENOUGH LAST YEAR.
I'M SO SORRY. THIS IS MY FAULT.

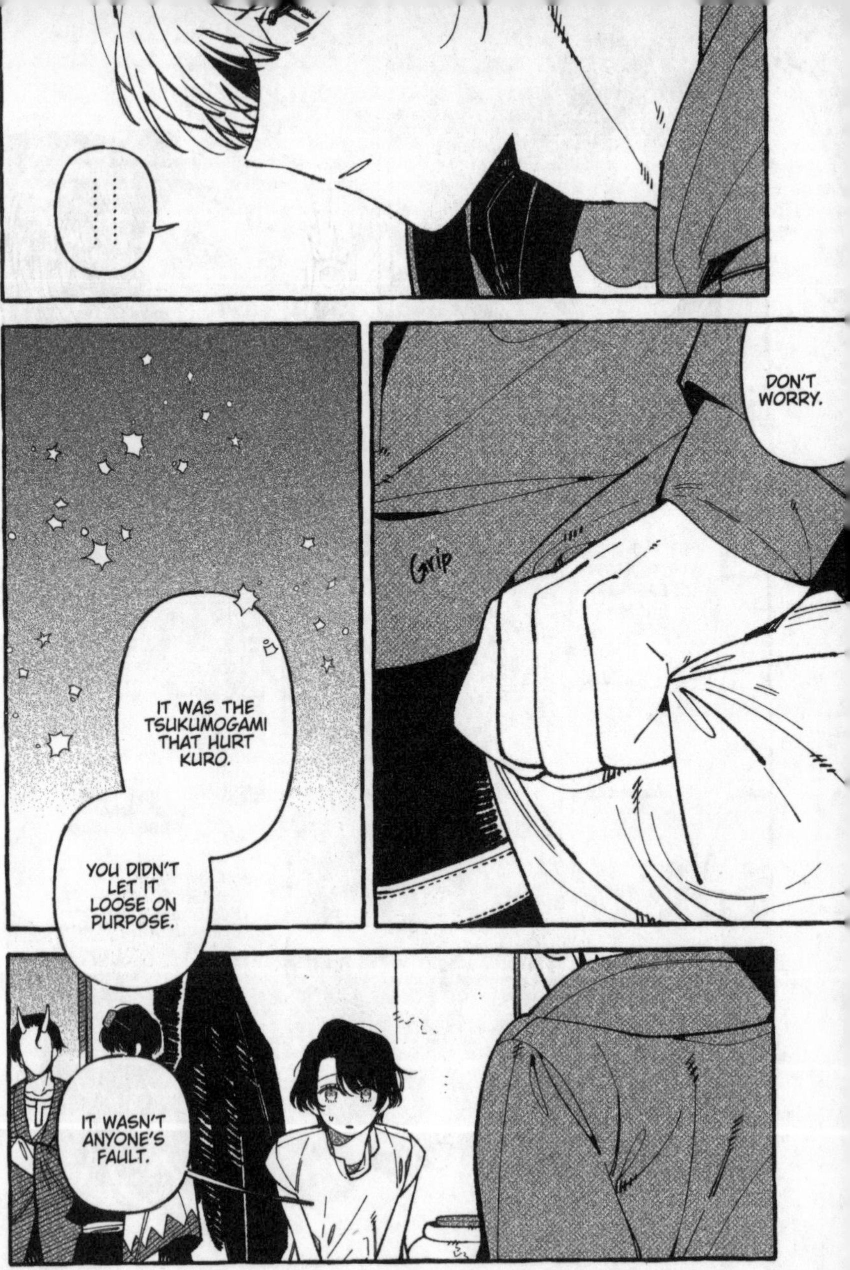
......
DON'T WORRY.
Grip
IT WAS THE TSUKUMOGAMI THAT HURT KURO.
YOU DIDN'T LET IT LOOSE ON PURPOSE.
IT WASN'T ANYONE'S FAULT.

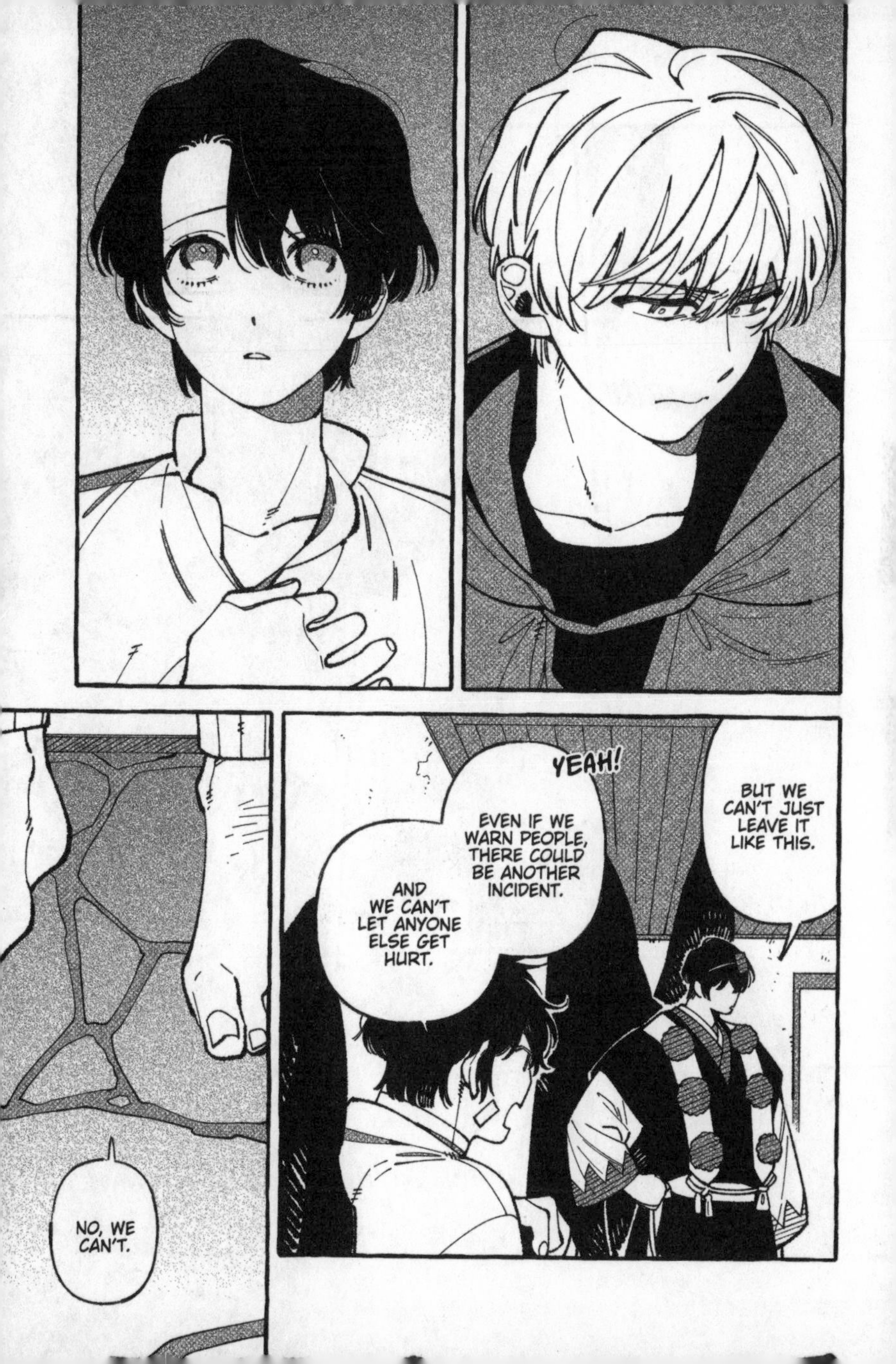
BUT WE CAN'T JUST LEAVE IT LIKE THIS.
YEAH!
EVEN IF WE WARN PEOPLE, THERE COULD BE ANOTHER INCIDENT.
AND WE CAN'T LET ANYONE ELSE GET HURT.
NO, WE CAN'T.

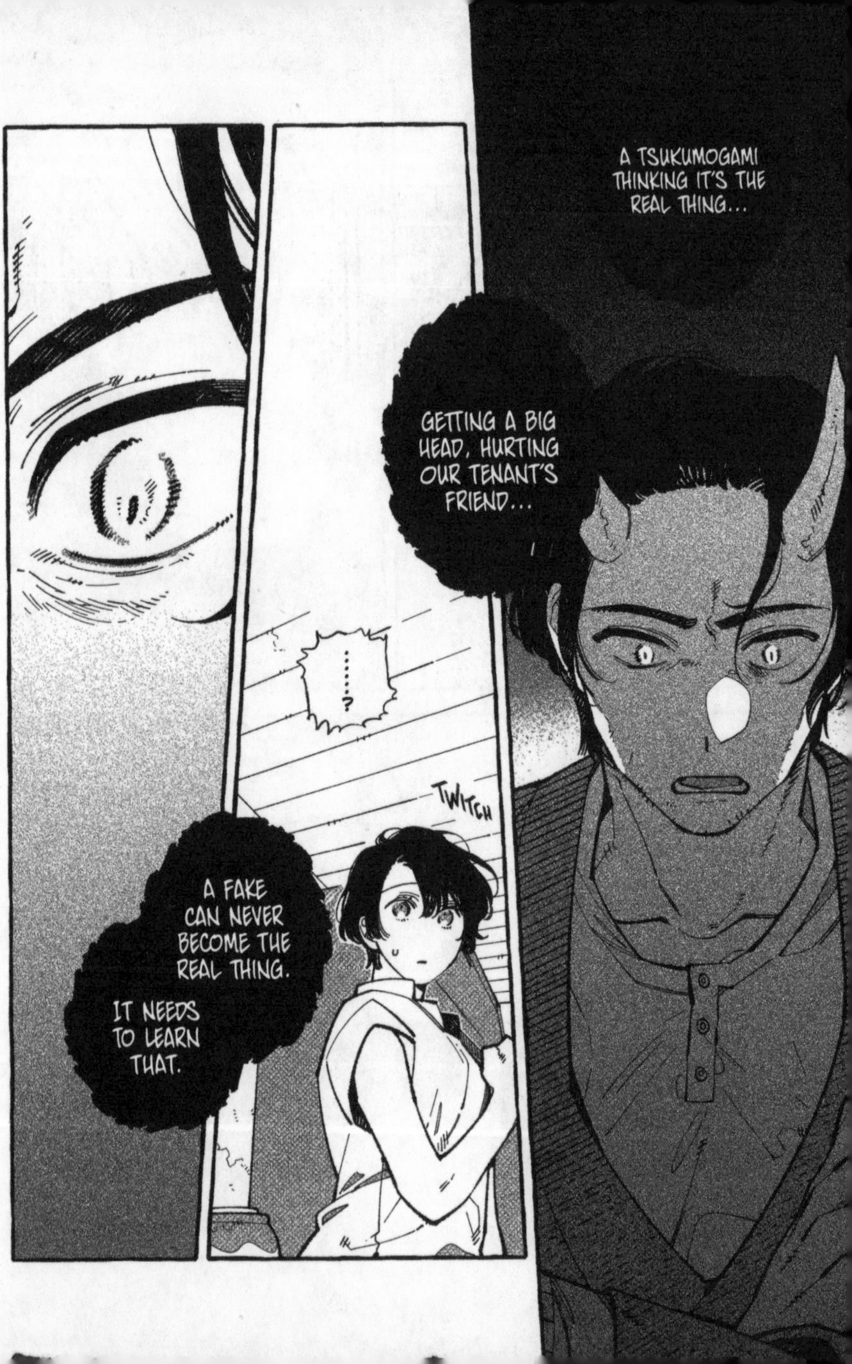
A TSUKUMOGAMI THINKING IT'S THE REAL THING...
GETTING A BIG HEAD, HURTING OUR TENANT'S FRIEND...
......?
TWITCH
A FAKE CAN NEVER BECOME THE REAL THING.
IT NEEDS TO LEARN THAT.

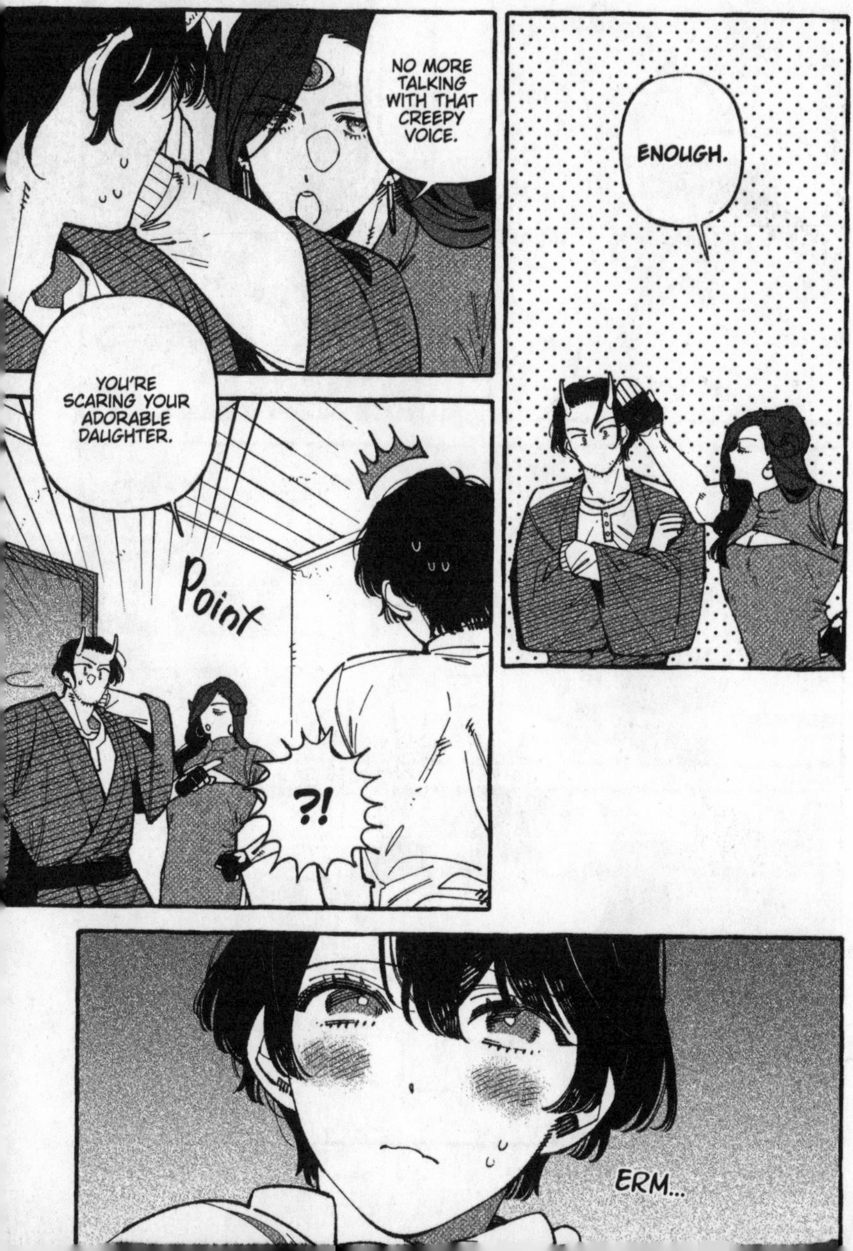
ENOUGH.
NO MORE TALKING WITH THAT CREEPY VOICE.
YOU'RE SCARING YOUR ADORABLE DAUGHTER.
Point
?!
ERM...

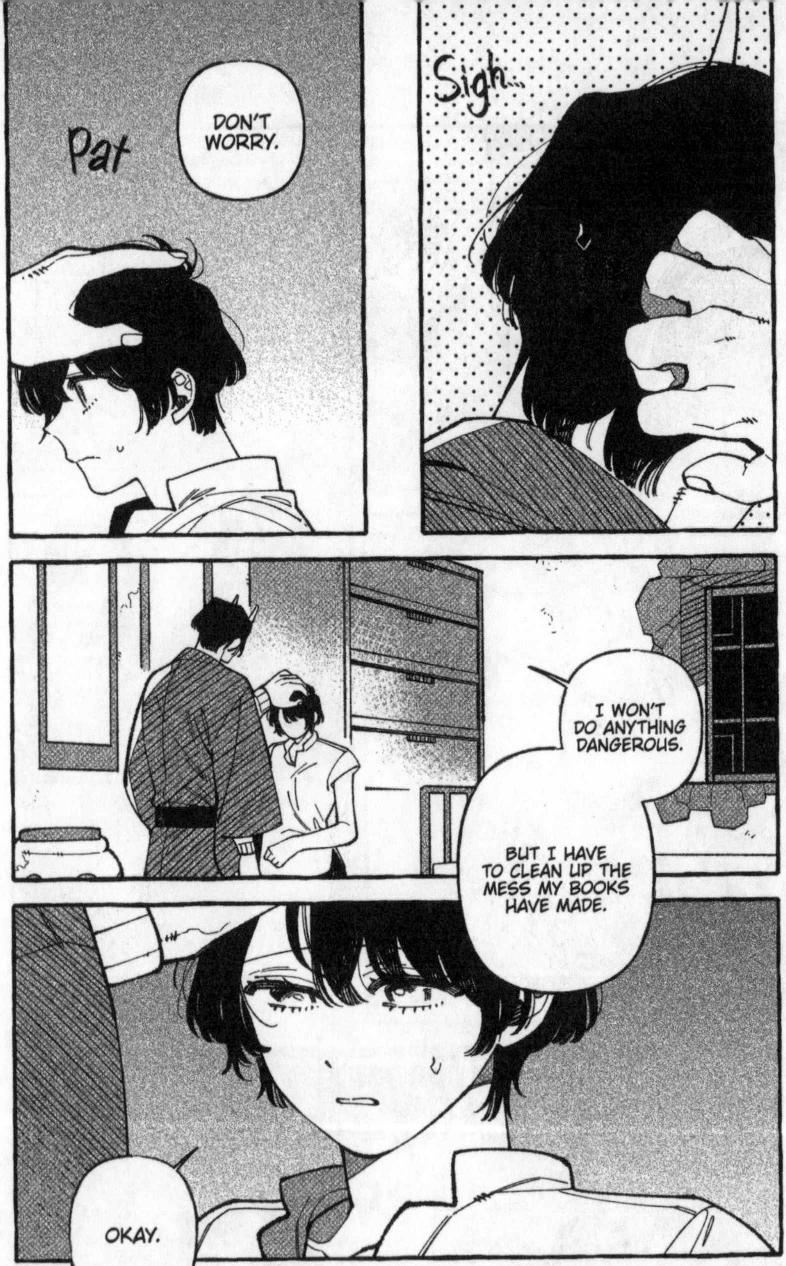
Sigh...
Pat
DON'T WORRY.
I WON'T DO ANYTHING DANGEROUS.
BUT I HAVE TO CLEAN UP THE MESS MY BOOKS HAVE MADE.
OKAY.

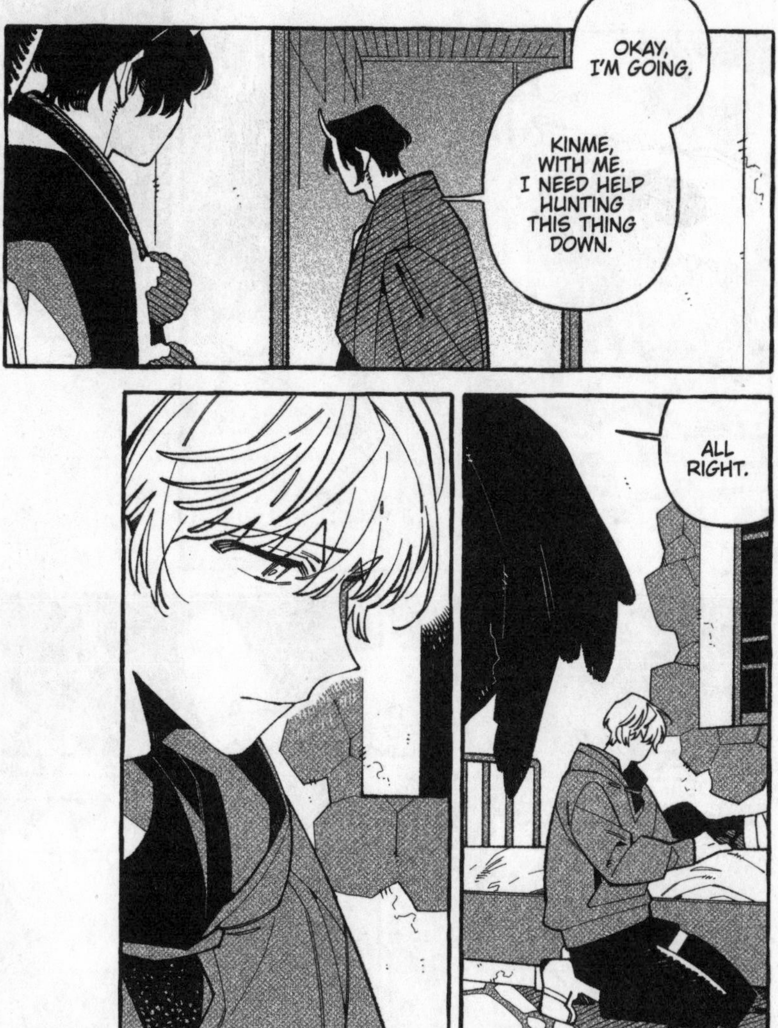
OKAY, I'M GOING.
KINME, WITH ME. I NEED HELP HUNTING THIS THING DOWN.
ALL RIGHT.

I'M SORRY FOR YELLING...

AND FOR ALL THE RUDE THINGS I SAID.

I'LL APOLOGIZE FOR THE REST LATER.

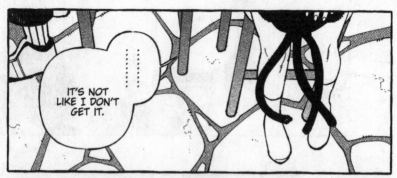

IT'S NOT LIKE I DON'T GET IT.

I THINK YOUR PANIC WAS NATURAL.

IT'S DANGEROUS OUT THERE. AND KURO WAS HURT.

KURO WAKES UP SOON.

I HOPE...

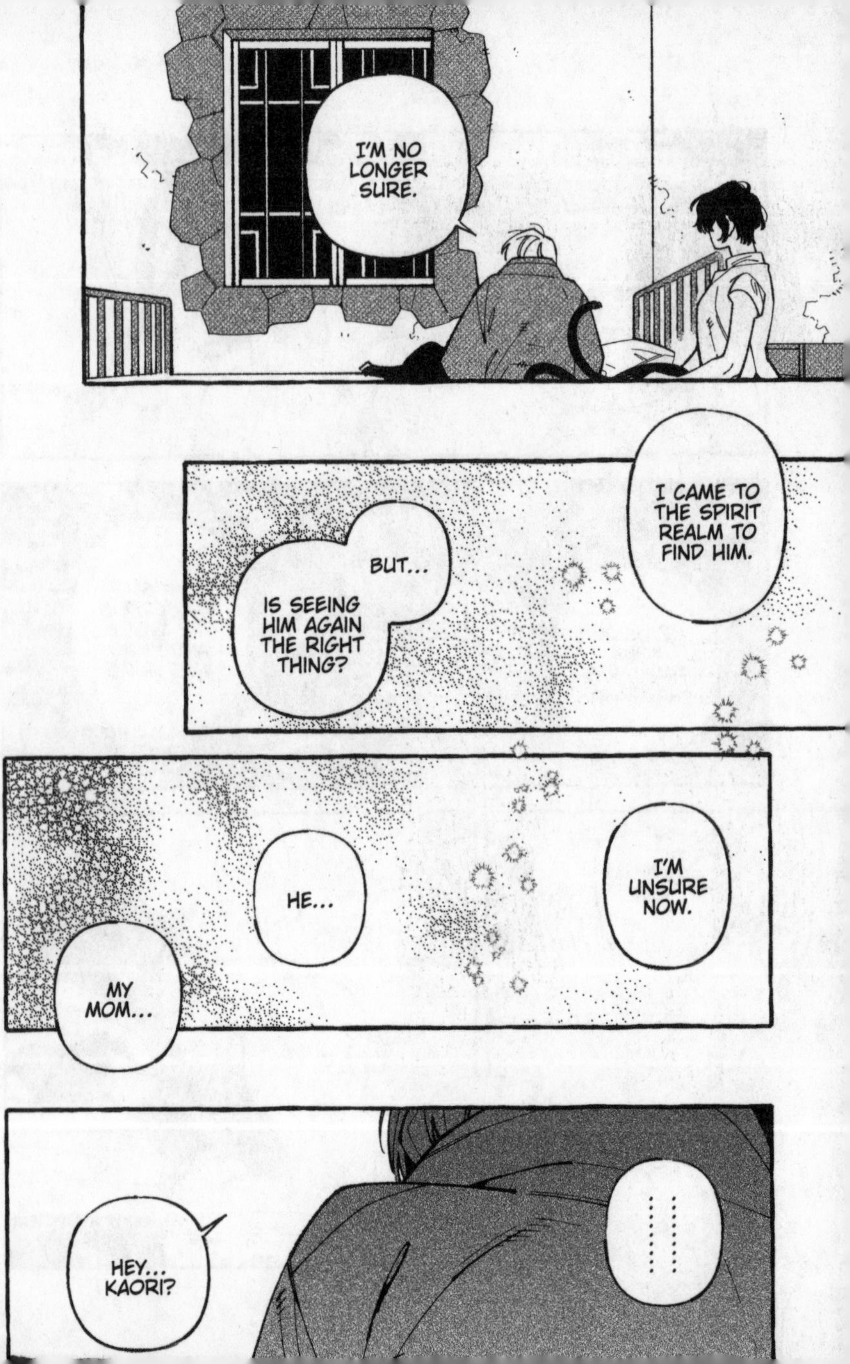
I'M NO LONGER SURE.
I CAME TO THE SPIRIT REALM TO FIND HIM.
BUT... IS SEEING HIM AGAIN THE RIGHT THING?
I'M UNSURE NOW.
HE...
MY MOM...
......
HEY... KAORI?

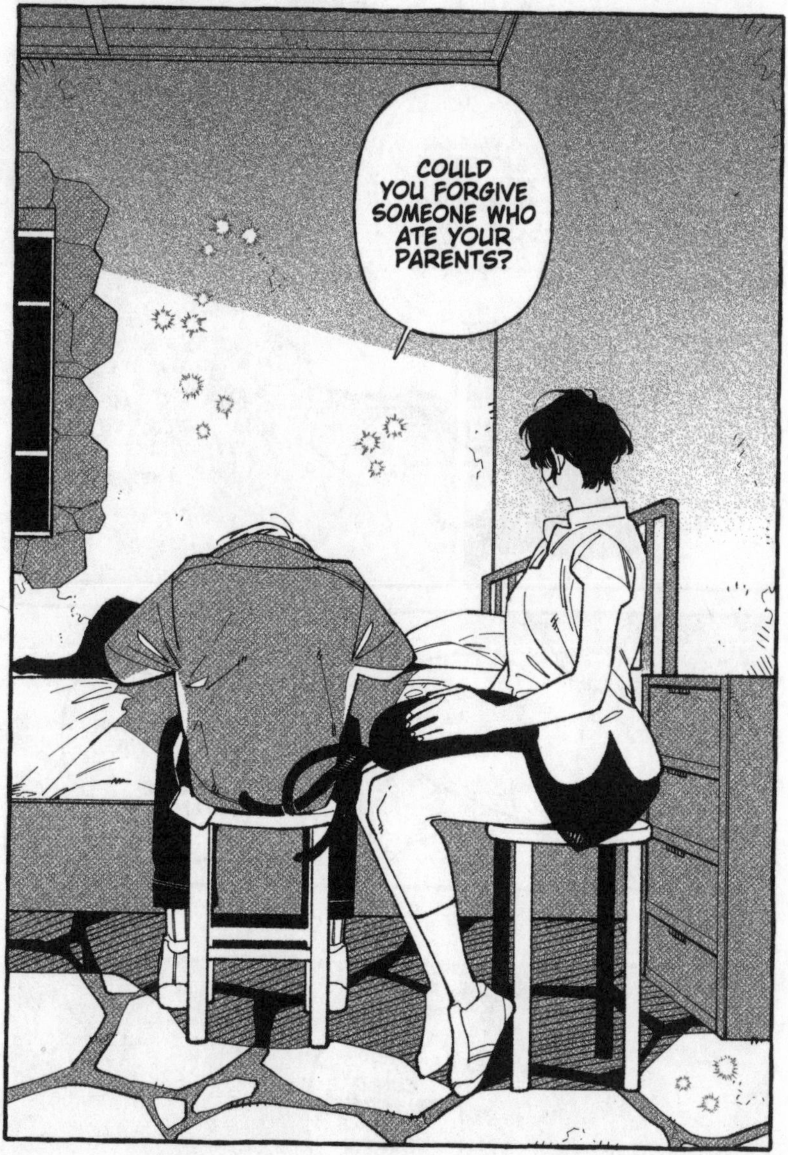
COULD YOU FORGIVE SOMEONE WHO ATE YOUR PARENTS?

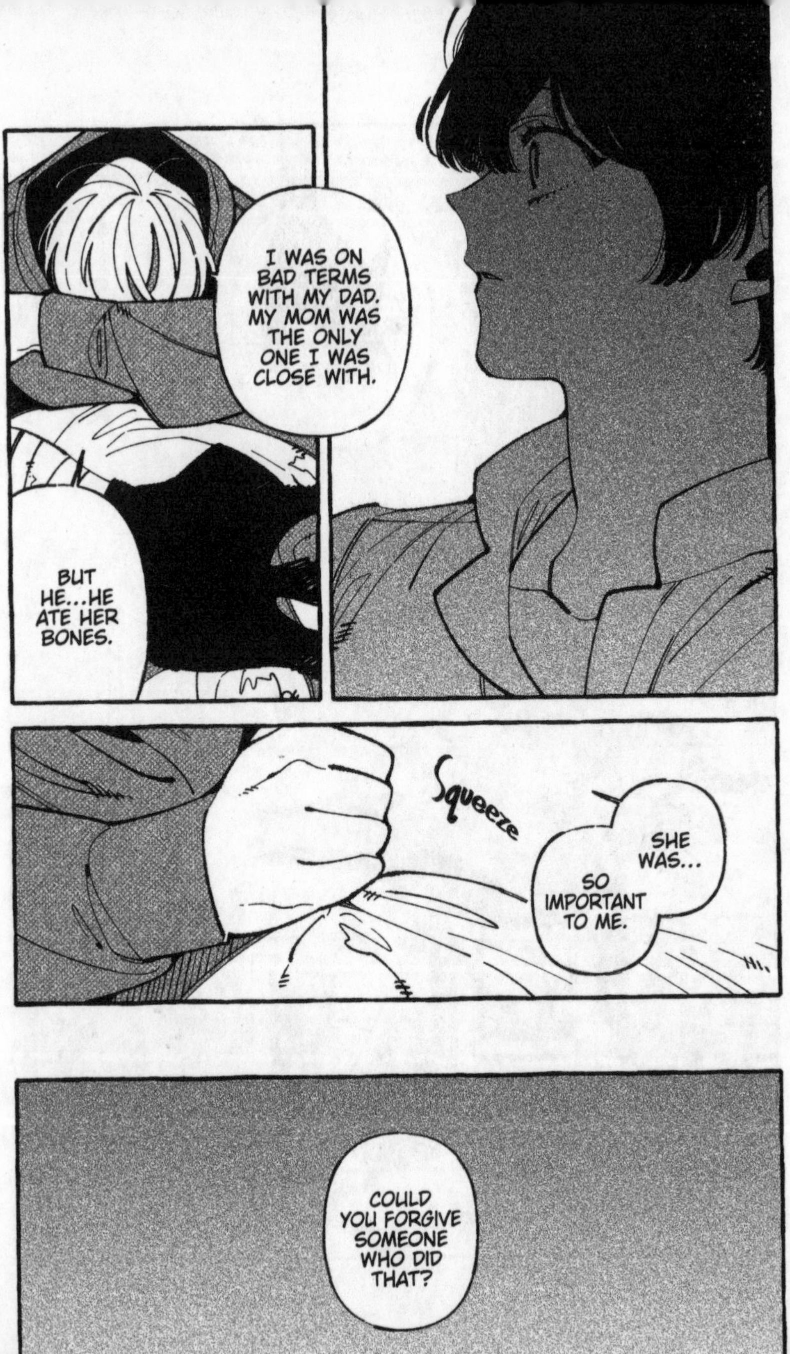
I WAS ON BAD TERMS WITH MY DAD. MY MOM WAS THE ONLY ONE I WAS CLOSE WITH.
BUT HE...HE ATE HER BONES.
Squeeze
SHE WAS... SO IMPORTANT TO ME.
COULD YOU FORGIVE SOMEONE WHO DID THAT?

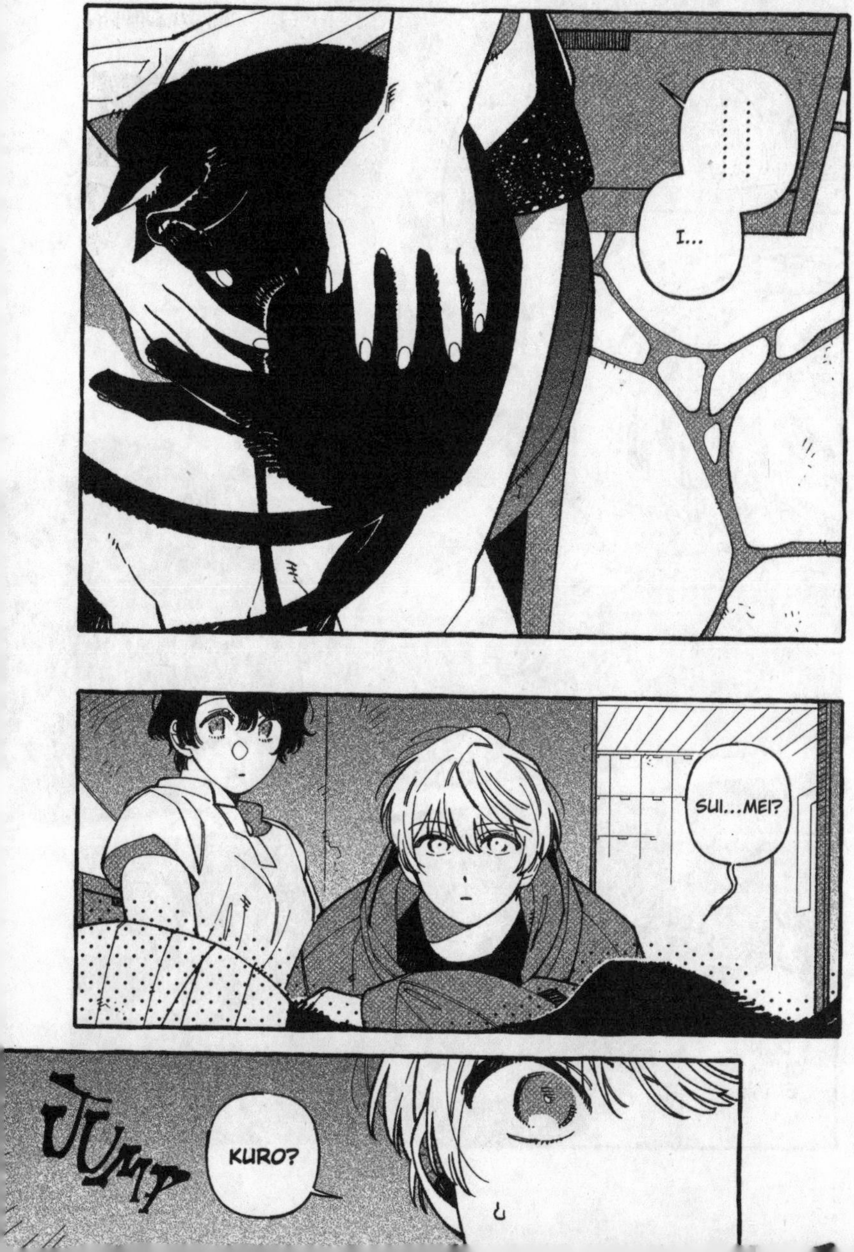
……
I...
SUI...MEI?
KURO?
JUMP

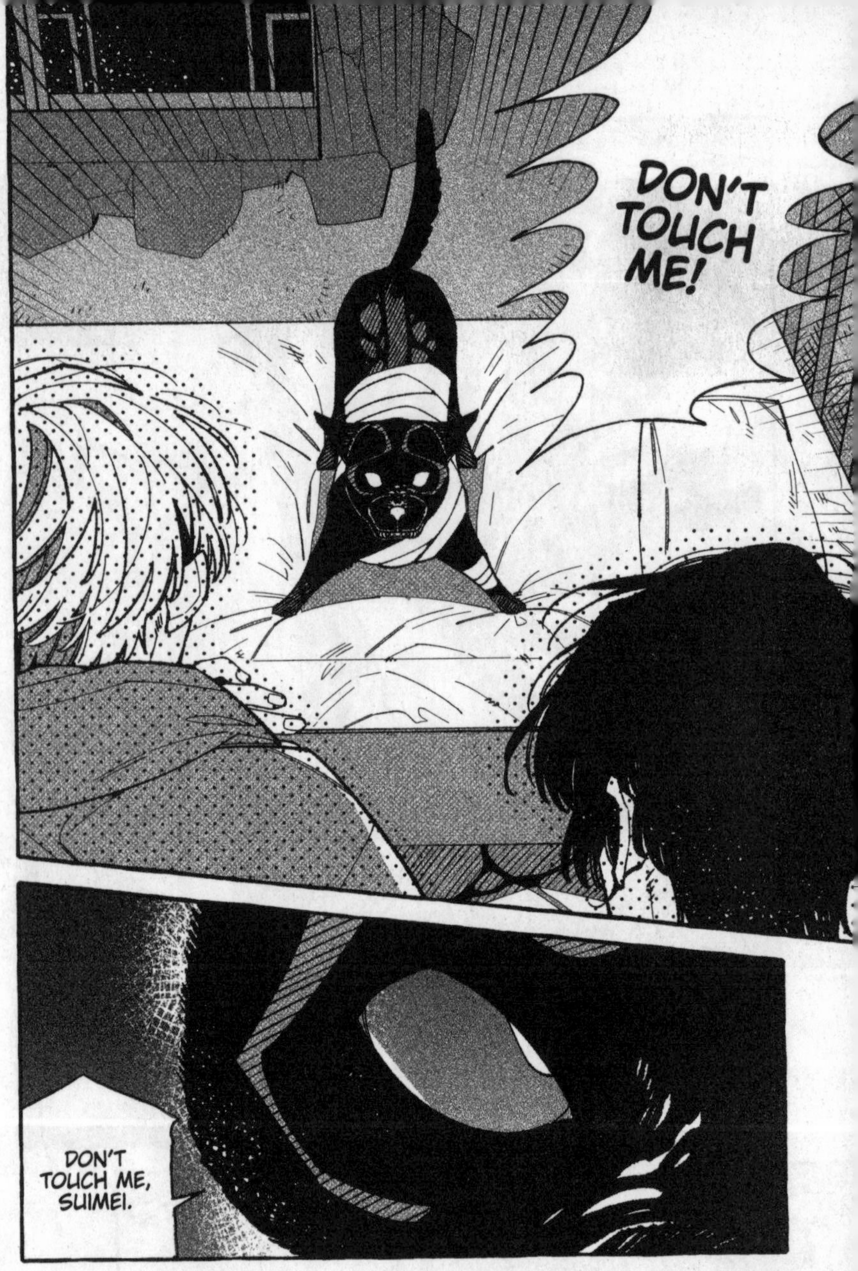
DON'T TOUCH ME!
DON'T TOUCH ME, SUIMEI.

THE HAUNTED BOOKSTORE

Gateway to a Parallel Universe

THE HAUNTED BOOKSTORE

Gateway to a Parallel Universe

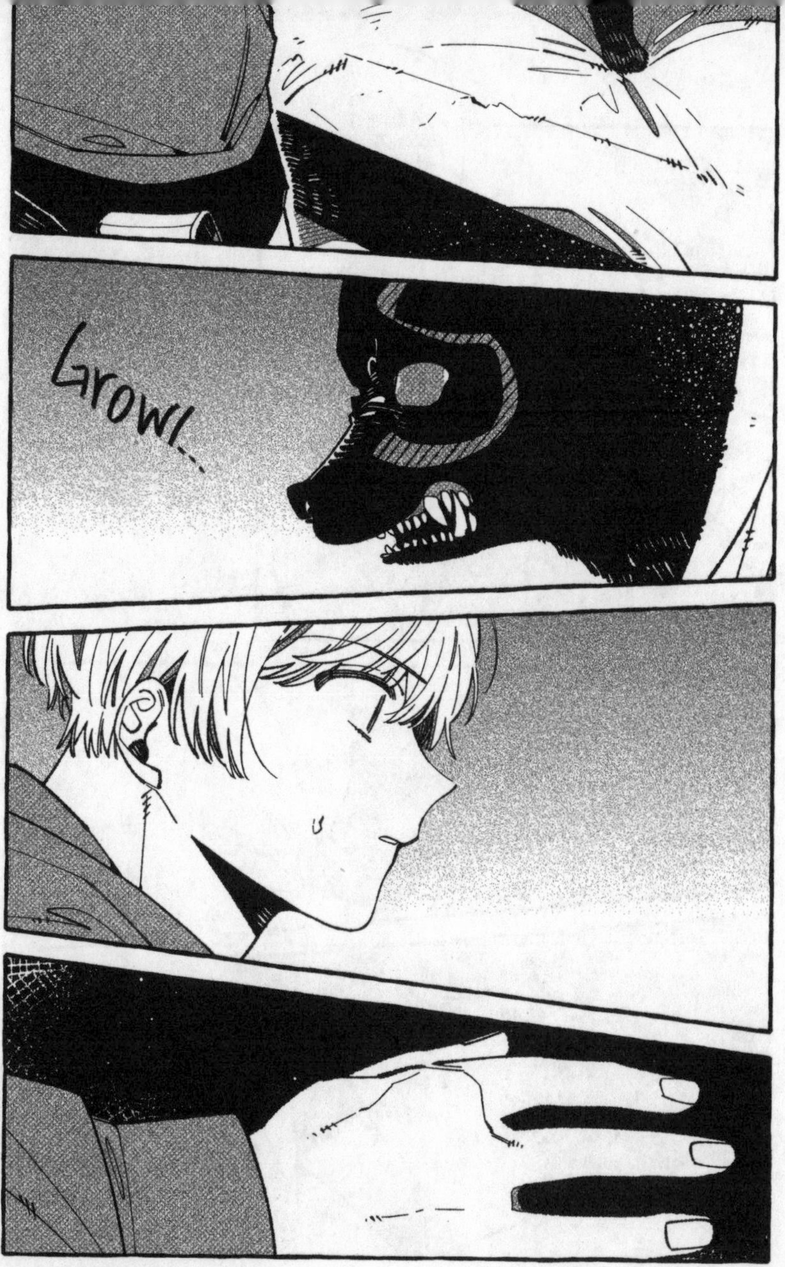
Growl...

CHAPTER 11
Humans and Spirits

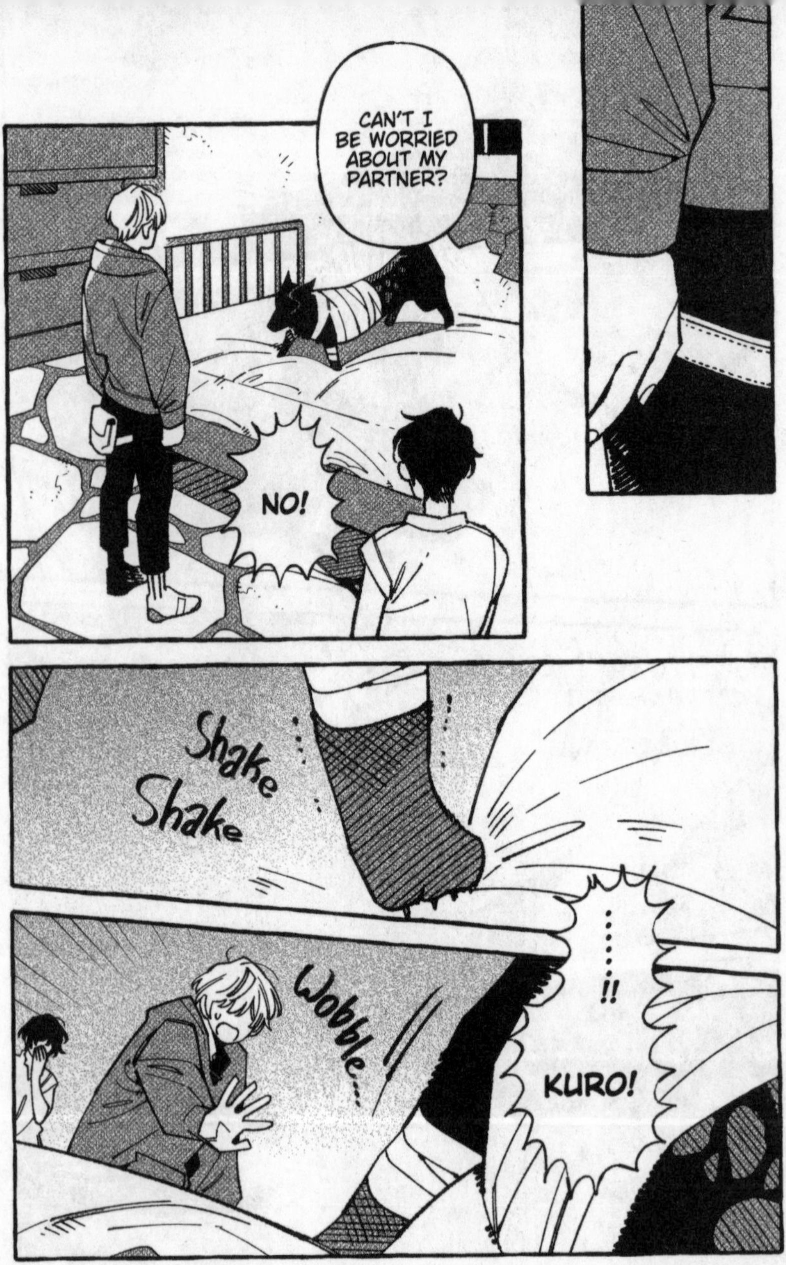
CAN'T I BE WORRIED ABOUT MY PARTNER?
NO!
......
Shake Shake
......
......!!
KURO!
Wobble...

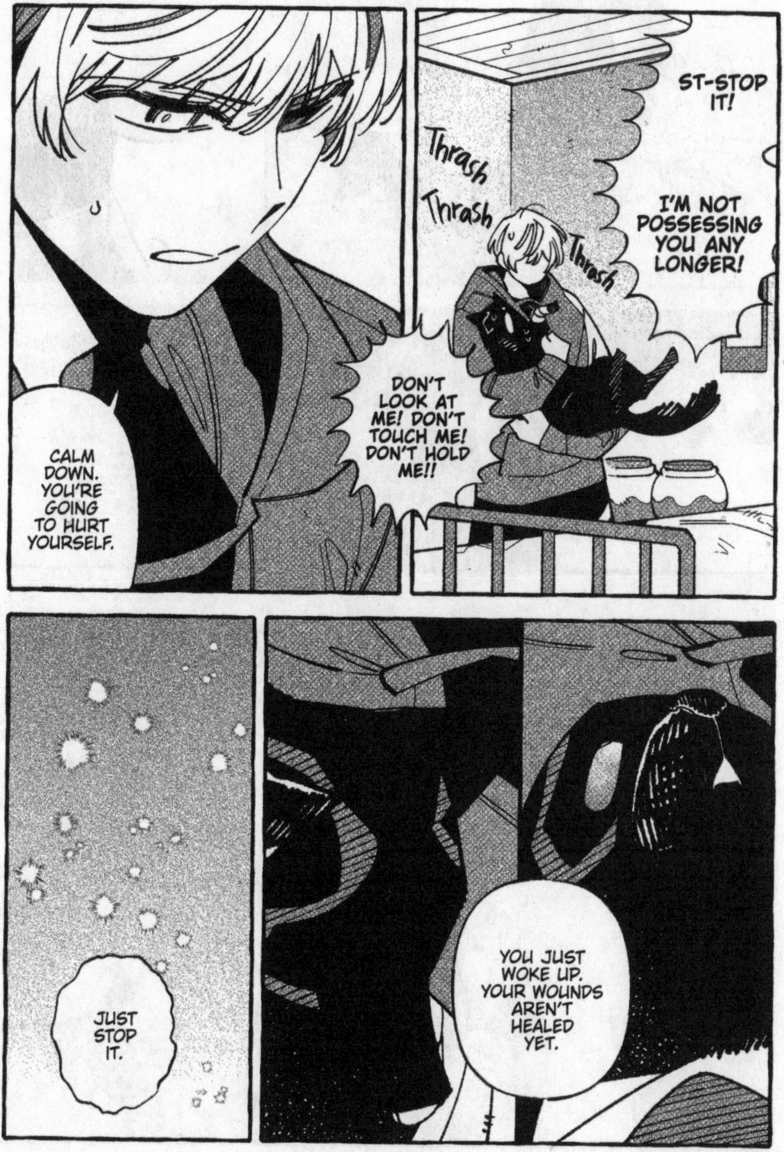
ST-STOP IT!
I'M NOT POSSESSING YOU ANY LONGER!
Thrash
Thrash
Thrash
DON'T LOOK AT ME! DON'T TOUCH ME! DON'T HOLD ME!!
CALM DOWN. YOU'RE GOING TO HURT YOURSELF.
YOU JUST WOKE UP. YOUR WOUNDS AREN'T HEALED YET.
JUST STOP IT.

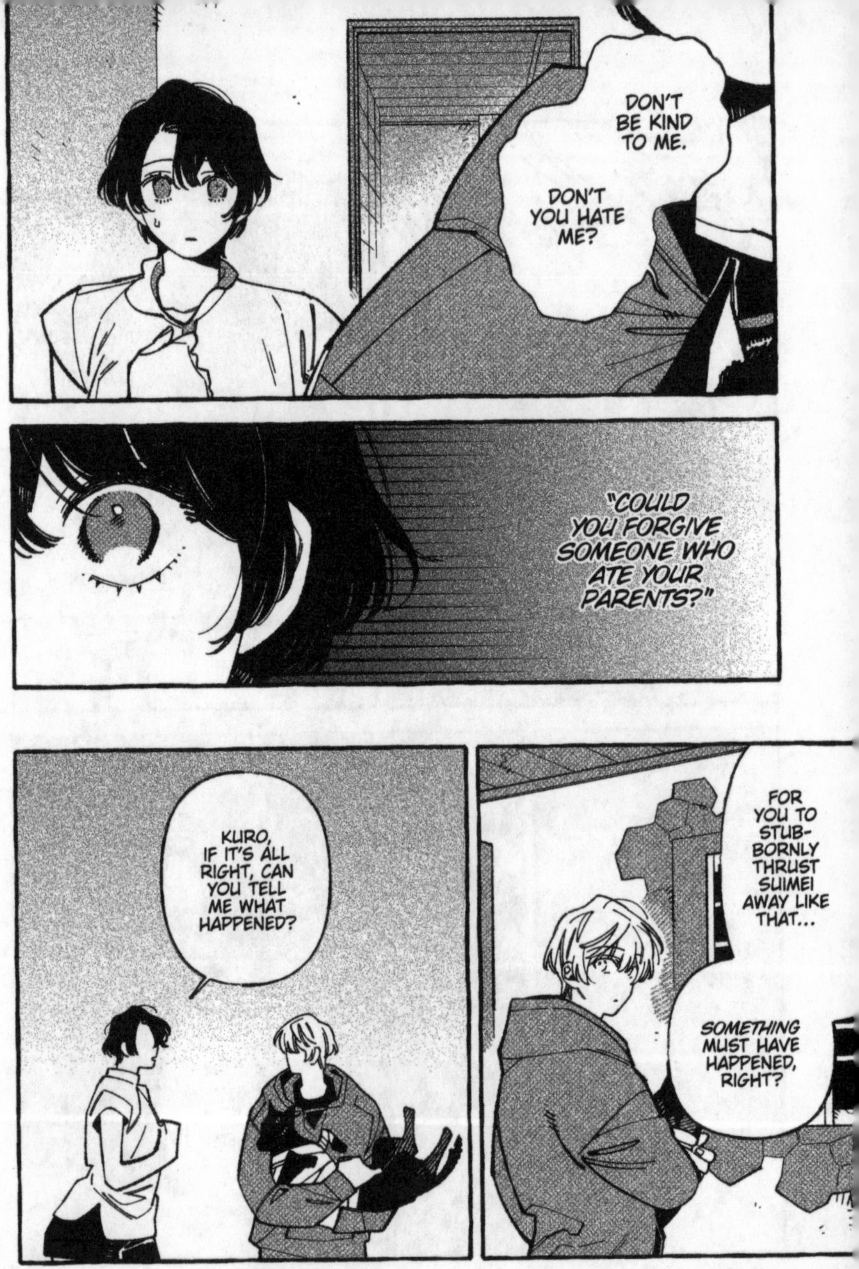
DON'T BE KIND TO ME.
DON'T YOU HATE ME?
"COULD YOU FORGIVE SOMEONE WHO ATE YOUR PARENTS?"
FOR YOU TO STUB-BORNLY THRUST SUIMEI AWAY LIKE THAT...
SOMETHING MUST HAVE HAPPENED, RIGHT?
KURO, IF IT'S ALL RIGHT, CAN YOU TELL ME WHAT HAPPENED?

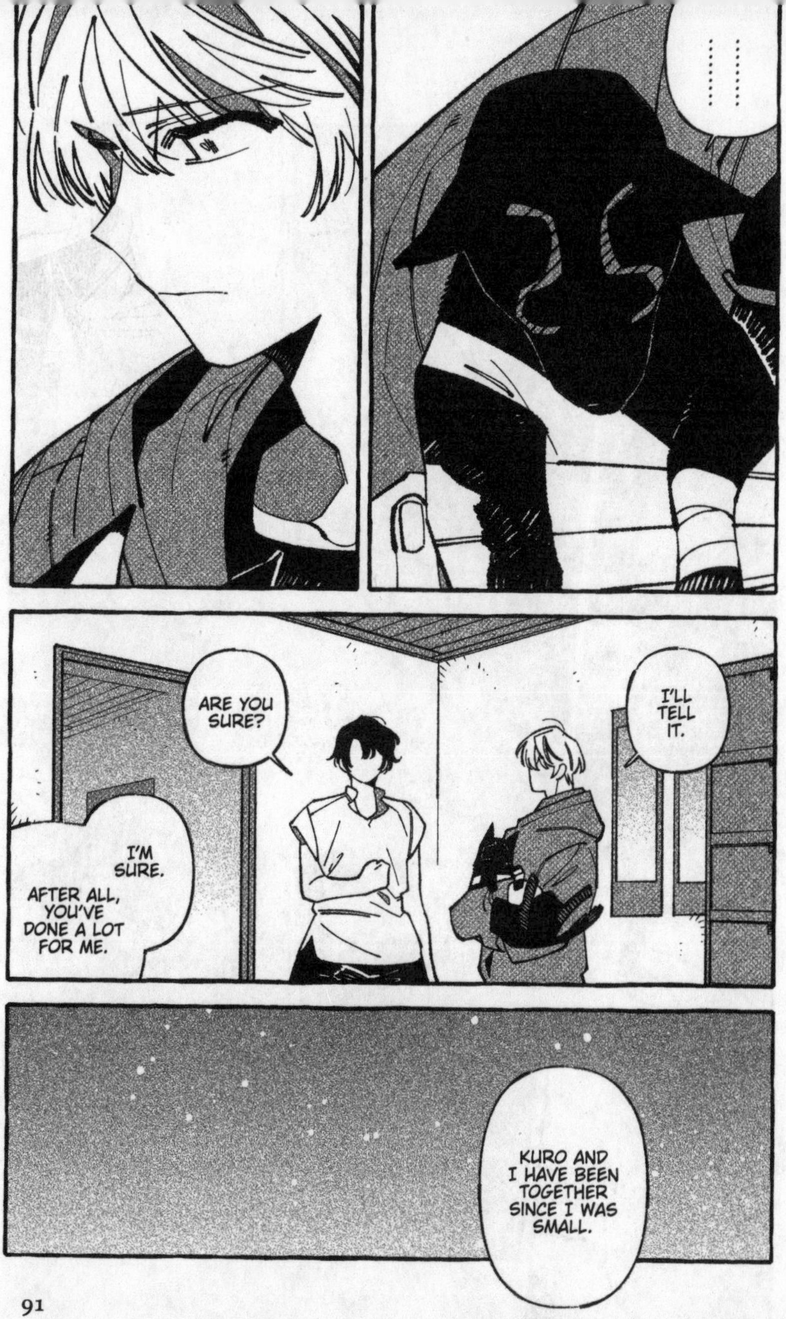
......
I'LL TELL IT.
ARE YOU SURE?
I'M SURE.
AFTER ALL, YOU'VE DONE A LOT FOR ME.
KURO AND I HAVE BEEN TOGETHER SINCE I WAS SMALL.

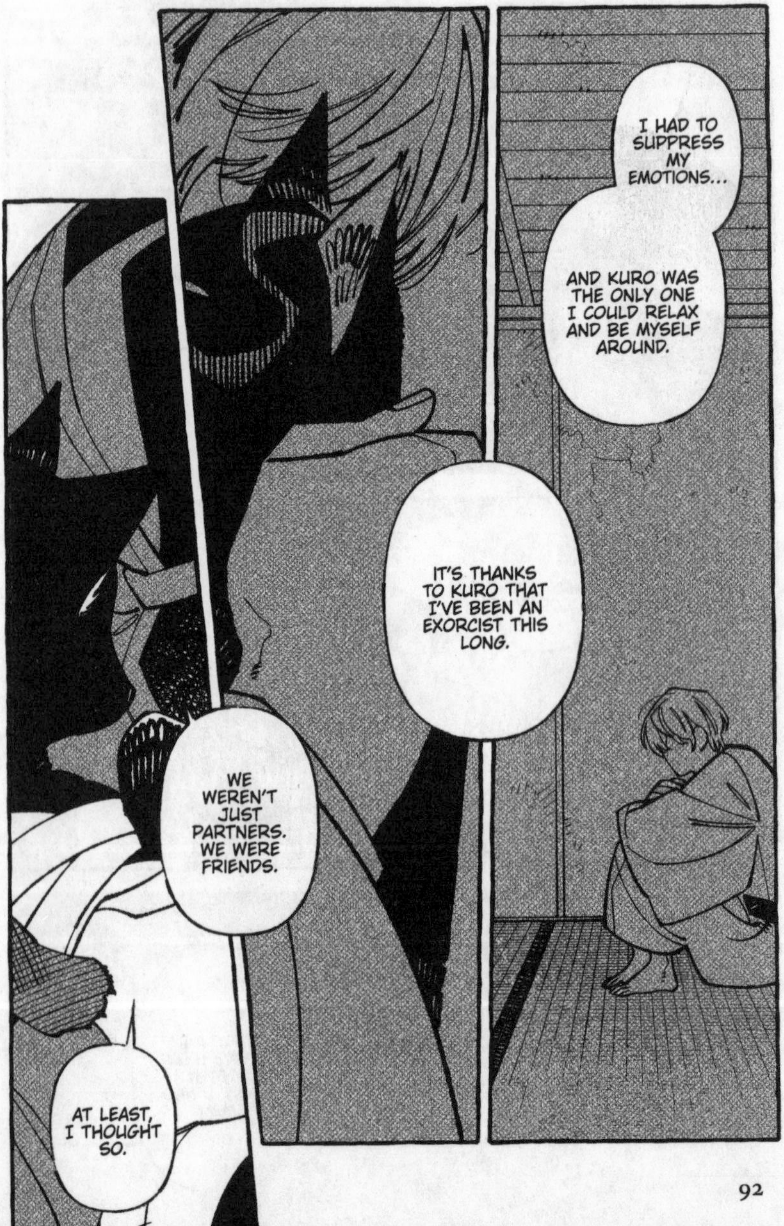
I HAD TO SUPPRESS MY EMOTIONS...
AND KURO WAS THE ONLY ONE I COULD RELAX AND BE MYSELF AROUND.
IT'S THANKS TO KURO THAT I'VE BEEN AN EXORCIST THIS LONG.
WE WEREN'T JUST PARTNERS. WE WERE FRIENDS.
AT LEAST, I THOUGHT SO.

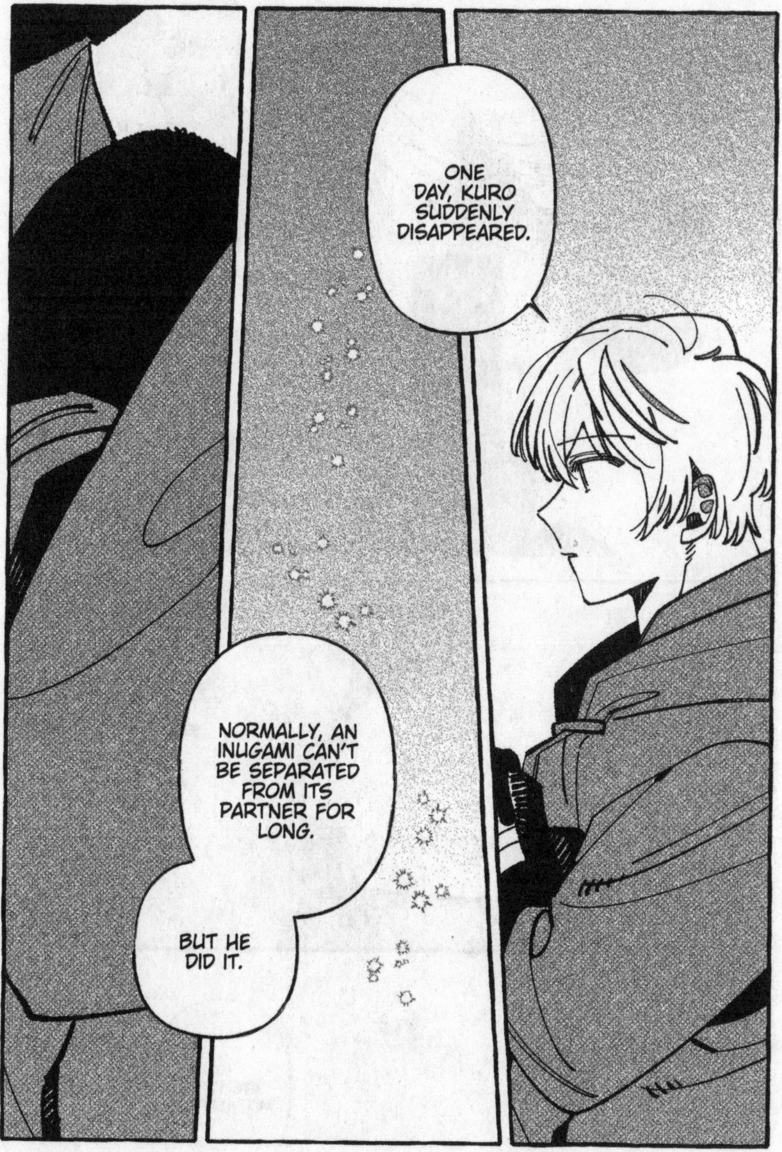
ONE DAY, KURO SUDDENLY DISAPPEARED.
NORMALLY, AN INUGAMI CAN'T BE SEPARATED FROM ITS PARTNER FOR LONG.
BUT HE DID IT.

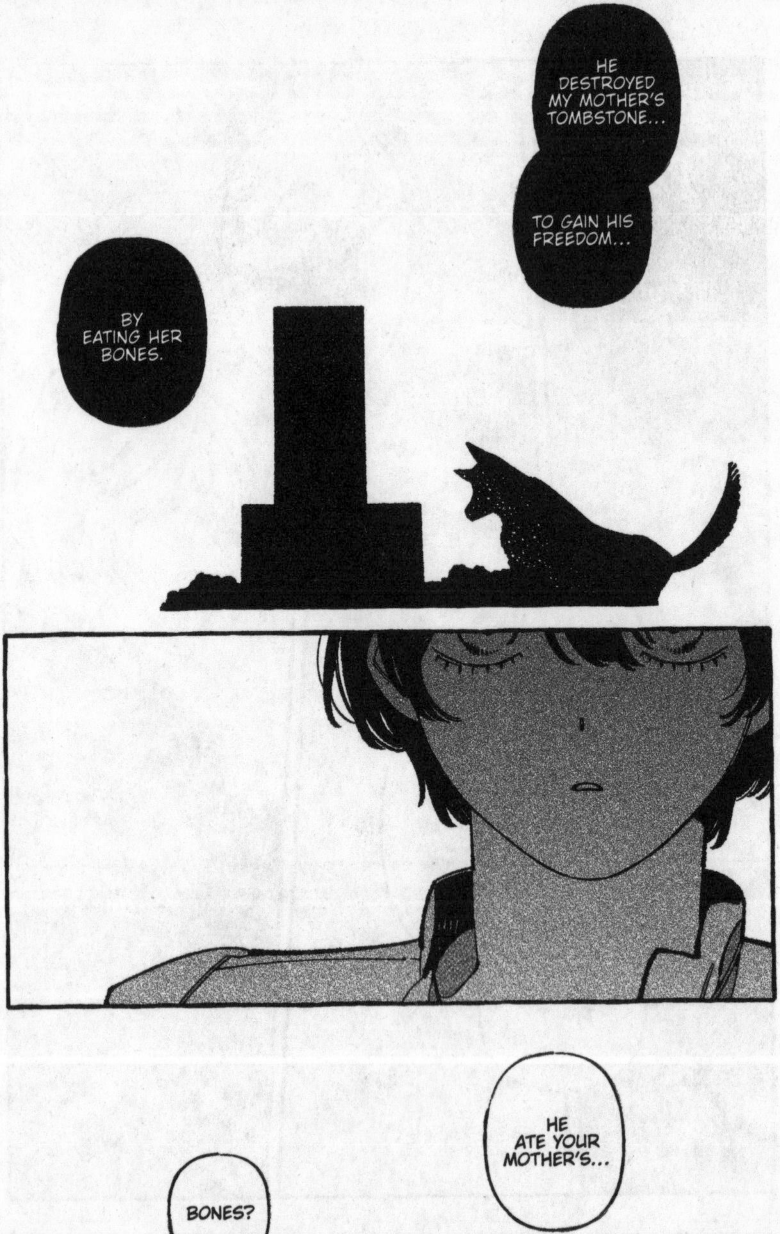
HE DESTROYED MY MOTHER'S TOMBSTONE...
TO GAIN HIS FREEDOM...
BY EATING HER BONES.
HE ATE YOUR MOTHER'S...
BONES?

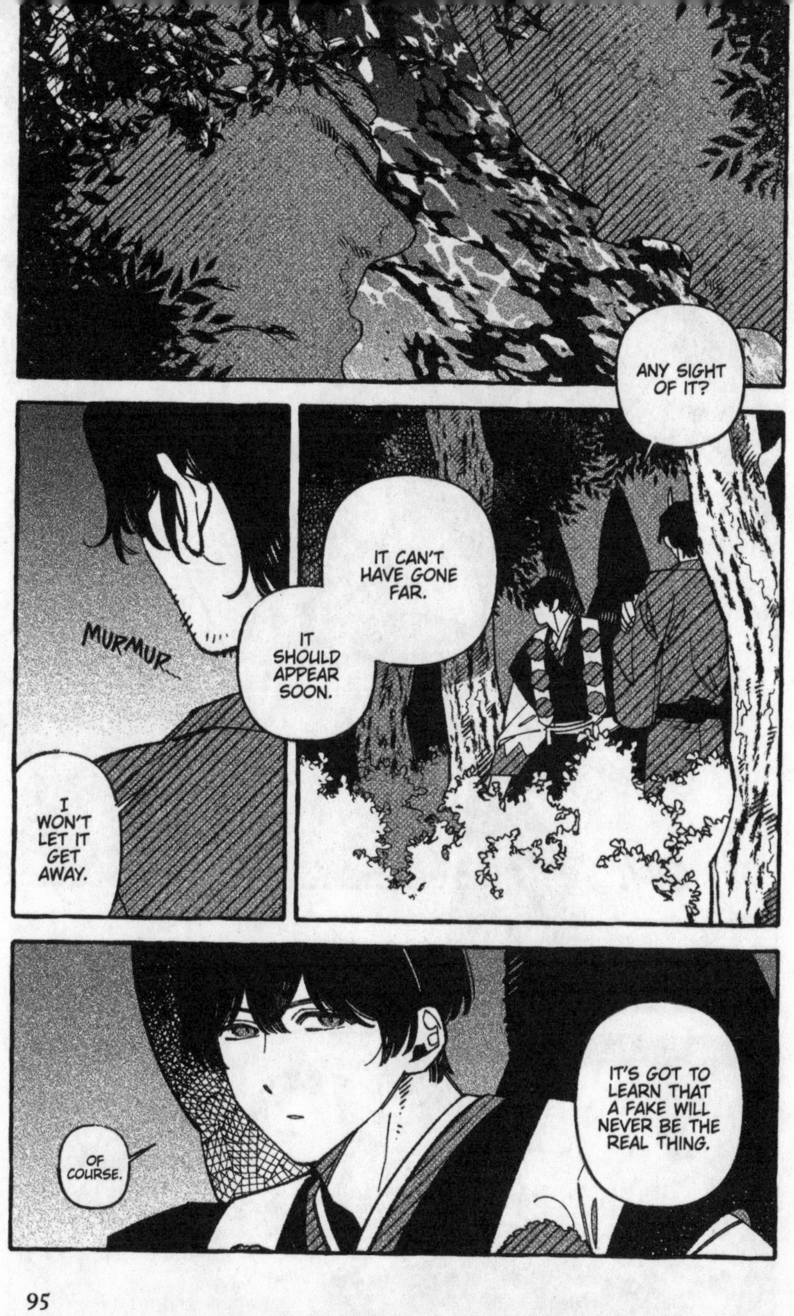
ANY SIGHT OF IT?
IT CAN'T HAVE GONE FAR.
IT SHOULD APPEAR SOON.
MURMUR
I WON'T LET IT GET AWAY.
IT'S GOT TO LEARN THAT A FAKE WILL NEVER BE THE REAL THING.
OF COURSE.

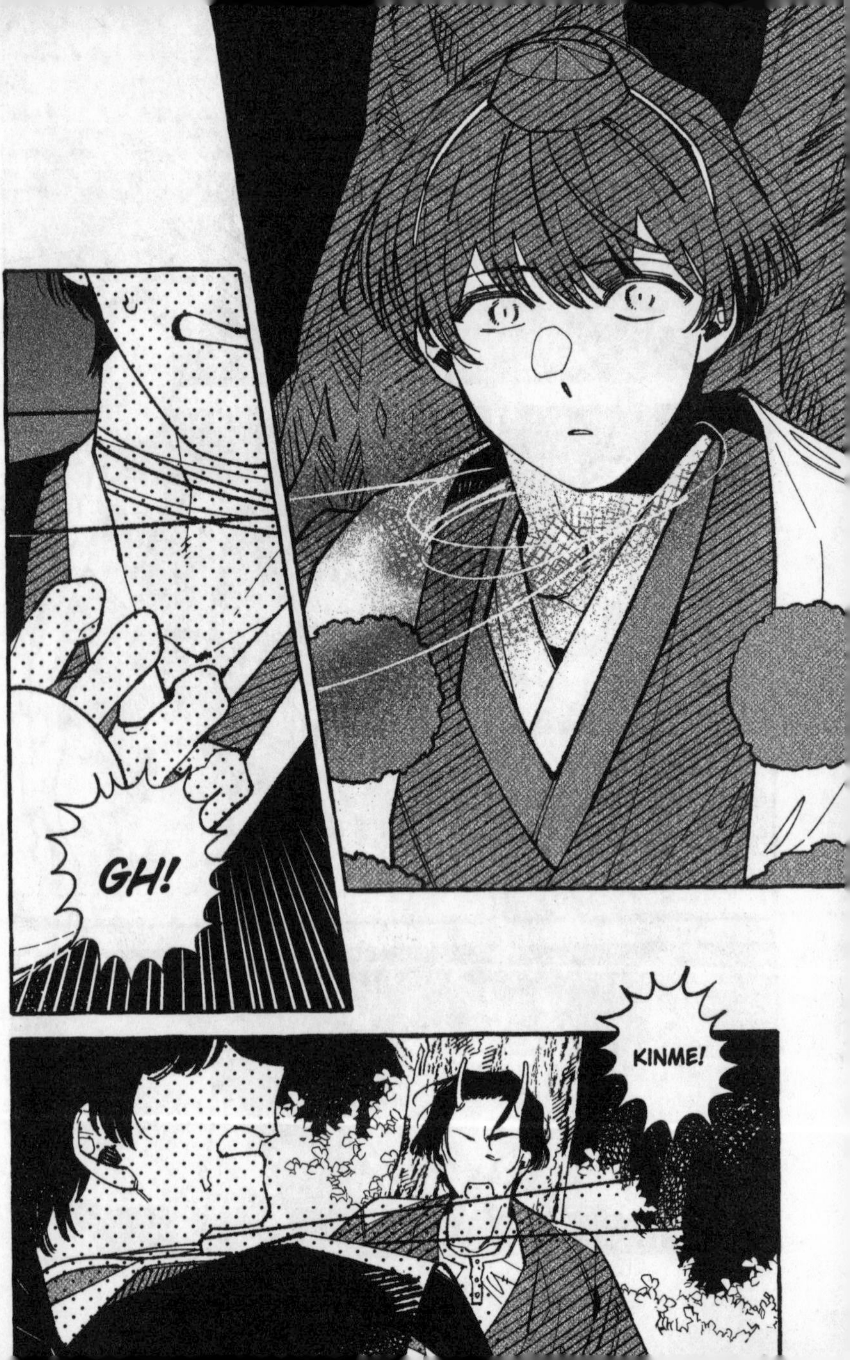
GH!
KINME!

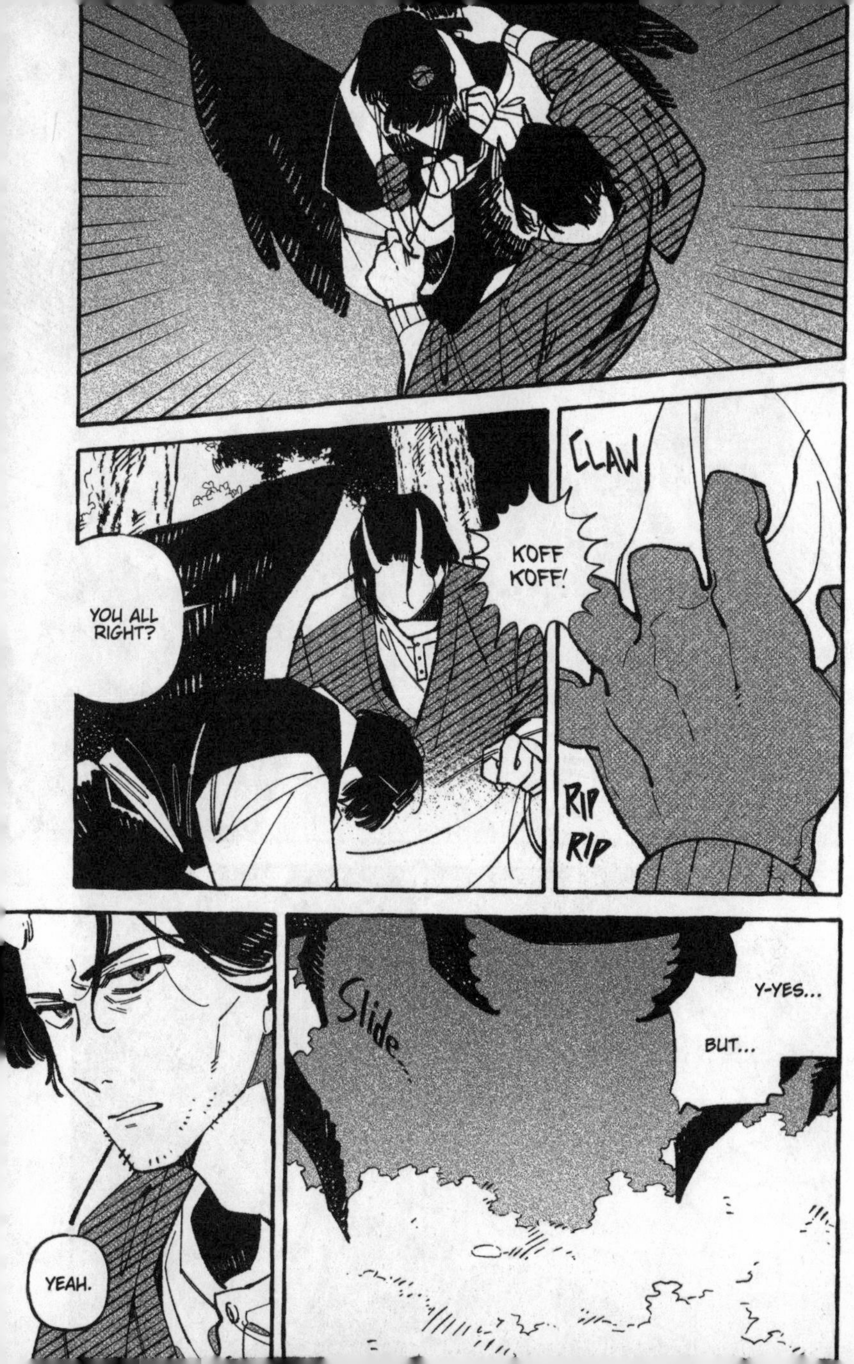
CLAW
RIP RIP
KOFF KOFF!
YOU ALL RIGHT?
Y-YES...
BUT...
Slide...
YEAH.

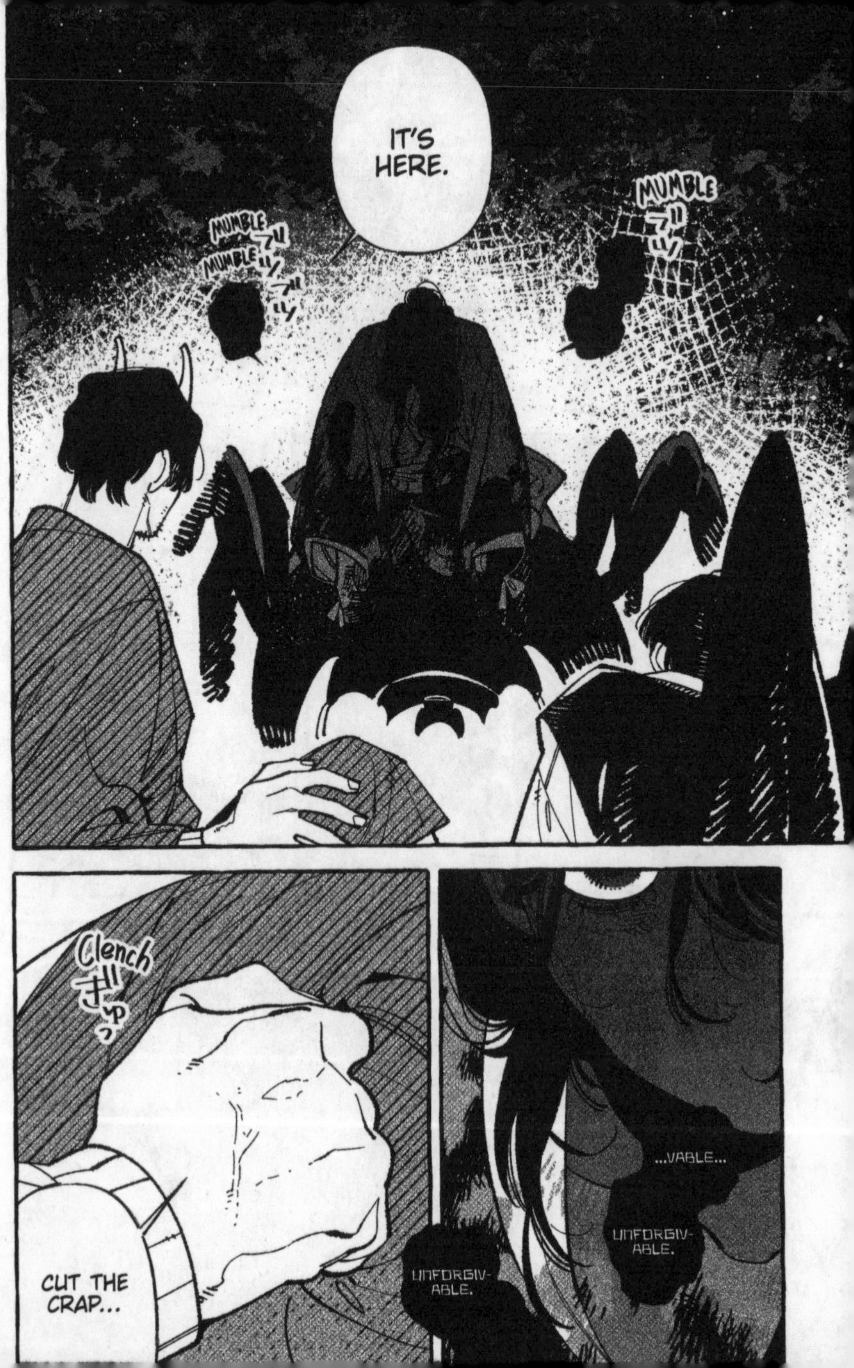
IT'S HERE.
MUMBLE
MUMBLE
MUMBLE
...VABLE...
UNFORGIV-ABLE.
UNFORGIV-ABLE.
Clench
CUT THE CRAP...

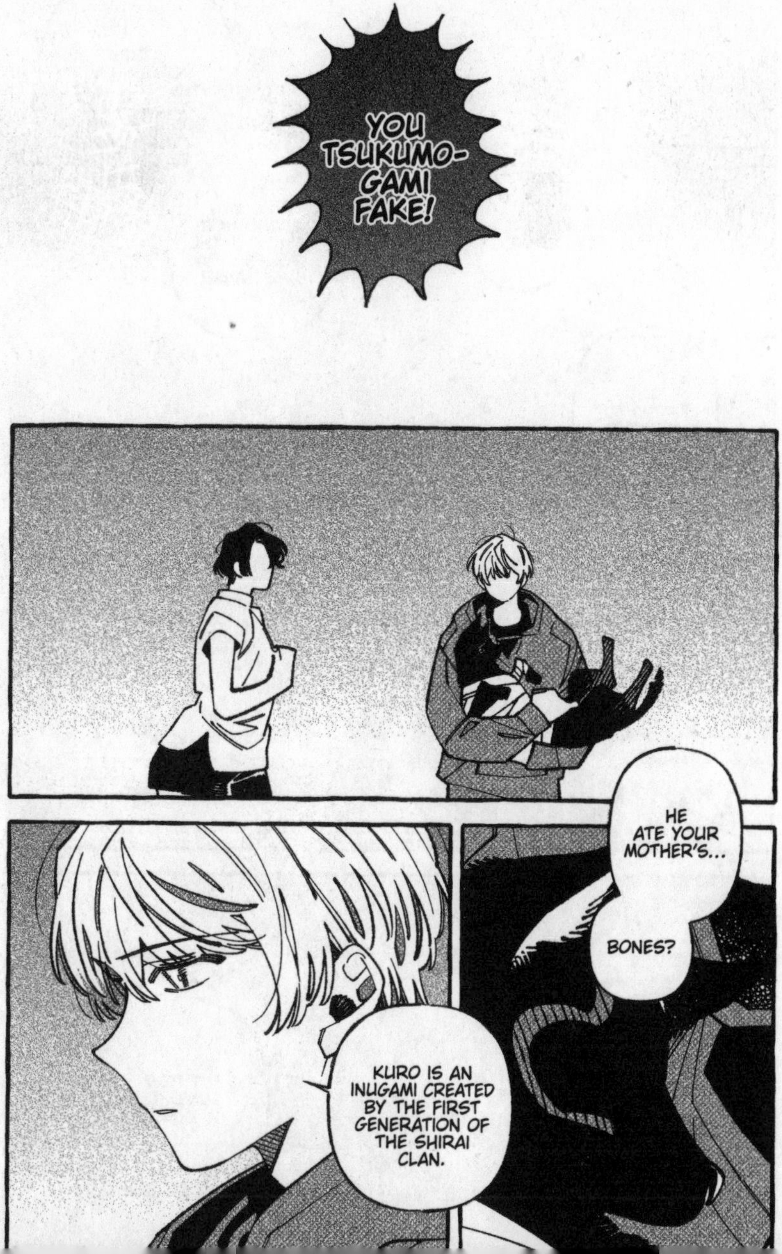
YOU TSUKUMO-GAMI FAKE!
HE ATE YOUR MOTHER'S...
BONES?
KURO IS AN INUGAMI CREATED BY THE FIRST GENERATION OF THE SHIRAI CLAN.

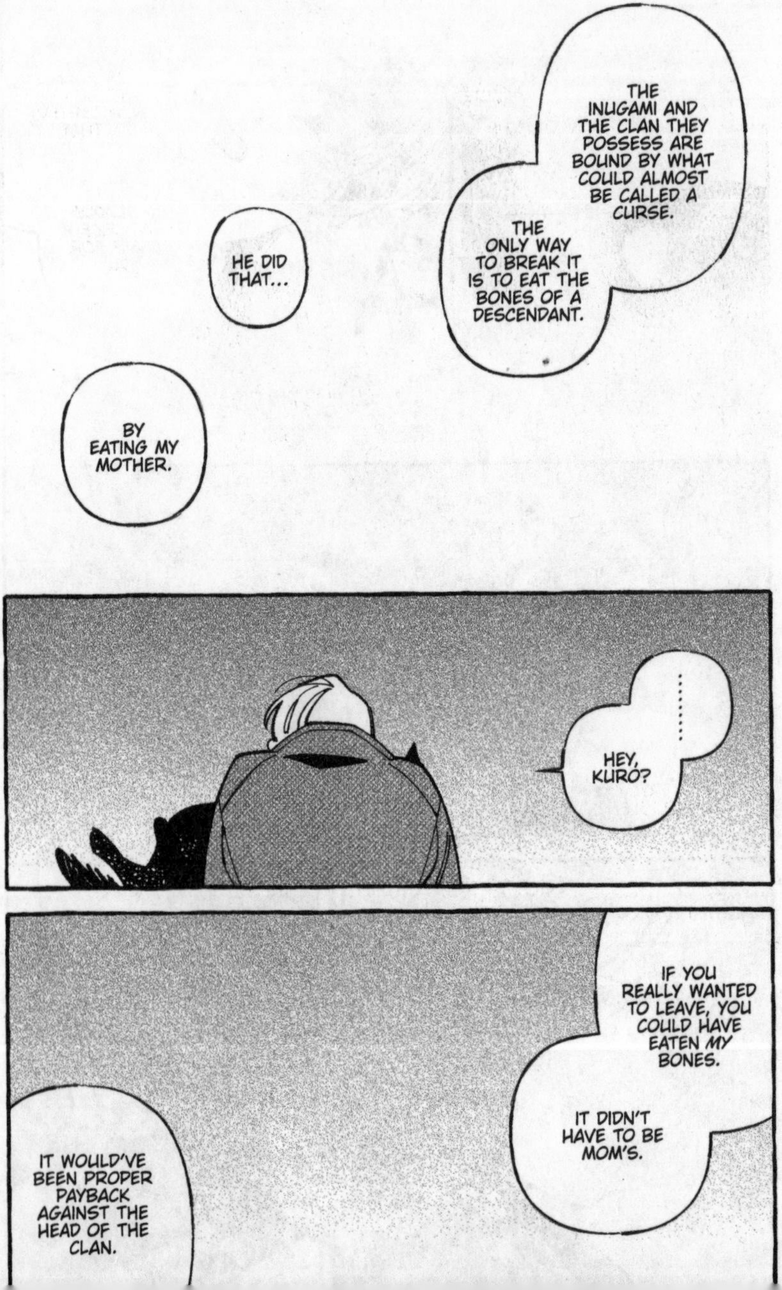
THE INUGAMI AND THE CLAN THEY POSSESS ARE BOUND BY WHAT COULD ALMOST BE CALLED A CURSE.
THE ONLY WAY TO BREAK IT IS TO EAT THE BONES OF A DESCENDANT.
HE DID THAT...
BY EATING MY MOTHER.
......
HEY, KURO?
IF YOU REALLY WANTED TO LEAVE, YOU COULD HAVE EATEN *MY* BONES.
IT DIDN'T HAVE TO BE MOM'S.
IT WOULD'VE BEEN PROPER PAYBACK AGAINST THE HEAD OF THE CLAN.

IF YOU WANTED TO BE FREE, I WOULD HAVE ACCEPTED THAT.

I'D GLADLY SACRIFICE MYSELF FOR YOU.

YOU'RE IMPORTANT TO ME.

SUIMEI...

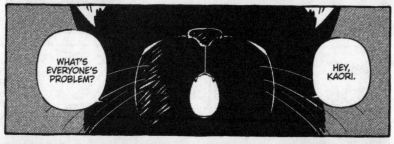

WHAT'S EVERYONE'S PROBLEM?

HEY, KAORI.

Turn

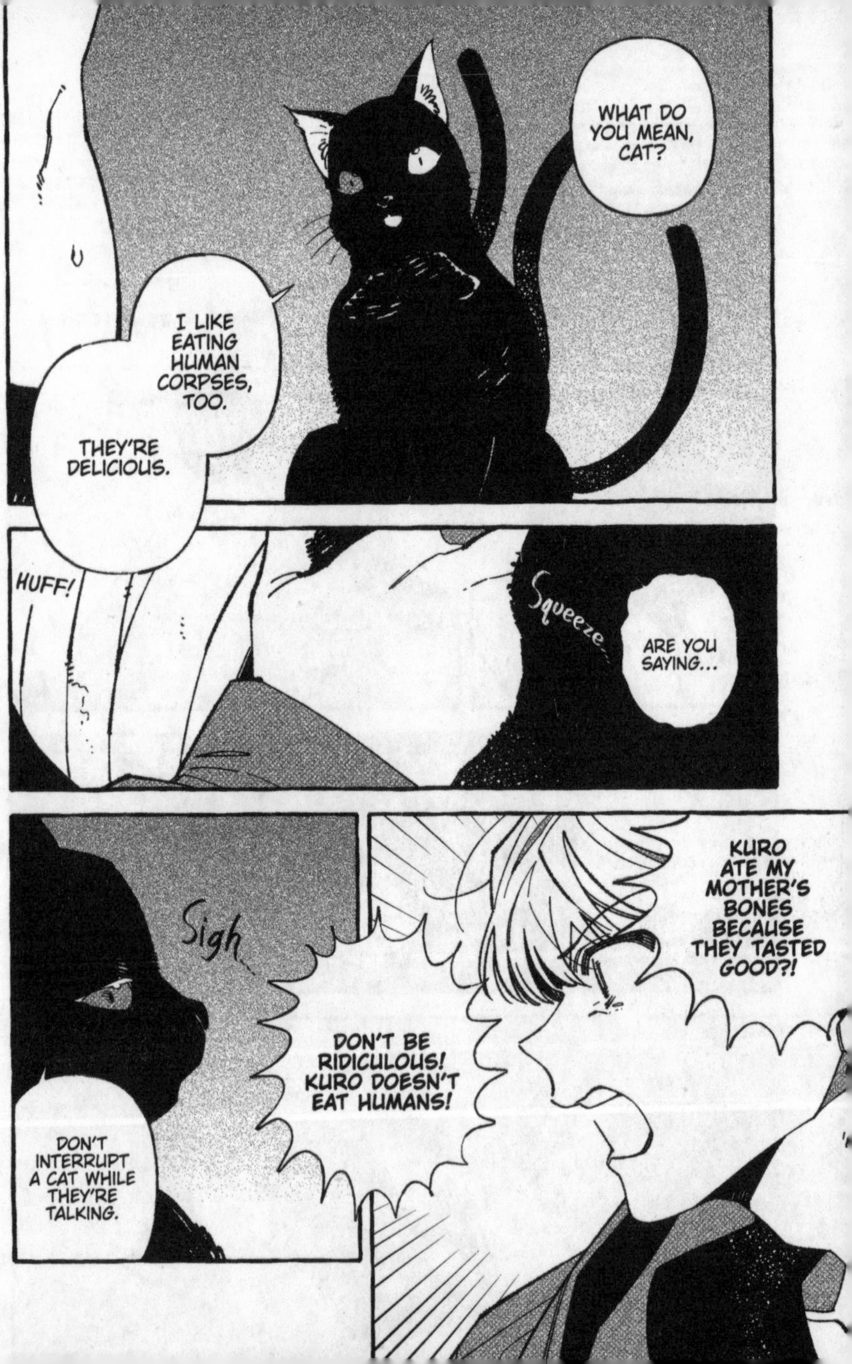
WHAT DO YOU MEAN, CAT?
I LIKE EATING HUMAN CORPSES, TOO.
THEY'RE DELICIOUS.
ARE YOU SAYING...
Squeeze...
HUFF!
KURO ATE MY MOTHER'S BONES BECAUSE THEY TASTED GOOD?!
DON'T BE RIDICULOUS! KURO DOESN'T EAT HUMANS!
Sigh...
DON'T INTERRUPT A CAT WHILE THEY'RE TALKING.

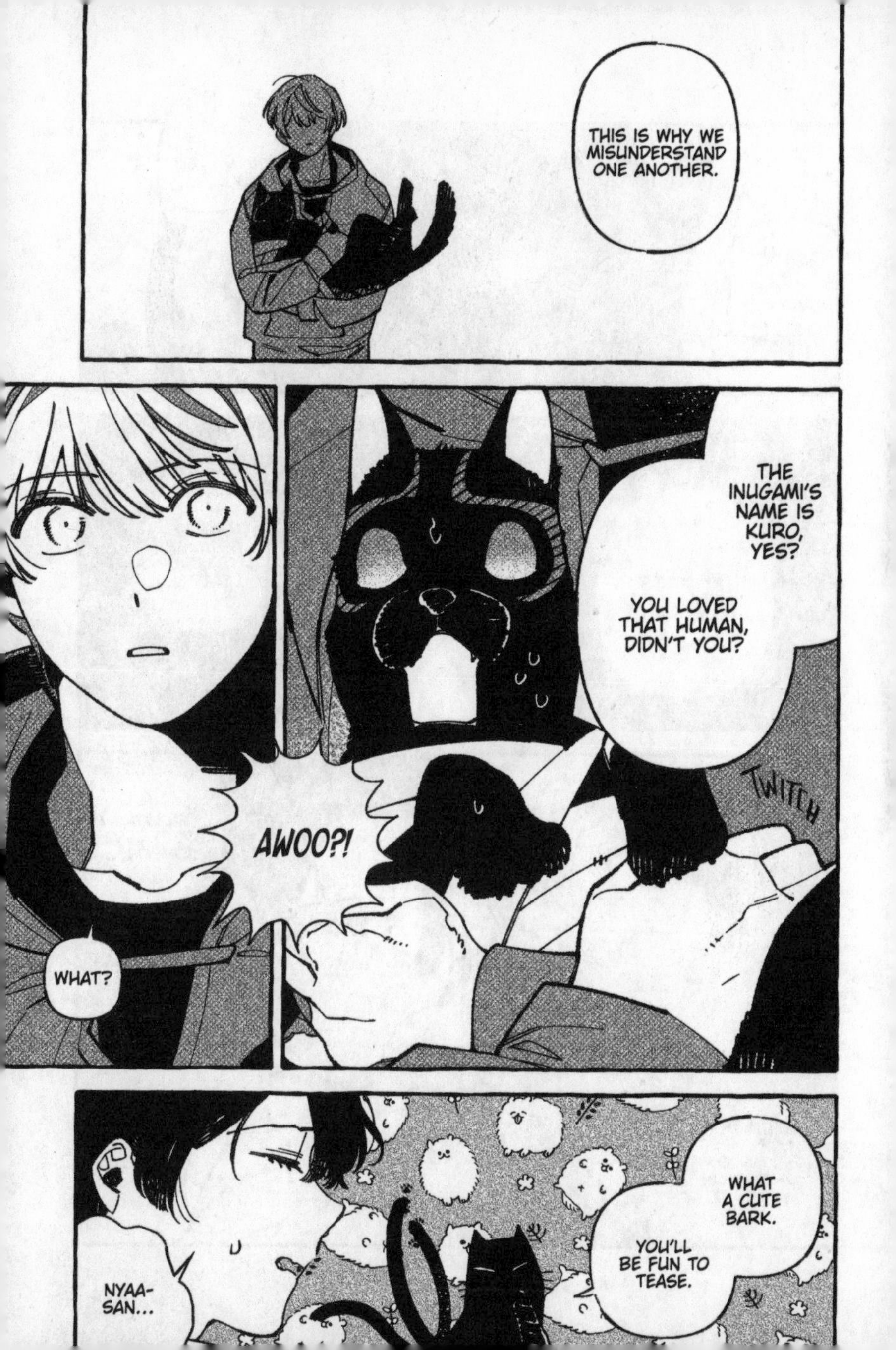
THIS IS WHY WE MISUNDERSTAND ONE ANOTHER.
THE INUGAMI'S NAME IS KURO, YES?
YOU LOVED THAT HUMAN, DIDN'T YOU?
TWITCH
AWOO?!
WHAT?
WHAT A CUTE BARK.
YOU'LL BE FUN TO TEASE.
NYAA-SAN...

WHEN I EAT HUMANS...
I DO IT FOR ONE OF TWO REASONS.
ONE IS BECAUSE THEY'RE TASTY.
THE OTHER IS BECAUSE I LOVE THEM.
THE MORE A SPIRIT LOVES SOMEONE...
THE STRONGER THE DESIRE TO EAT THEM.
I WANT TO CHEW THEIR INTESTINES, GNAW THEIR BONES, DRINK THEIR BLOOD.
I WANT THAT IMPORTANT PERSON TO BECOME PART OF ME.
DOING THAT HELPS KEEP THE MEMORY OF THEM IN MY HEART.

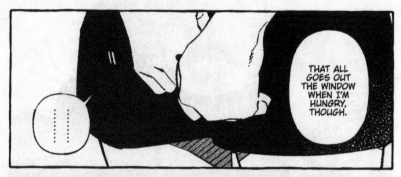

THAT ALL GOES OUT THE WINDOW WHEN I'M HUNGRY, THOUGH.

......

I ACTUALLY PROMISED NYAA-SAN THAT SHE GETS TO EAT ME WHEN I DIE.

WHAT?

PURR PURR

TO A HUMAN, EATING THEIR REMAINS MIGHT FEEL LIKE A BETRAYAL.

BUT IT MEANS SOMETHING DIFFERENT FOR A SPIRIT.

THAT'S WHY I THINK YOU AND KURO SHOULD TALK ABOUT THIS.

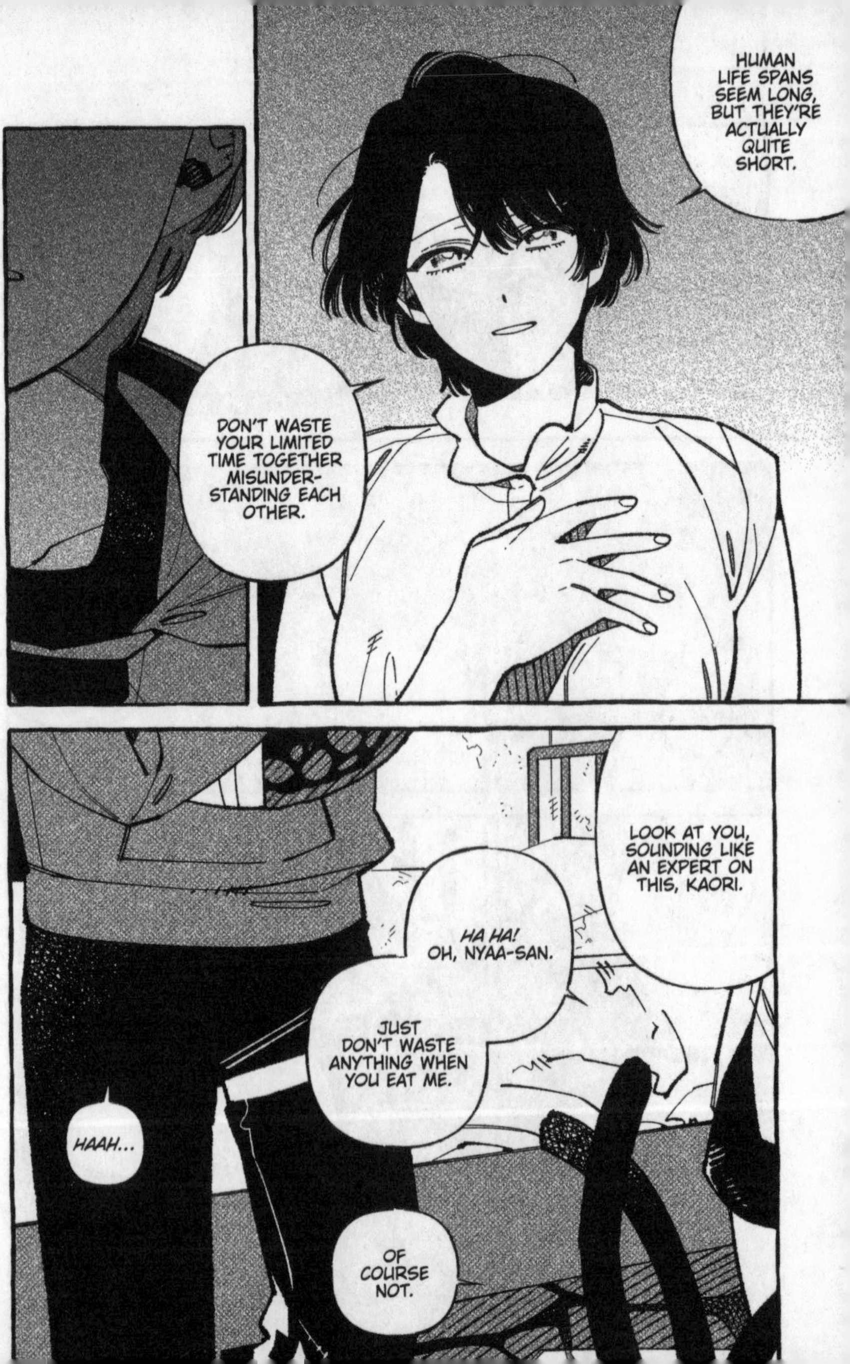
HUMAN LIFE SPANS SEEM LONG, BUT THEY'RE ACTUALLY QUITE SHORT.
DON'T WASTE YOUR LIMITED TIME TOGETHER MISUNDER-STANDING EACH OTHER.
LOOK AT YOU, SOUNDING LIKE AN EXPERT ON THIS, KAORI.
HA HA! OH, NYAA-SAN.
JUST DON'T WASTE ANYTHING WHEN YOU EAT ME.
HAAH...
OF COURSE NOT.

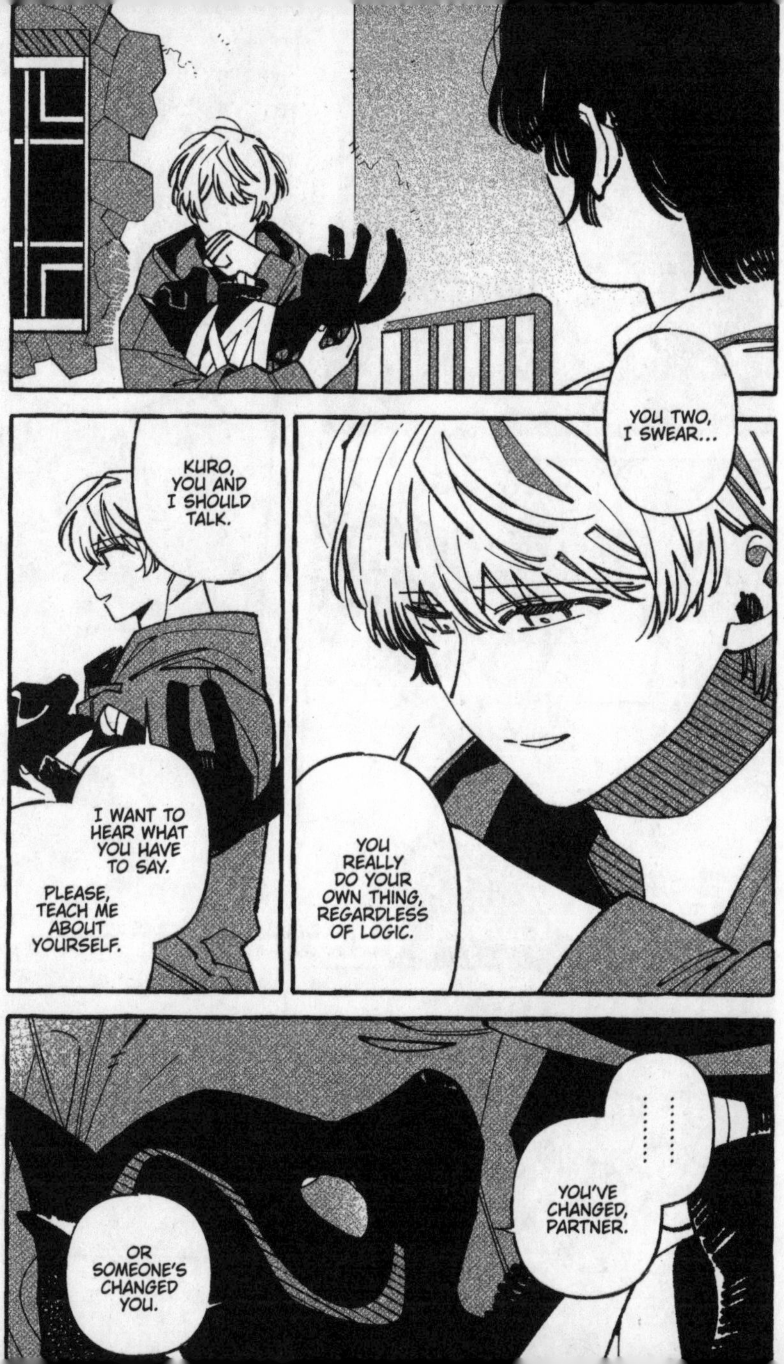
YOU TWO, I SWEAR...
YOU REALLY DO YOUR OWN THING, REGARDLESS OF LOGIC.
KURO, YOU AND I SHOULD TALK.
I WANT TO HEAR WHAT YOU HAVE TO SAY.
PLEASE, TEACH ME ABOUT YOURSELF.
......
YOU'VE CHANGED, PARTNER.
OR SOMEONE'S CHANGED YOU.

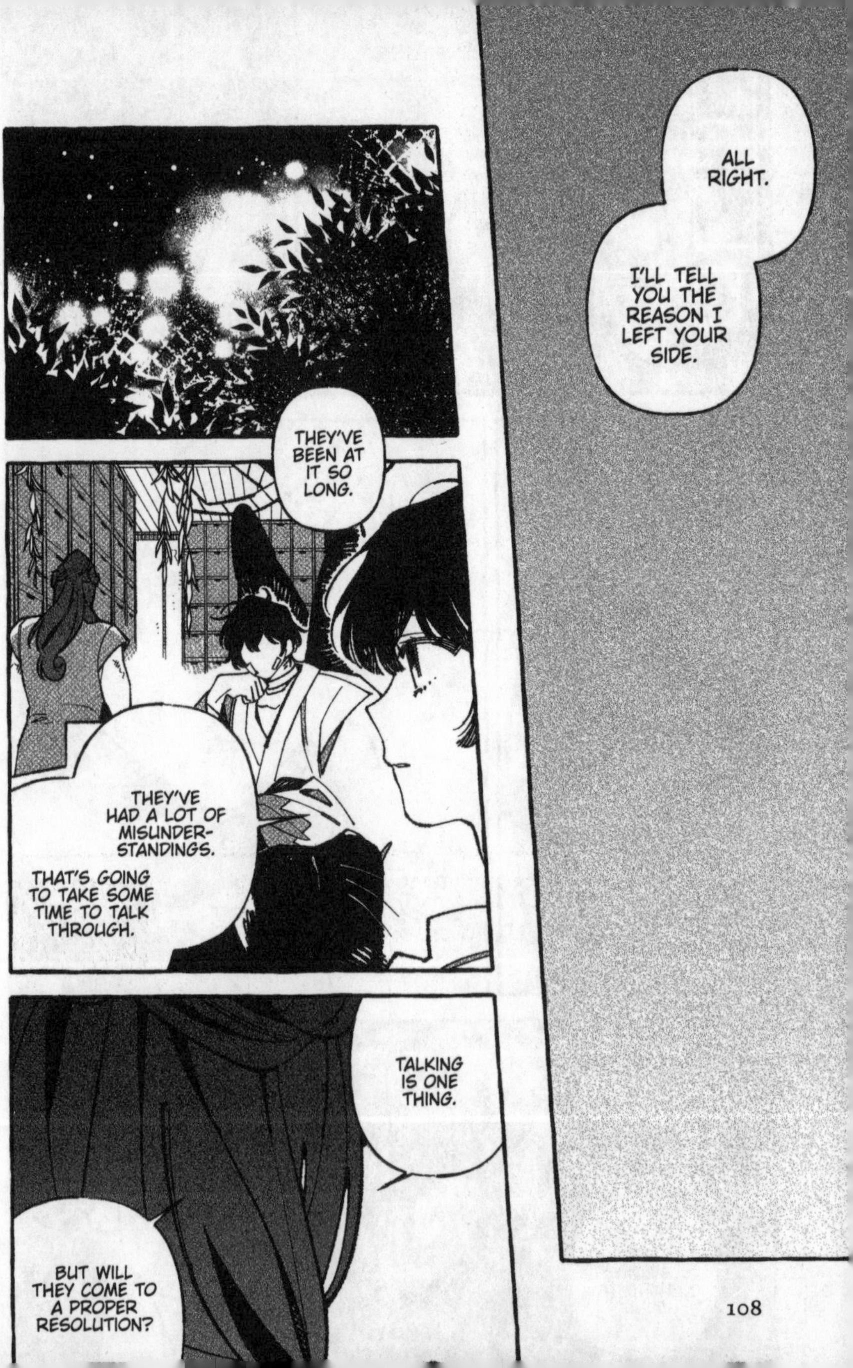
ALL RIGHT.
I'LL TELL YOU THE REASON I LEFT YOUR SIDE.
THEY'VE BEEN AT IT SO LONG.
THEY'VE HAD A LOT OF MISUNDER-STANDINGS.
THAT'S GOING TO TAKE SOME TIME TO TALK THROUGH.
TALKING IS ONE THING.
BUT WILL THEY COME TO A PROPER RESOLUTION?

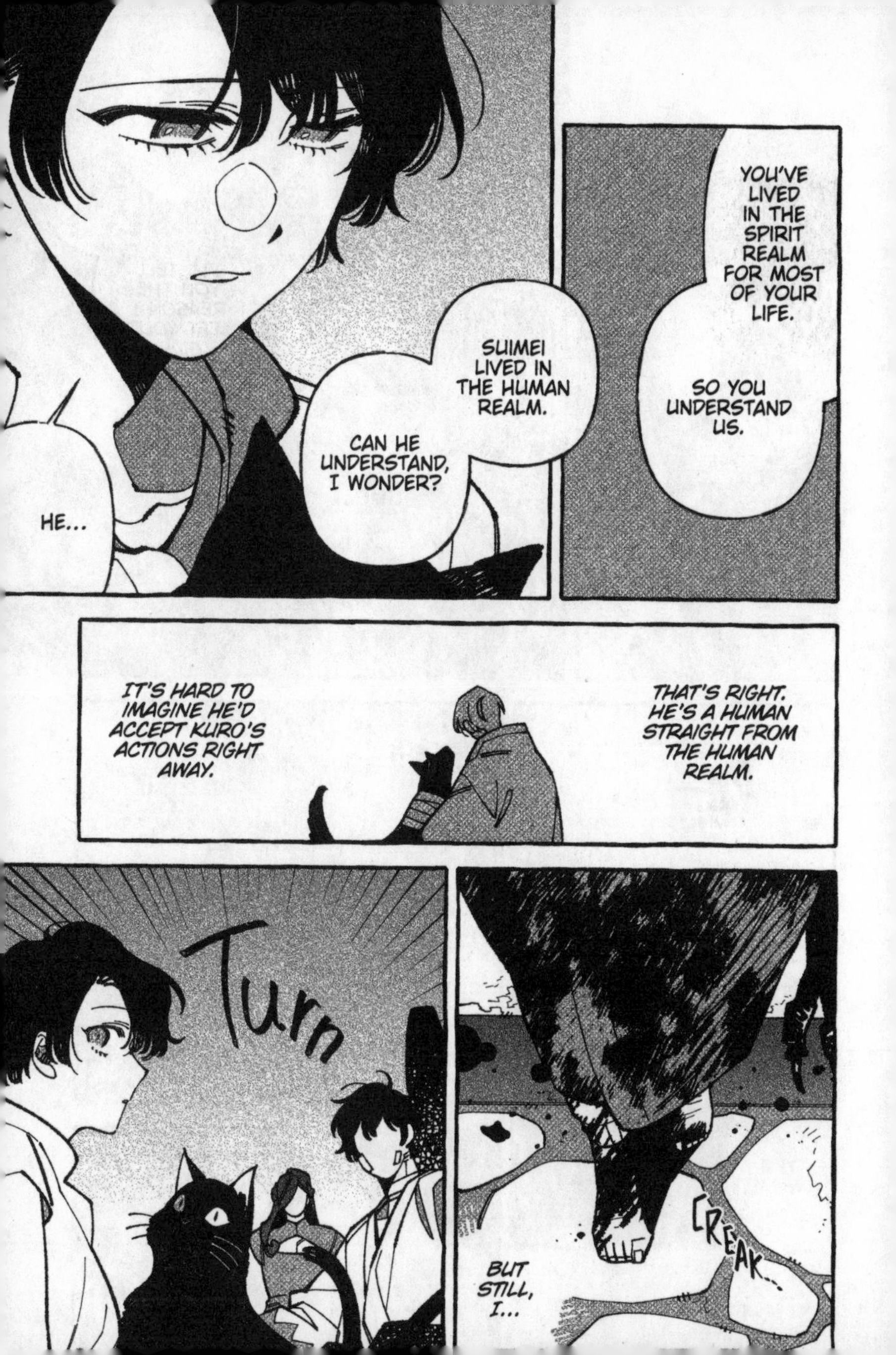
YOU'VE LIVED IN THE SPIRIT REALM FOR MOST OF YOUR LIFE.
SO YOU UNDERSTAND US.
SUIMEI LIVED IN THE HUMAN REALM.
CAN HE UNDERSTAND, I WONDER?
HE...
THAT'S RIGHT. HE'S A HUMAN STRAIGHT FROM THE HUMAN REALM.
IT'S HARD TO IMAGINE HE'D ACCEPT KURO'S ACTIONS RIGHT AWAY.
CREAK...
BUT STILL, I...
Turn

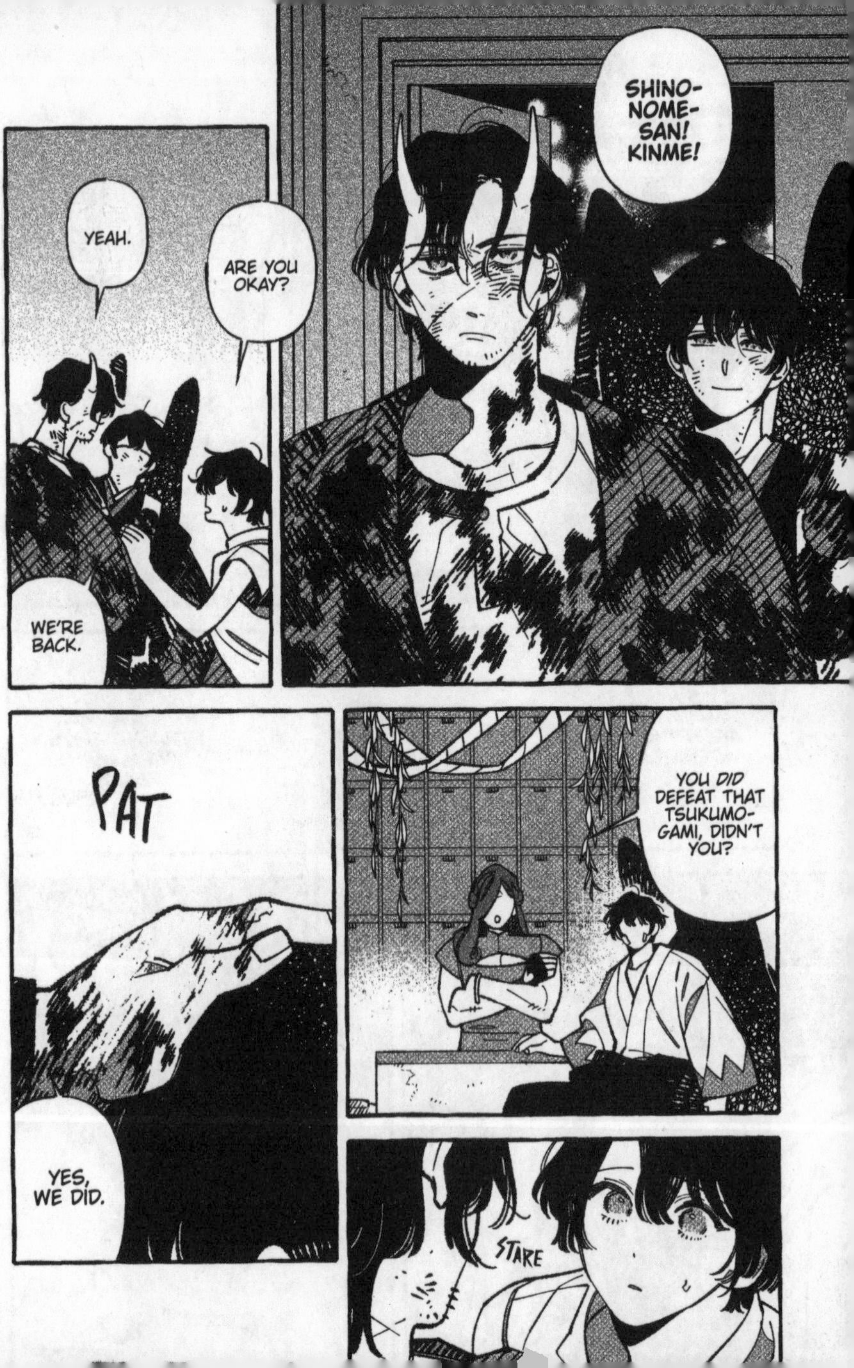
SHINO-NOME-SAN! KINME!
ARE YOU OKAY?
YEAH.
WE'RE BACK.
YOU *DID* DEFEAT THAT TSUKUMO-GAMI, DIDN'T YOU?
STARE
PAT
YES, WE DID.

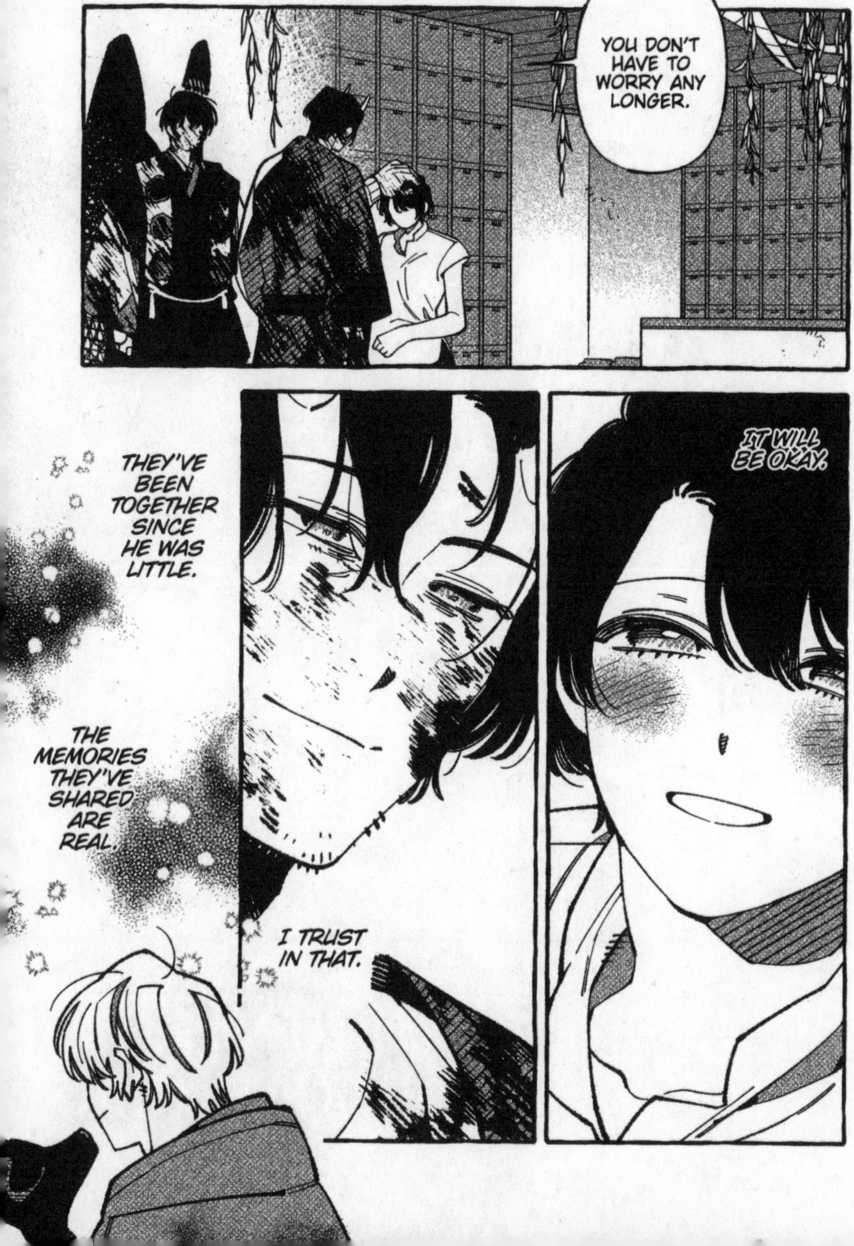
YOU DON'T HAVE TO WORRY ANY LONGER.
IT WILL BE OKAY.
THEY'VE BEEN TOGETHER SINCE HE WAS LITTLE.
THE MEMORIES THEY'VE SHARED ARE REAL.
I TRUST IN THAT.

THE HAUNTED BOOKSTORE

Gateway to a Parallel Universe

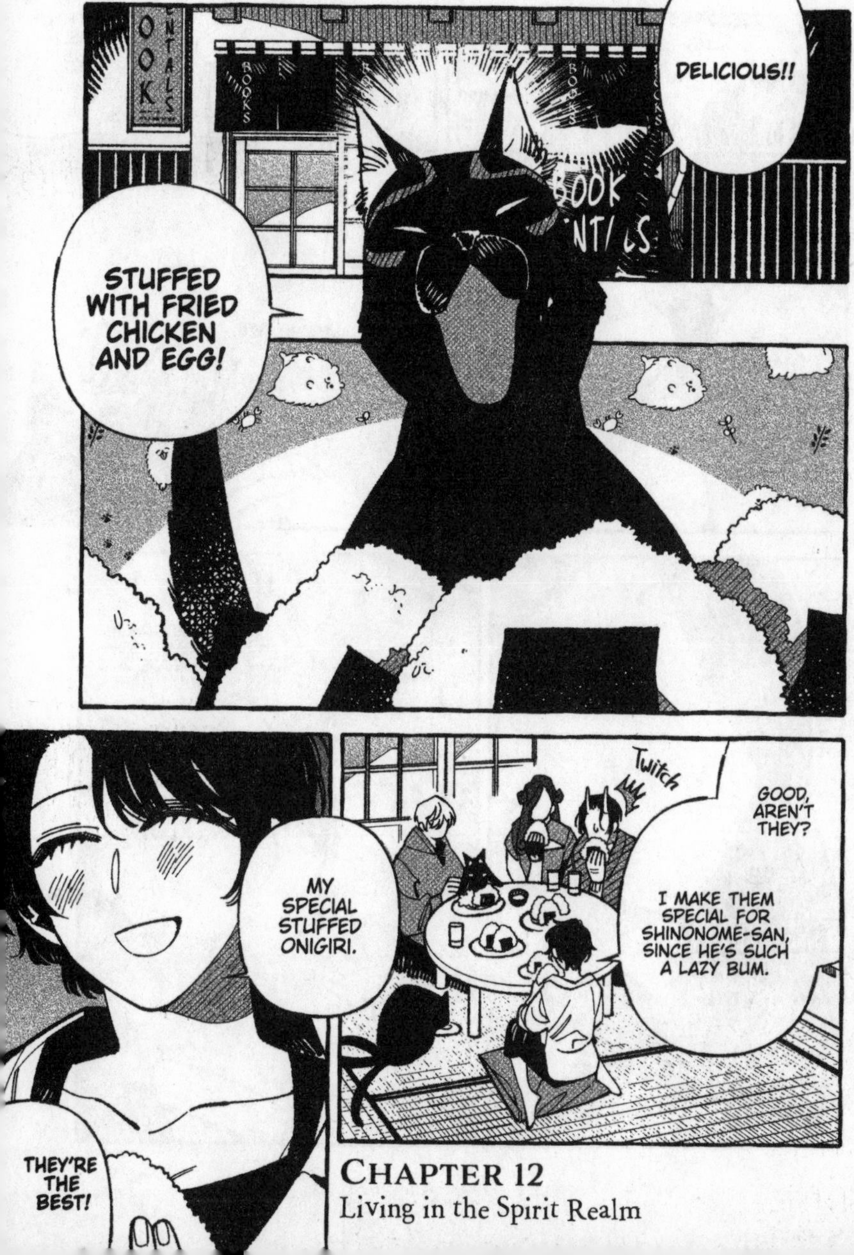
DELICIOUS!!
STUFFED WITH FRIED CHICKEN AND EGG!
Twitch
GOOD, AREN'T THEY?
I MAKE THEM SPECIAL FOR SHINONOME-SAN, SINCE HE'S SUCH A LAZY BUM.
MY SPECIAL STUFFED ONIGIRI.
THEY'RE THE BEST!

CHAPTER 12
Living in the Spirit Realm

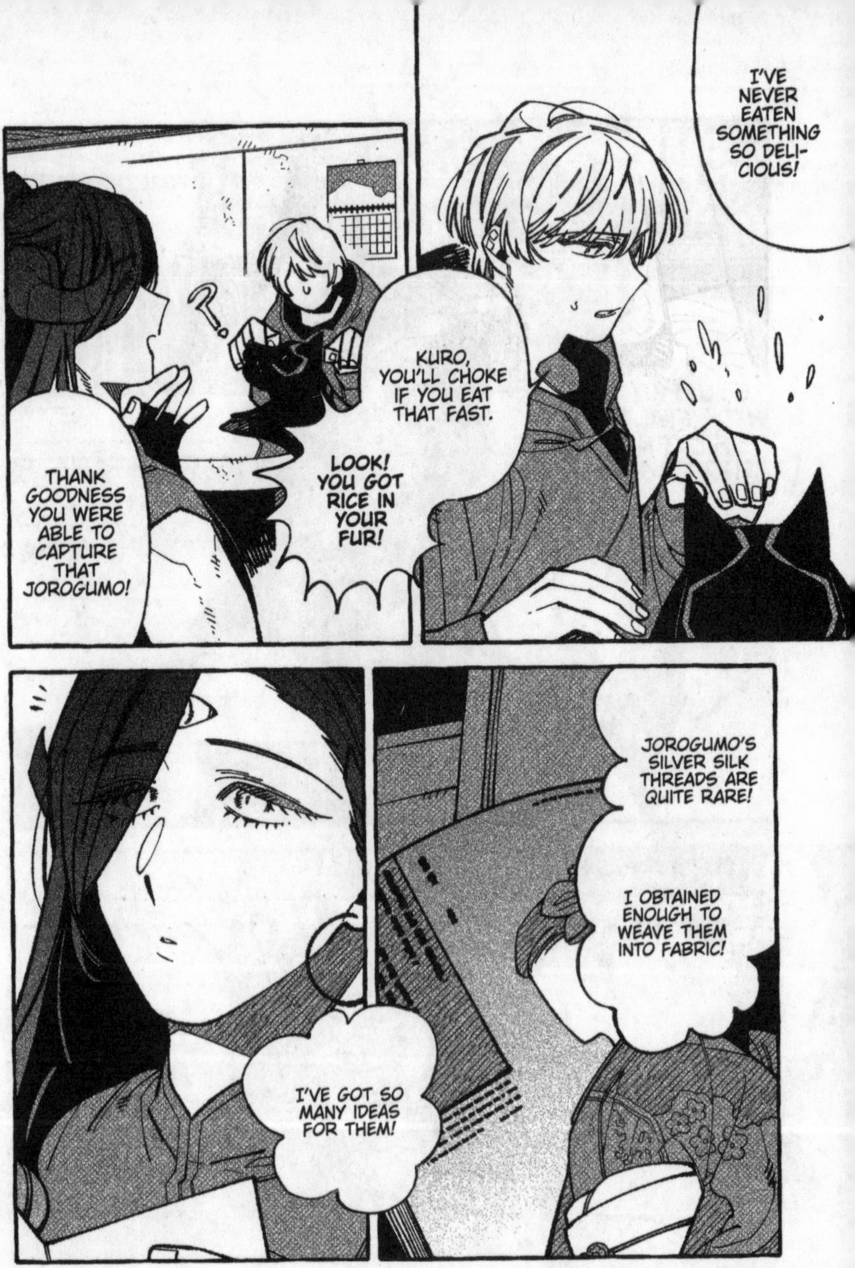
I'VE NEVER EATEN SOMETHING SO DELI- CIOUS!
KURO, YOU'LL CHOKE IF YOU EAT THAT FAST.
LOOK! YOU GOT RICE IN YOUR FUR!
THANK GOODNESS YOU WERE ABLE TO CAPTURE THAT JOROGUMO!
JOROGUMO'S SILVER SILK THREADS ARE QUITE RARE!
I OBTAINED ENOUGH TO WEAVE THEM INTO FABRIC!
I'VE GOT SO MANY IDEAS FOR THEM!

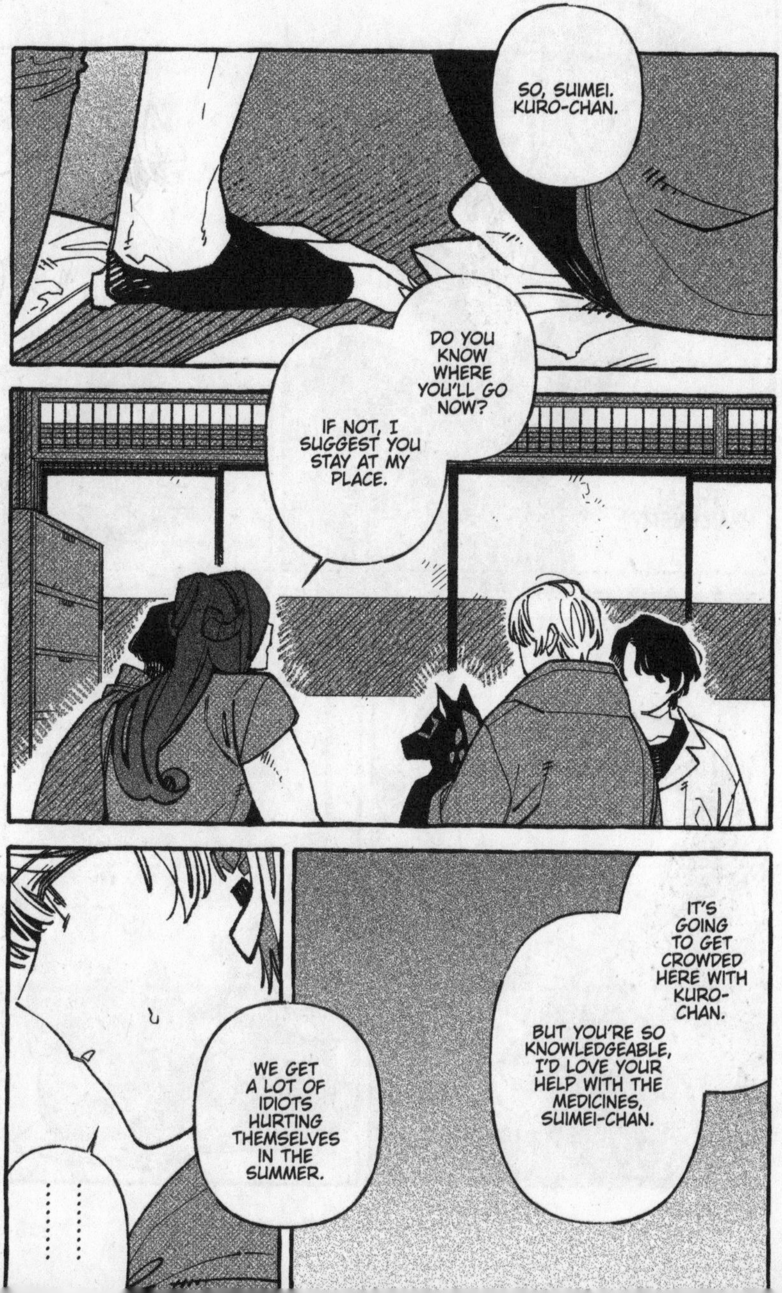
SO, SUIMEI. KURO-CHAN.
DO YOU KNOW WHERE YOU'LL GO NOW?
IF NOT, I SUGGEST YOU STAY AT MY PLACE.
IT'S GOING TO GET CROWDED HERE WITH KURO-CHAN.
BUT YOU'RE SO KNOWLEDGEABLE, I'D LOVE YOUR HELP WITH THE MEDICINES, SUIMEI-CHAN.
WE GET A LOT OF IDIOTS HURTING THEMSELVES IN THE SUMMER.
......

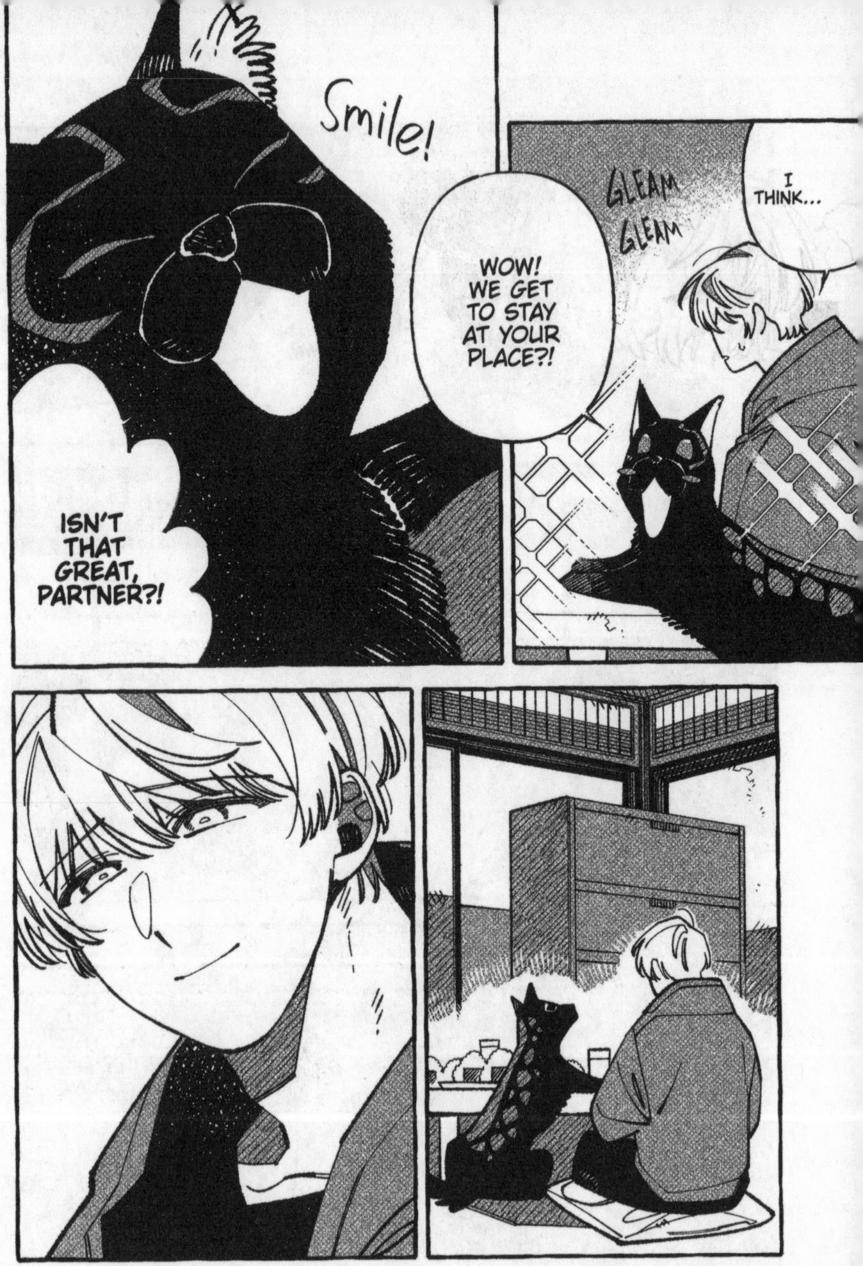
I THINK...
GLEAM GLEAM
WOW! WE GET TO STAY AT YOUR PLACE?!
Smile!
ISN'T THAT GREAT, PARTNER?!

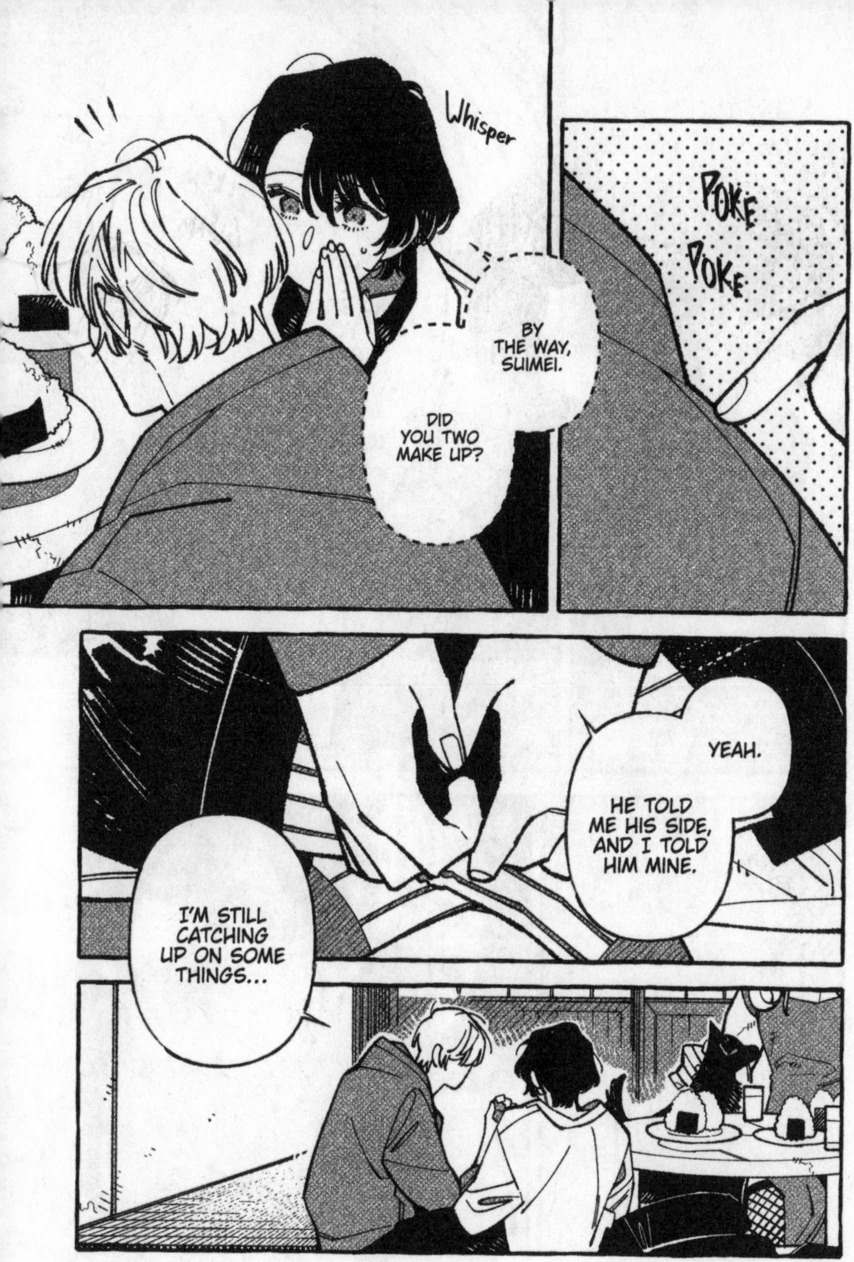
POKE
POKE
Whisper
BY THE WAY, SUIMEI.
DID YOU TWO MAKE UP?
YEAH.
HE TOLD ME HIS SIDE, AND I TOLD HIM MINE.
I'M STILL CATCHING UP ON SOME THINGS...

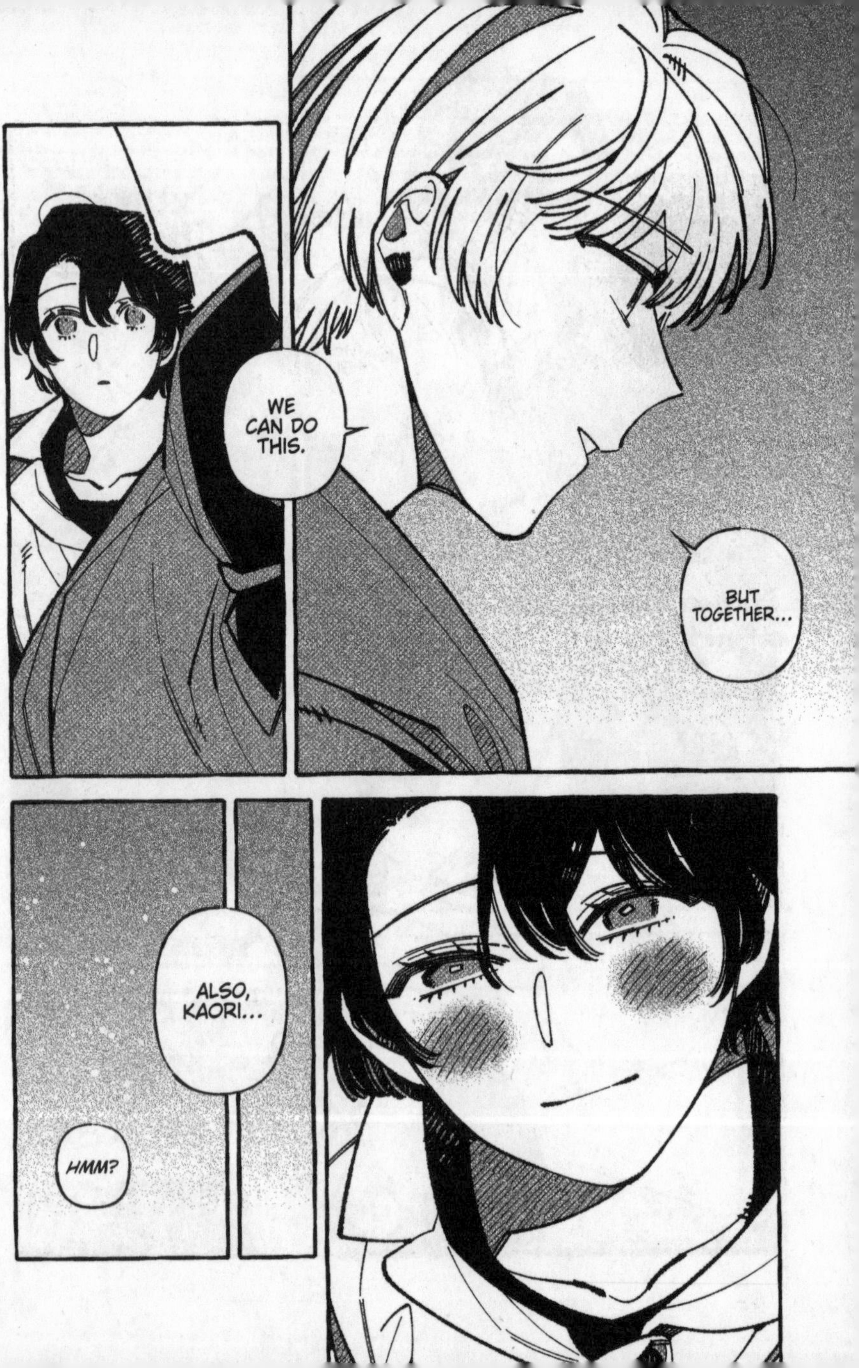
BUT TOGETHER...
WE CAN DO THIS.
ALSO, KAORI...
HMM?

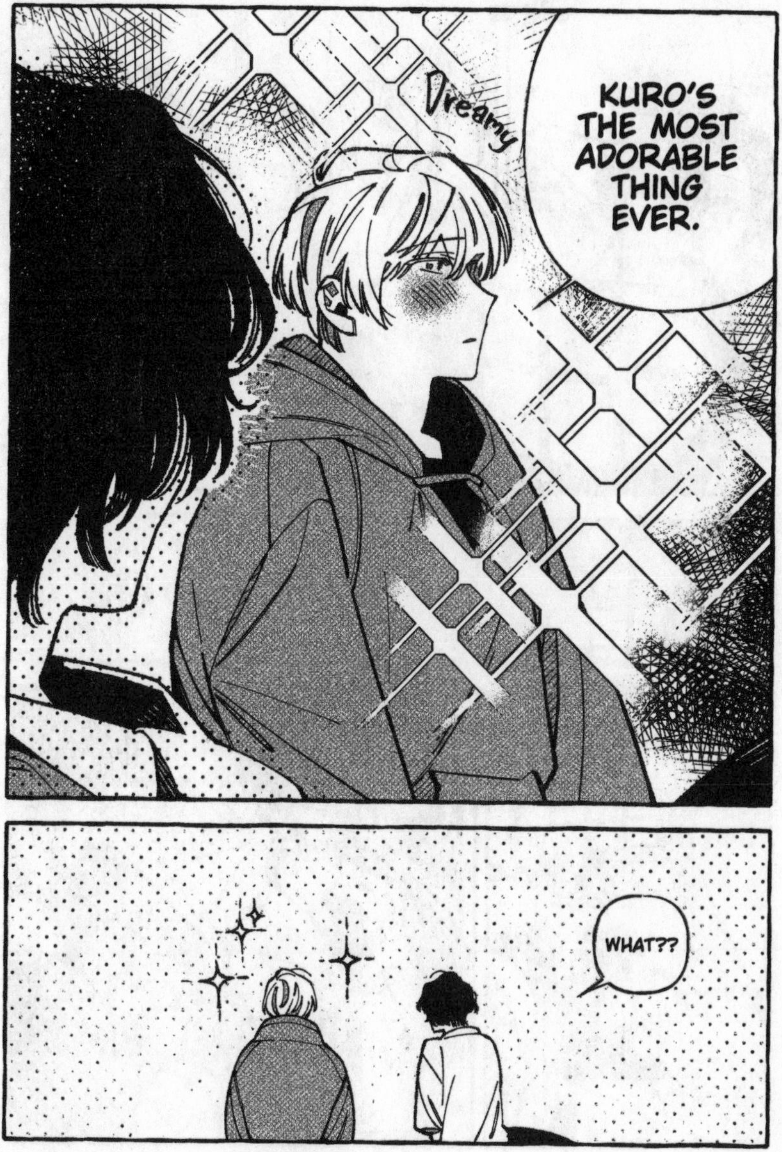
KURO'S THE MOST ADORABLE THING EVER.
Dreamy
WHAT??

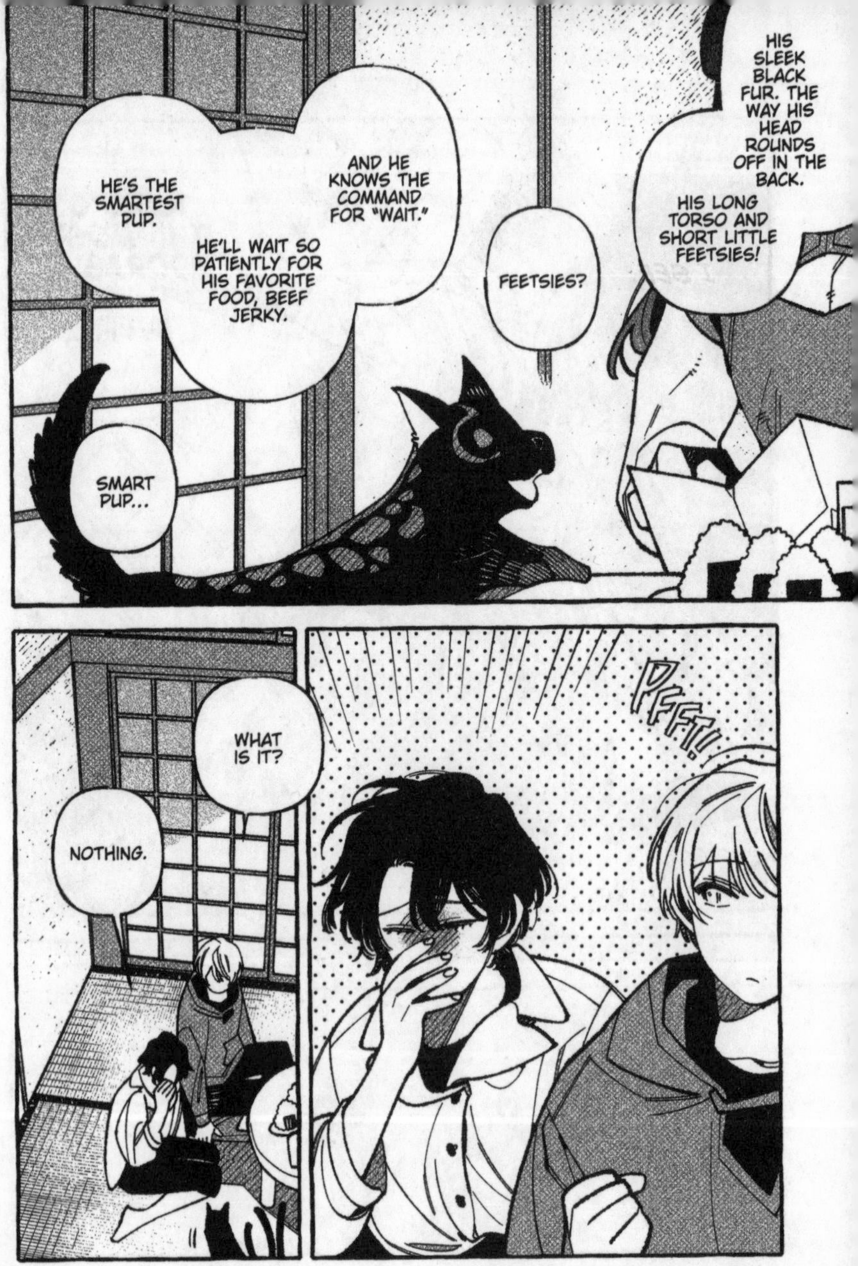
HIS SLEEK BLACK FUR. THE WAY HIS HEAD ROUNDS OFF IN THE BACK.
HIS LONG TORSO AND SHORT LITTLE FEETSIES!
FEETSIES?
HE'S THE SMARTEST PUP.
AND HE KNOWS THE COMMAND FOR "WAIT."
HE'LL WAIT SO PATIENTLY FOR HIS FAVORITE FOOD, BEEF JERKY.
SMART PUP...
PFFT!!
WHAT IS IT?
NOTHING.

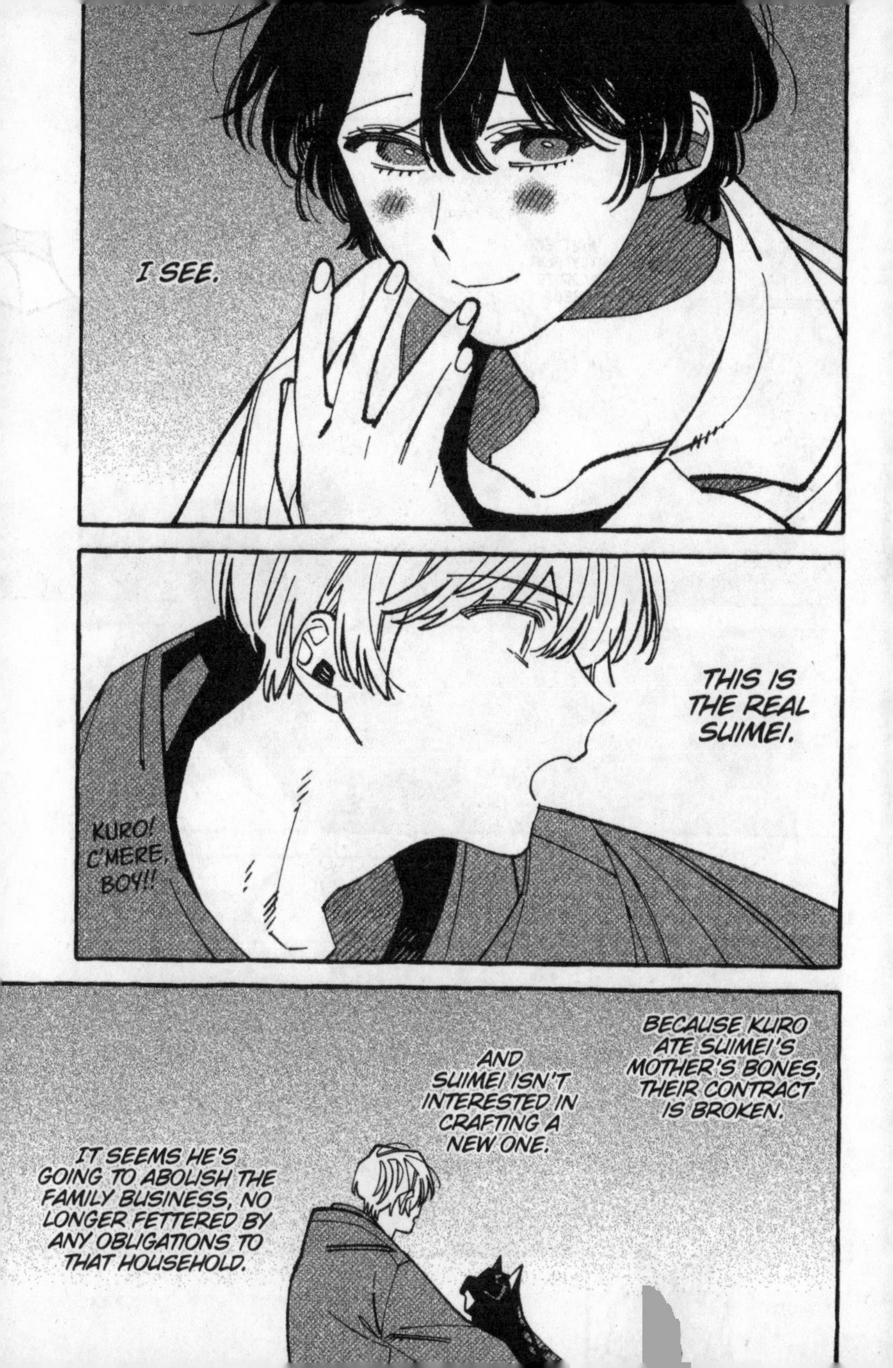
I SEE.
THIS IS THE REAL SUIMEI.
KURO! C'MERE, BOY!!
BECAUSE KURO ATE SUIMEI'S MOTHER'S BONES, THEIR CONTRACT IS BROKEN.
AND SUIMEI ISN'T INTERESTED IN CRAFTING A NEW ONE.
IT SEEMS HE'S GOING TO ABOLISH THE FAMILY BUSINESS, NO LONGER FETTERED BY ANY OBLIGATIONS TO THAT HOUSEHOLD.

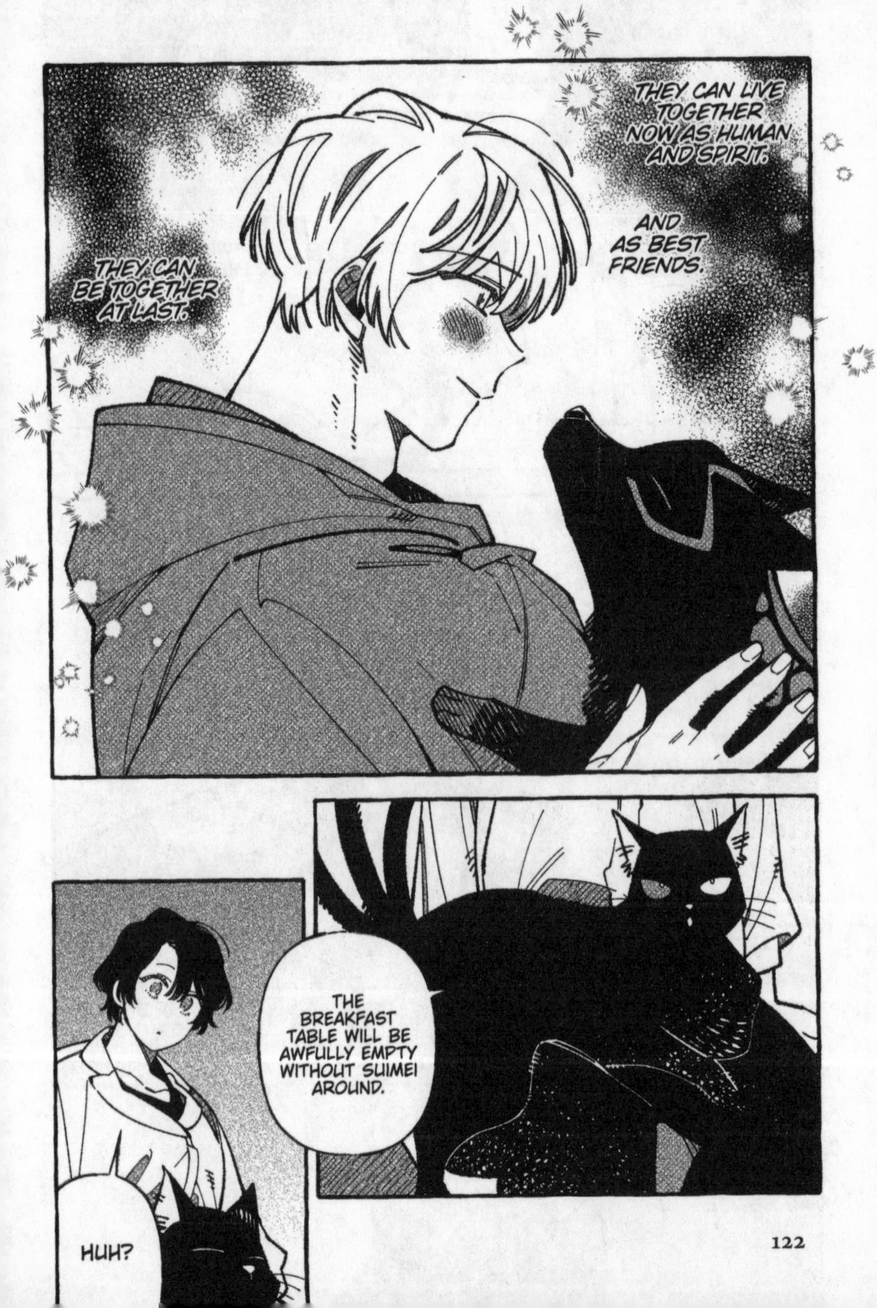
THEY CAN LIVE TOGETHER NOW AS HUMAN AND SPIRIT.
AND AS BEST FRIENDS.
THEY CAN BE TOGETHER AT LAST.
THE BREAKFAST TABLE WILL BE AWFULLY EMPTY WITHOUT SUIMEI AROUND.
HUH?

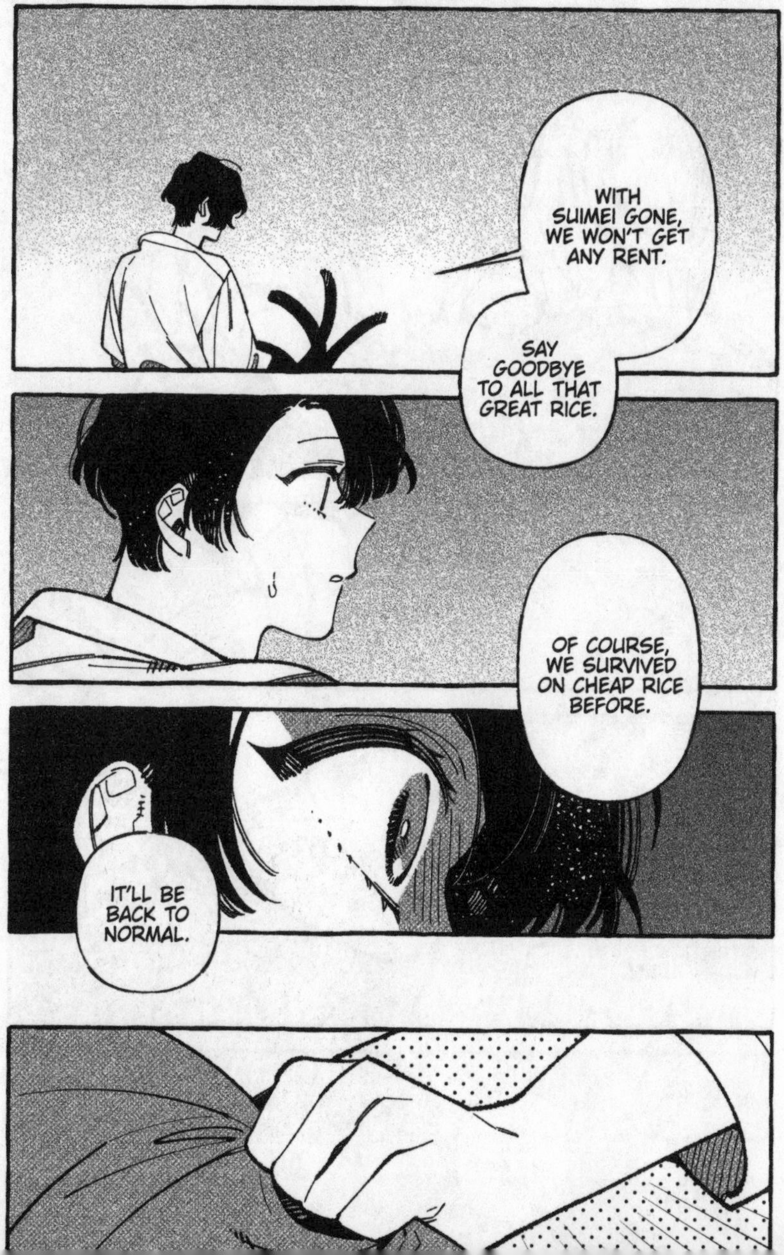
WITH SUIMEI GONE, WE WON'T GET ANY RENT.
SAY GOODBYE TO ALL THAT GREAT RICE.
OF COURSE, WE SURVIVED ON CHEAP RICE BEFORE.
IT'LL BE BACK TO NORMAL.

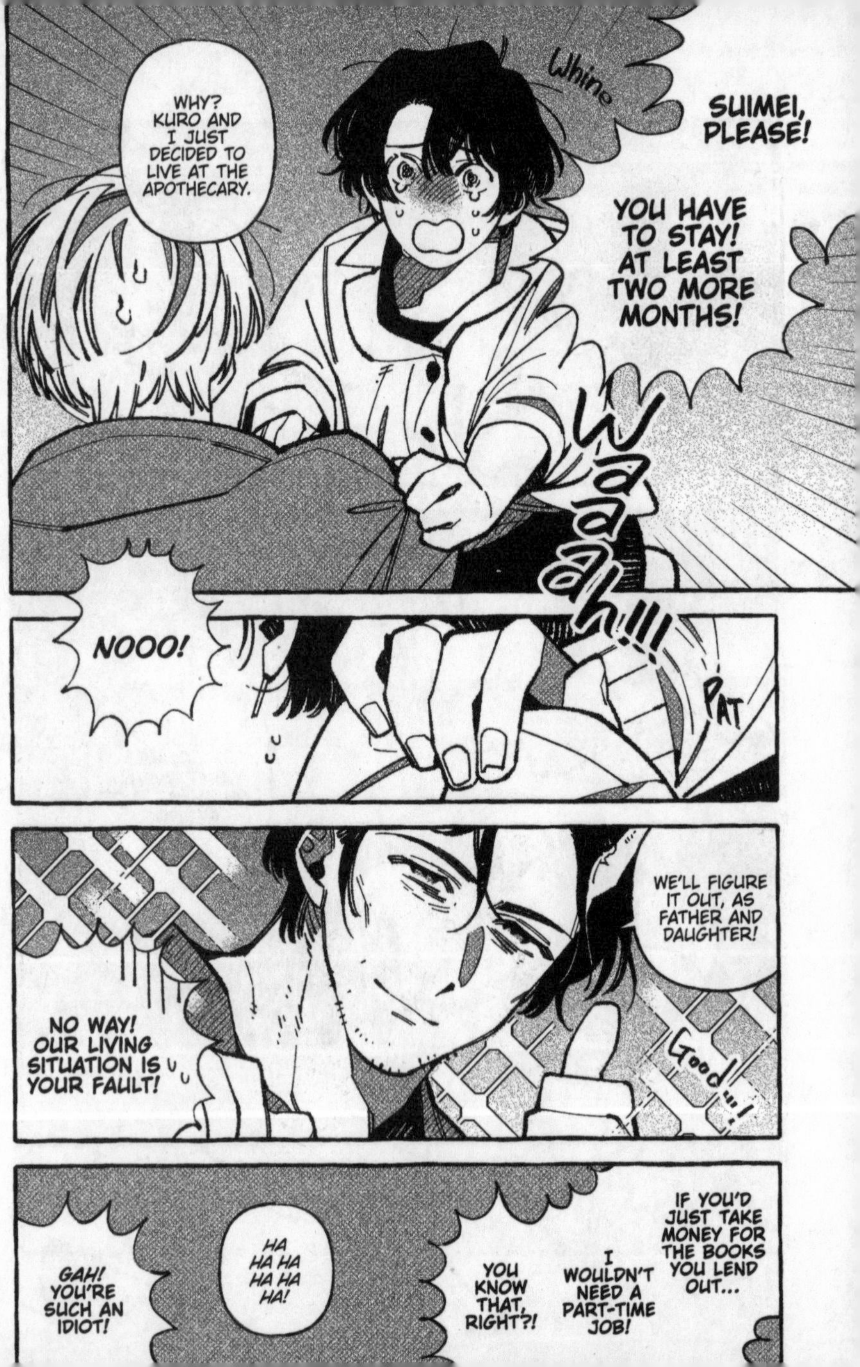
SUIMEI, PLEASE!
YOU HAVE TO STAY! AT LEAST TWO MORE MONTHS!
Whine
WHY? KURO AND I JUST DECIDED TO LIVE AT THE APOTHECARY.
Waaaah!!!
PAT
NOOO!
WE'LL FIGURE IT OUT, AS FATHER AND DAUGHTER!
Good...!
NO WAY! OUR LIVING SITUATION IS YOUR FAULT!
IF YOU'D JUST TAKE MONEY FOR THE BOOKS YOU LEND OUT...
I WOULDN'T NEED A PART-TIME JOB!
YOU KNOW THAT, RIGHT?!
HA HA HA HA HA HA HA!
GAH! YOU'RE SUCH AN IDIOT!

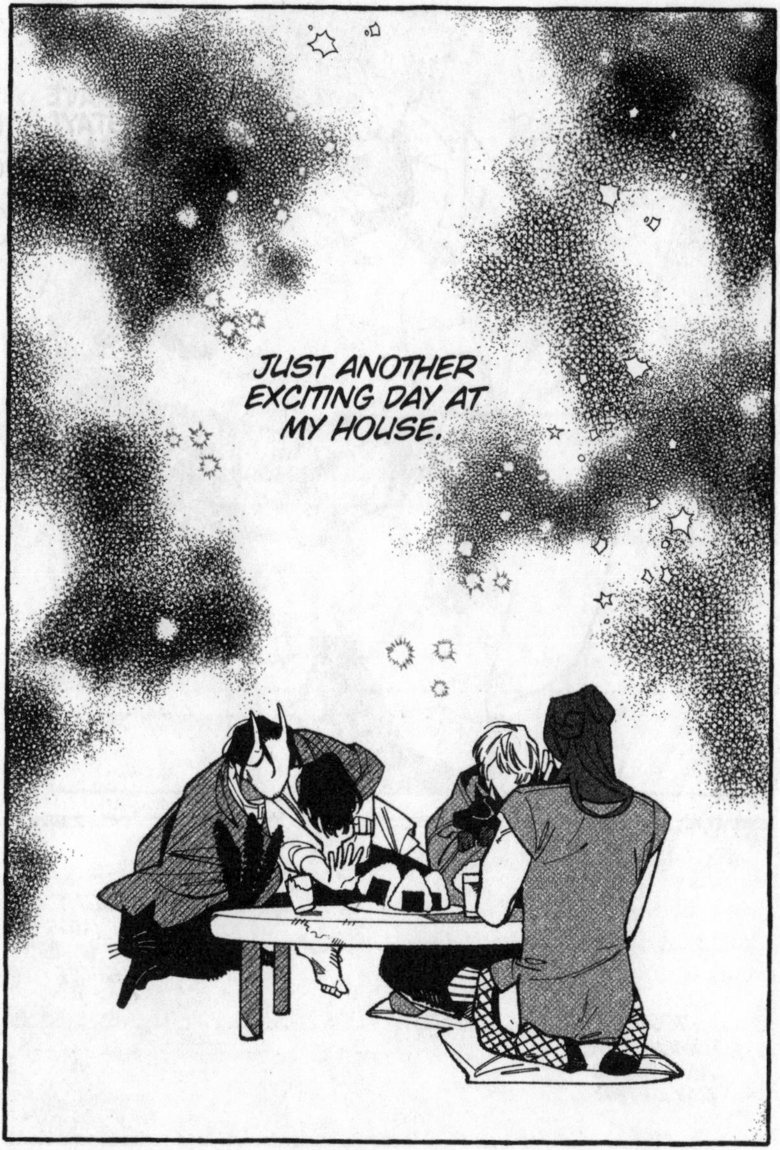
JUST ANOTHER EXCITING DAY AT MY HOUSE.

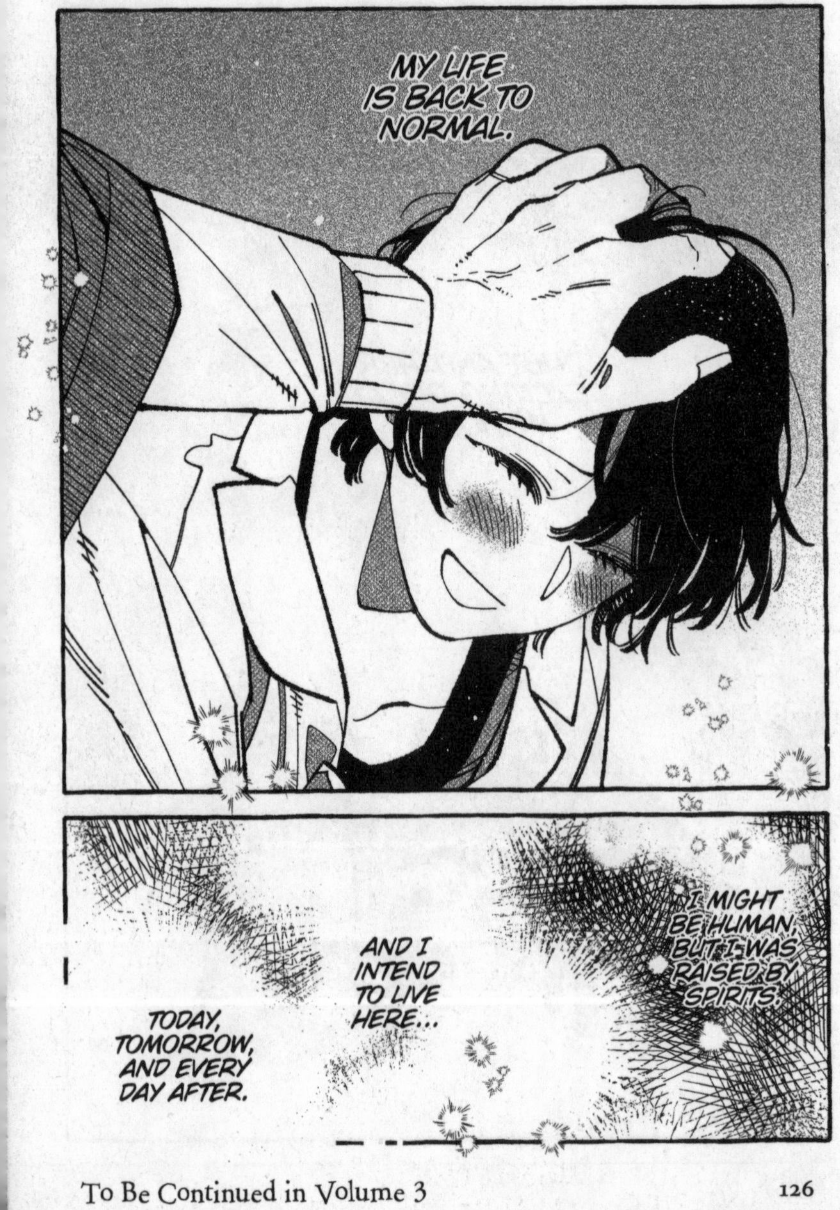
MY LIFE IS BACK TO NORMAL.
I MIGHT BE HUMAN, BUT I WAS RAISED BY SPIRITS.
AND I INTEND TO LIVE HERE...
TODAY, TOMORROW, AND EVERY DAY AFTER.

To Be Continued in Volume 3

THE
HAUNTED
BOOKSTORE
Gateway to a
Parallel Universe

THE HAUNTED BOOKSTORE
Gateway to a Parallel Universe

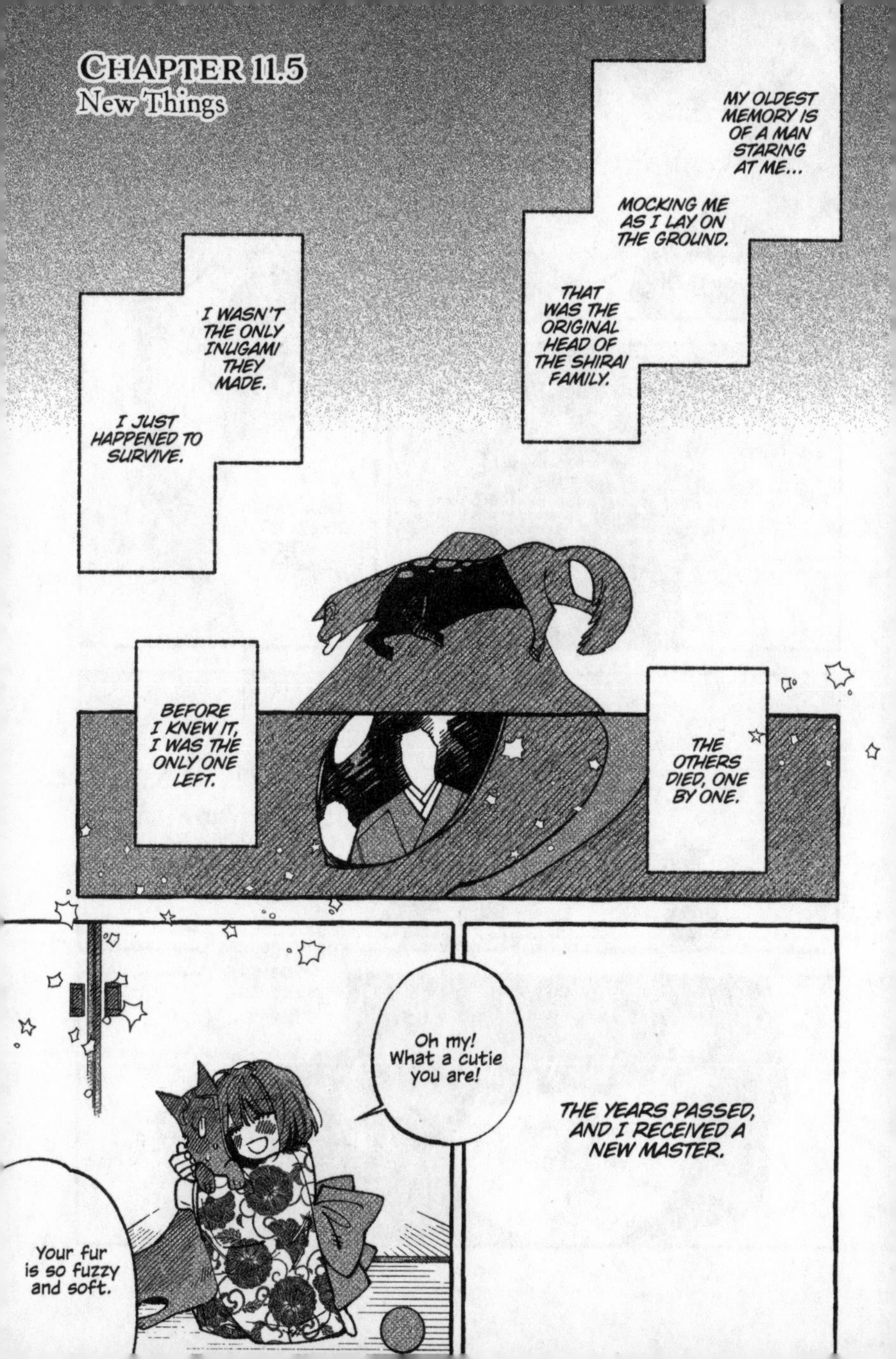
CHAPTER 11.5
New Things
MY OLDEST MEMORY IS OF A MAN STARING AT ME...
MOCKING ME AS I LAY ON THE GROUND.
THAT WAS THE ORIGINAL HEAD OF THE SHIRAI FAMILY.
I WASN'T THE ONLY INUGAMI THEY MADE.
I JUST HAPPENED TO SURVIVE.
THE OTHERS DIED, ONE BY ONE.
BEFORE I KNEW IT, I WAS THE ONLY ONE LEFT.
THE YEARS PASSED, AND I RECEIVED A NEW MASTER.
Oh my! What a cutie you are!
Your fur is so fuzzy and soft.

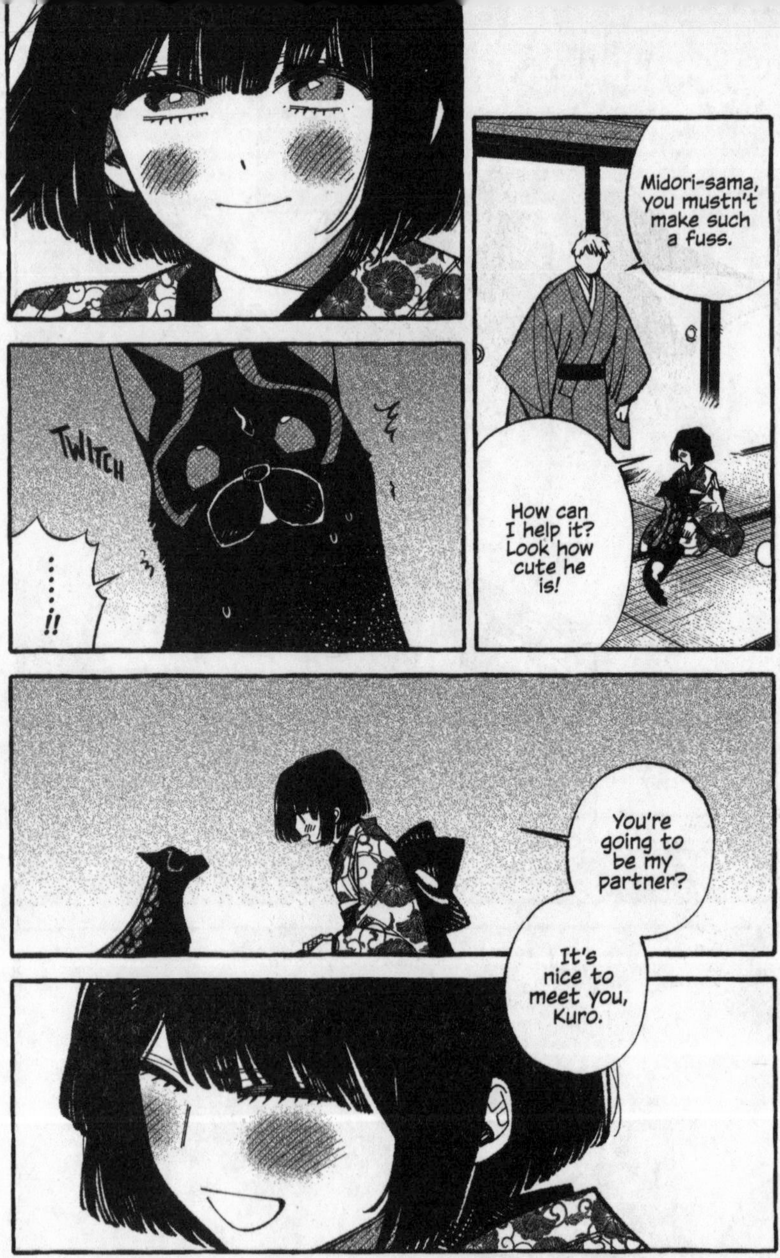
Midori-sama, you mustn't make such a fuss.
How can I help it? Look how cute he is!
TWITCH
......!!
You're going to be my partner?
It's nice to meet you, Kuro.

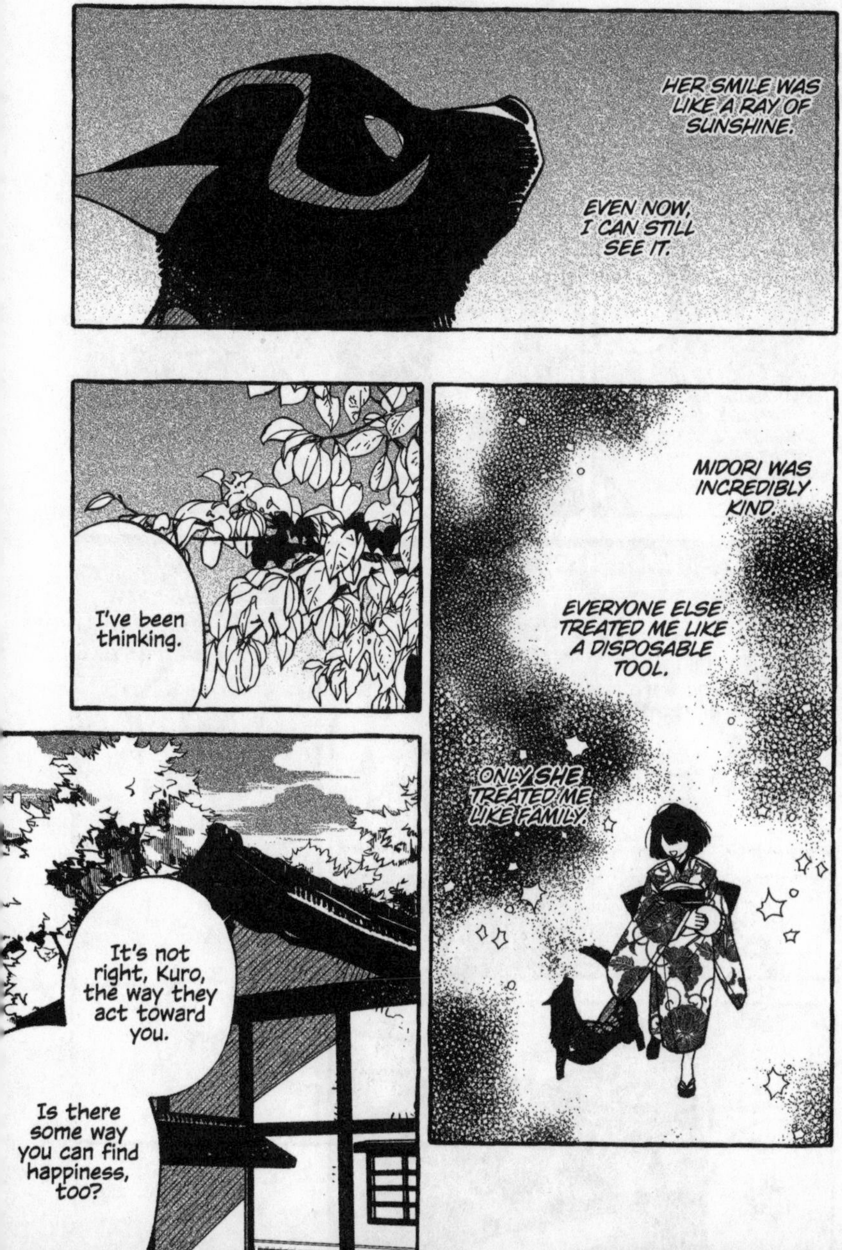
HER SMILE WAS LIKE A RAY OF SUNSHINE.
EVEN NOW, I CAN STILL SEE IT.
MIDORI WAS INCREDIBLY KIND.
EVERYONE ELSE TREATED ME LIKE A DISPOSABLE TOOL.
ONLY SHE TREATED ME LIKE FAMILY.
I've been thinking.
It's not right, Kuro, the way they act toward you.
Is there some way you can find happiness, too?

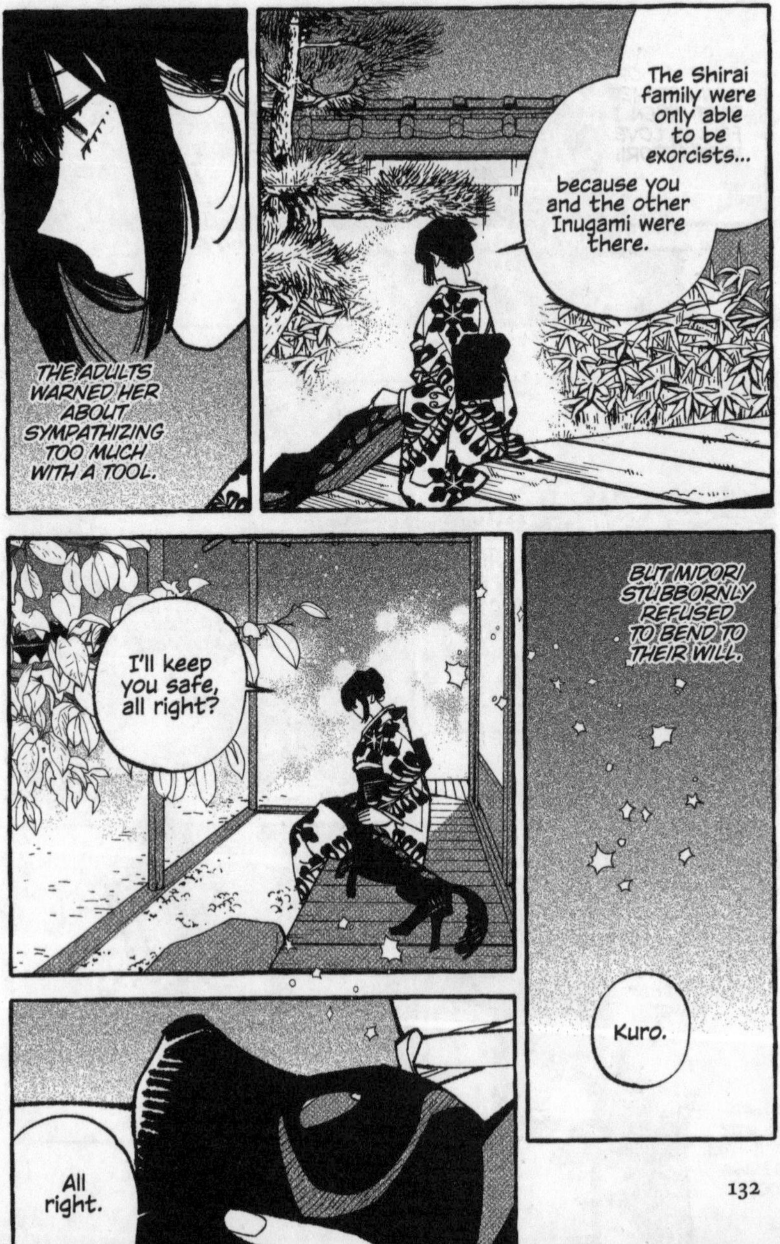
The Shirai family were only able to be exorcists...
because you and the other Inugami were there.
THE ADULTS WARNED HER ABOUT SYMPATHIZING TOO MUCH WITH A TOOL.
BUT MIDORI STUBBORNLY REFUSED TO BEND TO THEIR WILL.
Kuro.
I'll keep you safe, all right?
All right.

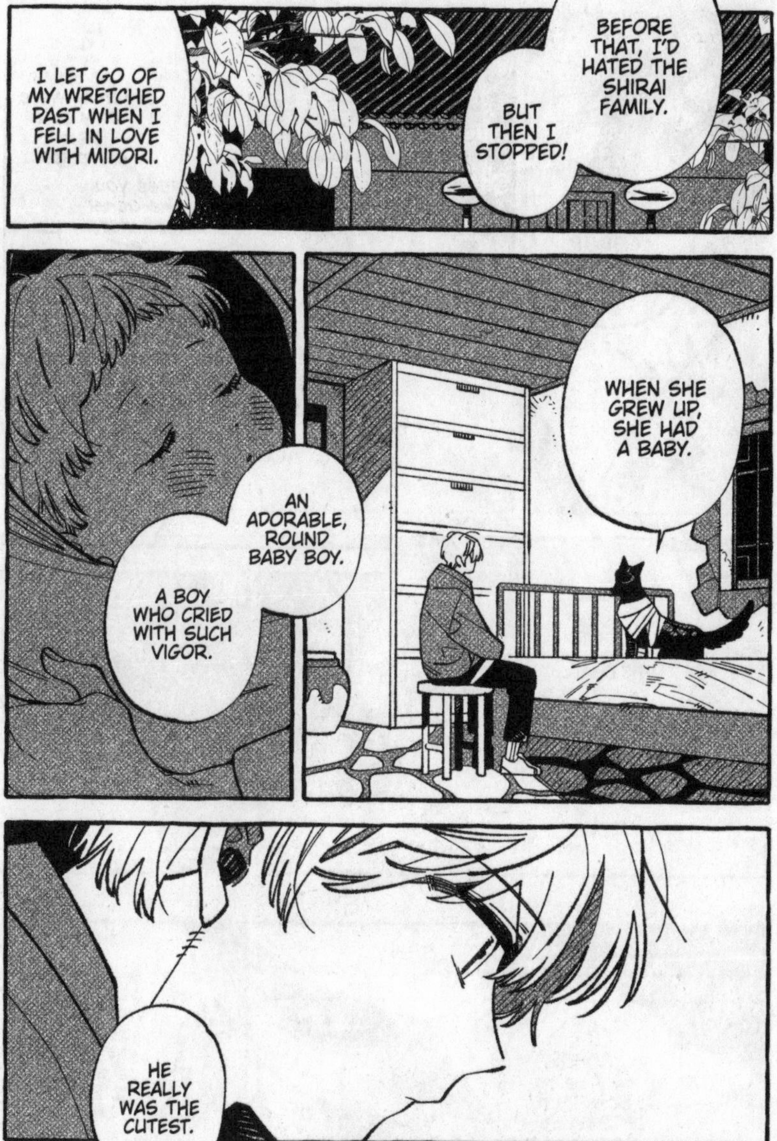
BEFORE THAT, I'D HATED THE SHIRAI FAMILY.
BUT THEN I STOPPED!
I LET GO OF MY WRETCHED PAST WHEN I FELL IN LOVE WITH MIDORI.
WHEN SHE GREW UP, SHE HAD A BABY.
AN ADORABLE, ROUND BABY BOY.
A BOY WHO CRIED WITH SUCH VIGOR.
HE REALLY WAS THE CUTEST.

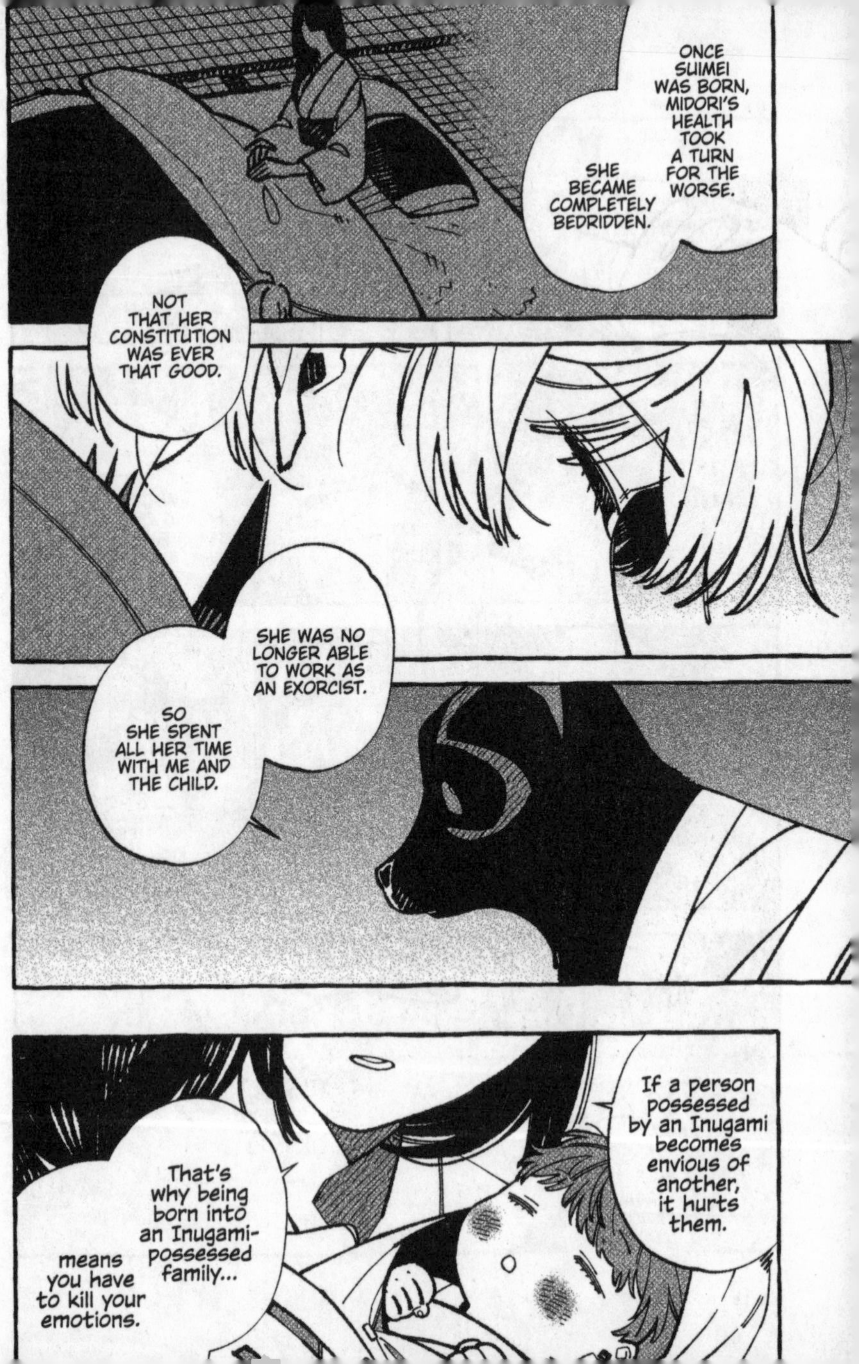
ONCE SUIMEI WAS BORN, MIDORI'S HEALTH TOOK A TURN FOR THE WORSE.
SHE BECAME COMPLETELY BEDRIDDEN.
NOT THAT HER CONSTITUTION WAS EVER THAT GOOD.
SHE WAS NO LONGER ABLE TO WORK AS AN EXORCIST.
SO SHE SPENT ALL HER TIME WITH ME AND THE CHILD.
If a person possessed by an Inugami becomes envious of another, it hurts them.
That's why being born into an Inugami-possessed family...
means you have to kill your emotions.

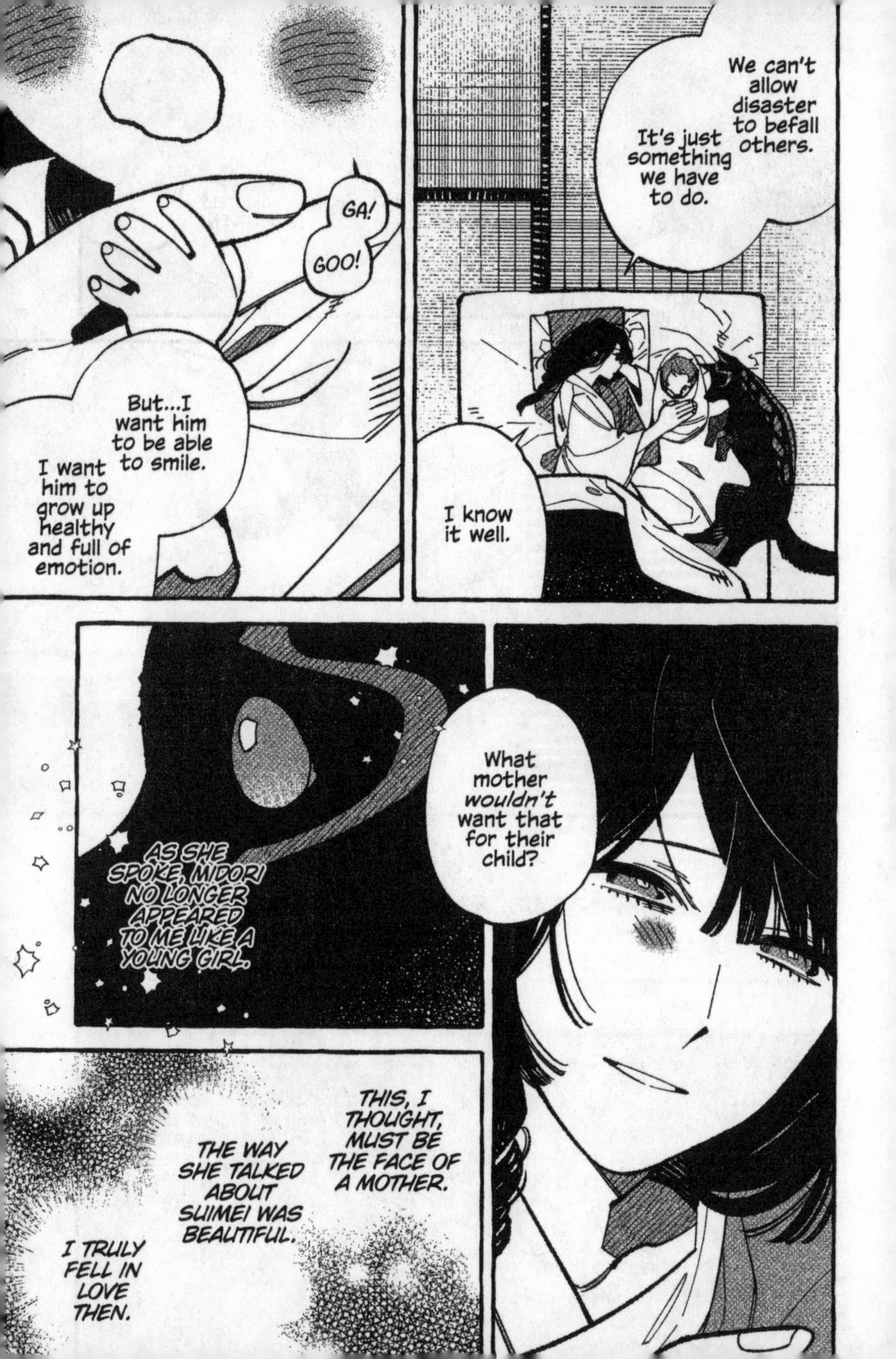

We can't allow disaster to befall others.
It's just something we have to do.
I know it well.
GA!
GOO!
But...I want him to be able to smile.
I want him to grow up healthy and full of emotion.
What mother *wouldn't* want that for their child?
AS SHE SPOKE, MIDORI NO LONGER APPEARED TO ME LIKE A YOUNG GIRL.
THIS, I THOUGHT, MUST BE THE FACE OF A MOTHER.
THE WAY SHE TALKED ABOUT SUIMEI WAS BEAUTIFUL.
I TRULY FELL IN LOVE THEN.

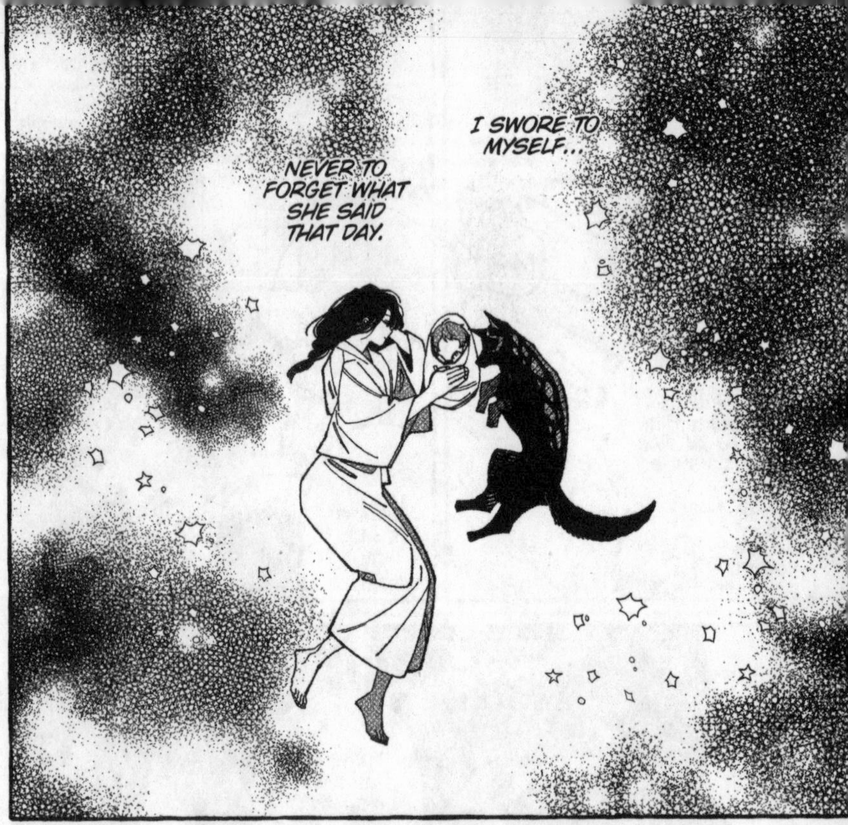
I SWORE TO MYSELF...
NEVER TO FORGET WHAT SHE SAID THAT DAY.

WHEN MY PARTNER...WHEN SUIMEI TURNED THREE, HIS EXORCIST EDUCATION BEGAN.

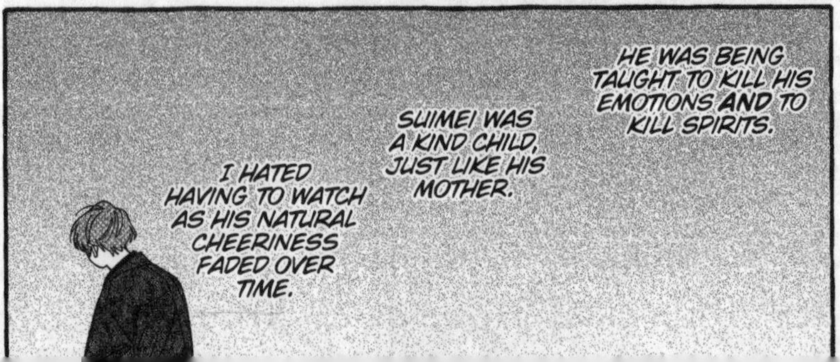
HE WAS BEING TAUGHT TO KILL HIS EMOTIONS AND TO KILL SPIRITS.
SUIMEI WAS A KIND CHILD, JUST LIKE HIS MOTHER.
I HATED HAVING TO WATCH AS HIS NATURAL CHEERINESS FADED OVER TIME.

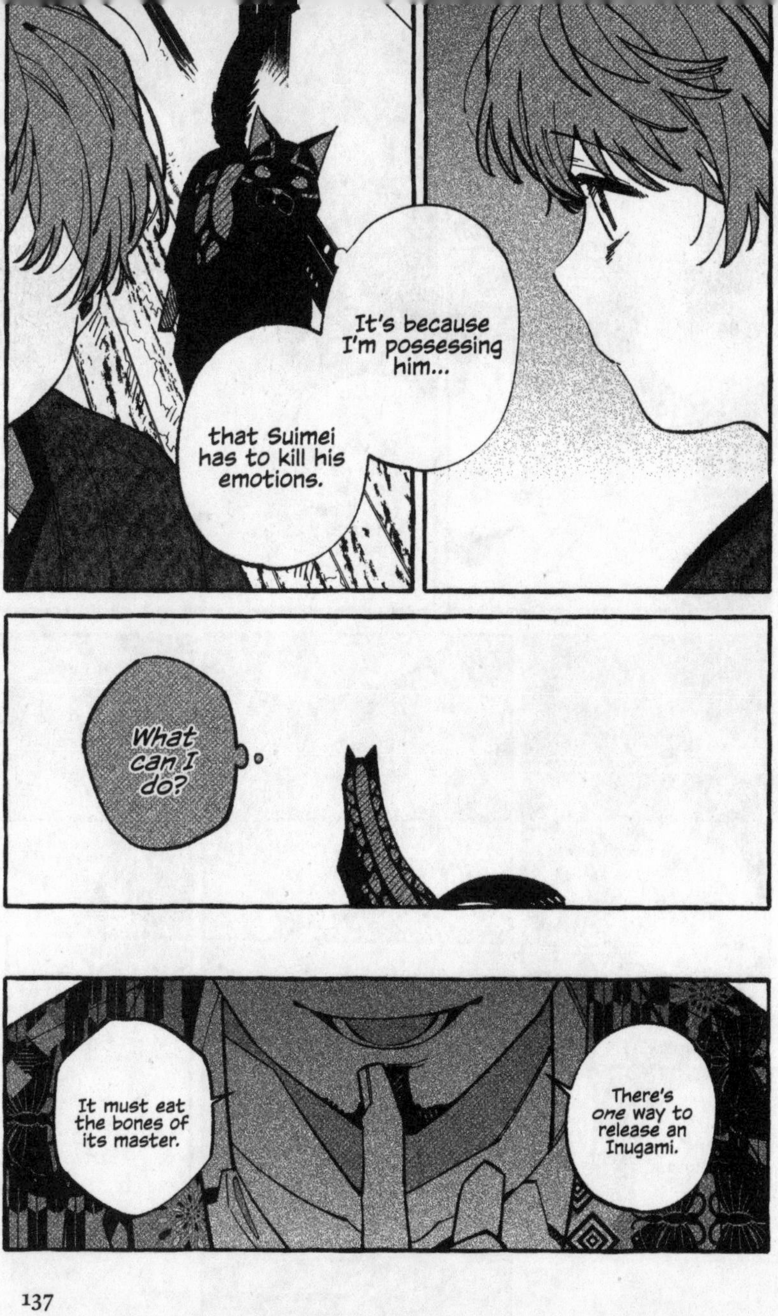
It's because I'm possessing him...
that Suimei has to kill his emotions.
What can I do?
There's *one* way to release an Inugami.
It must eat the bones of its master.

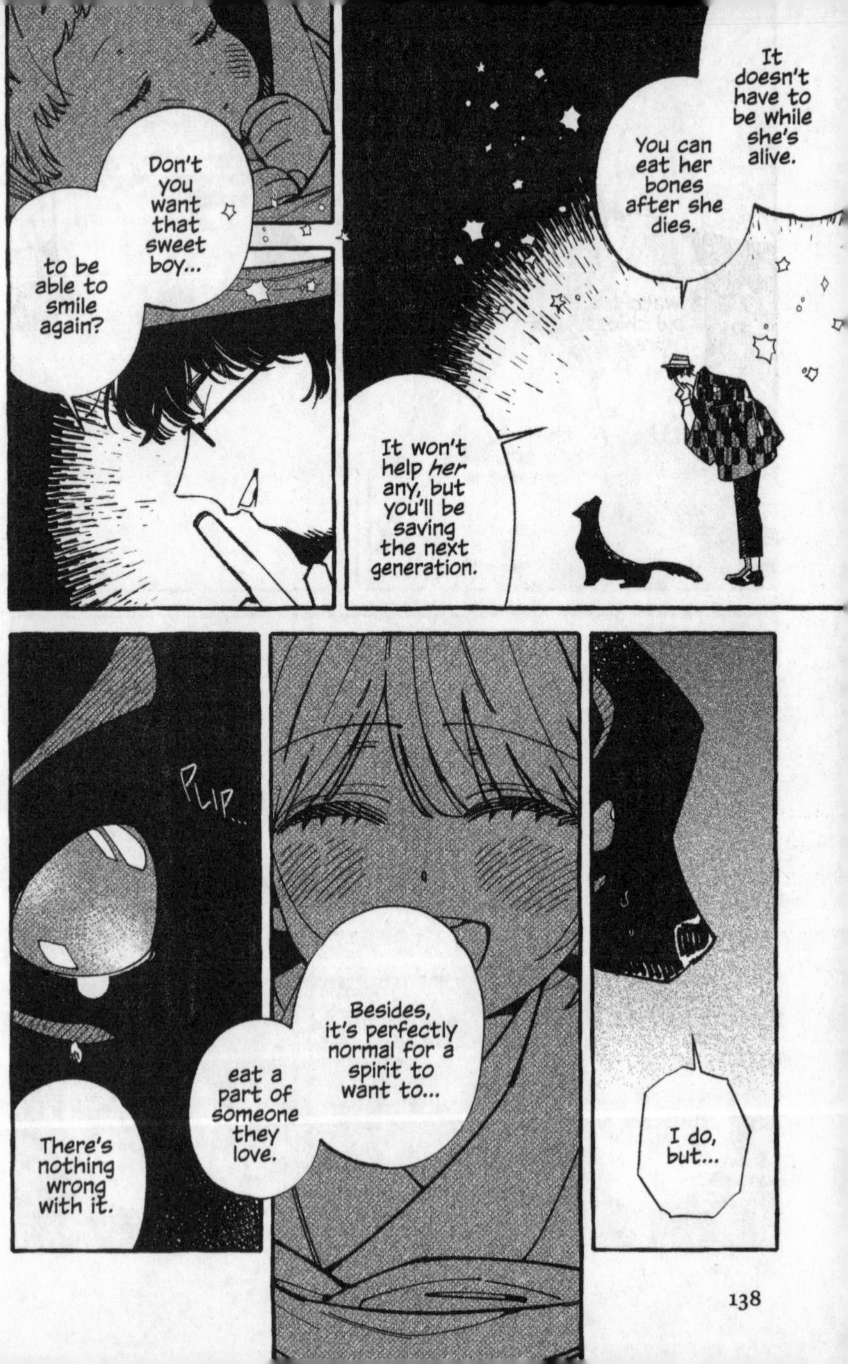
It doesn't have to be while she's alive.
You can eat her bones after she dies.
It won't help *her* any, but you'll be saving the next generation.
Don't you want that sweet boy...
to be able to smile again?
I do, but...
Besides, it's perfectly normal for a spirit to want to...
eat a part of someone they love.
PLIP...
There's nothing wrong with it.

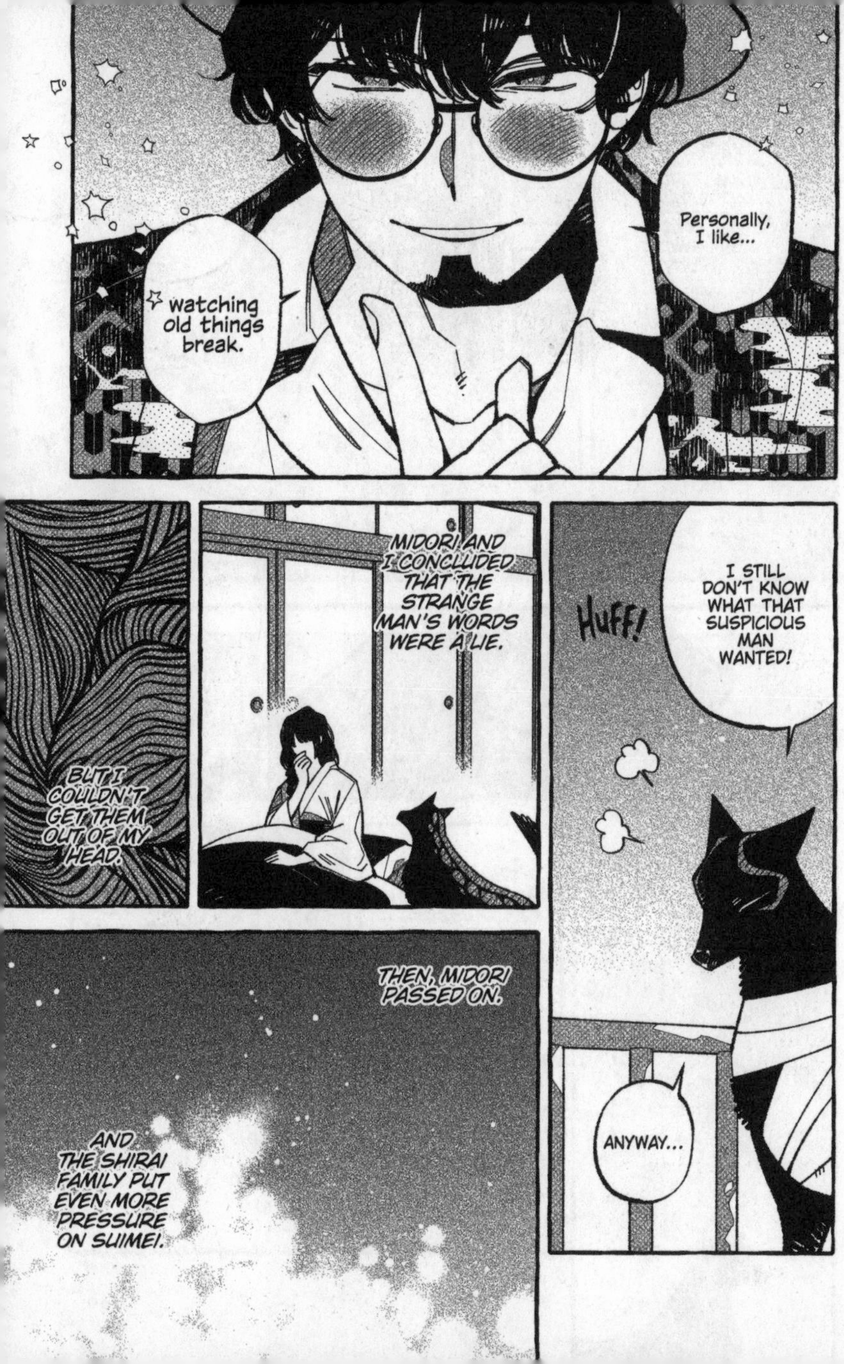
Personally, I like...
watching old things break.
I STILL DON'T KNOW WHAT THAT SUSPICIOUS MAN WANTED!
HUFF!
ANYWAY...
MIDORI AND I CONCLUDED THAT THE STRANGE MAN'S WORDS WERE A LIE.
BUT I COULDN'T GET THEM OUT OF MY HEAD.
THEN, MIDORI PASSED ON.
AND THE SHIRAI FAMILY PUT EVEN MORE PRESSURE ON SUIMEI.

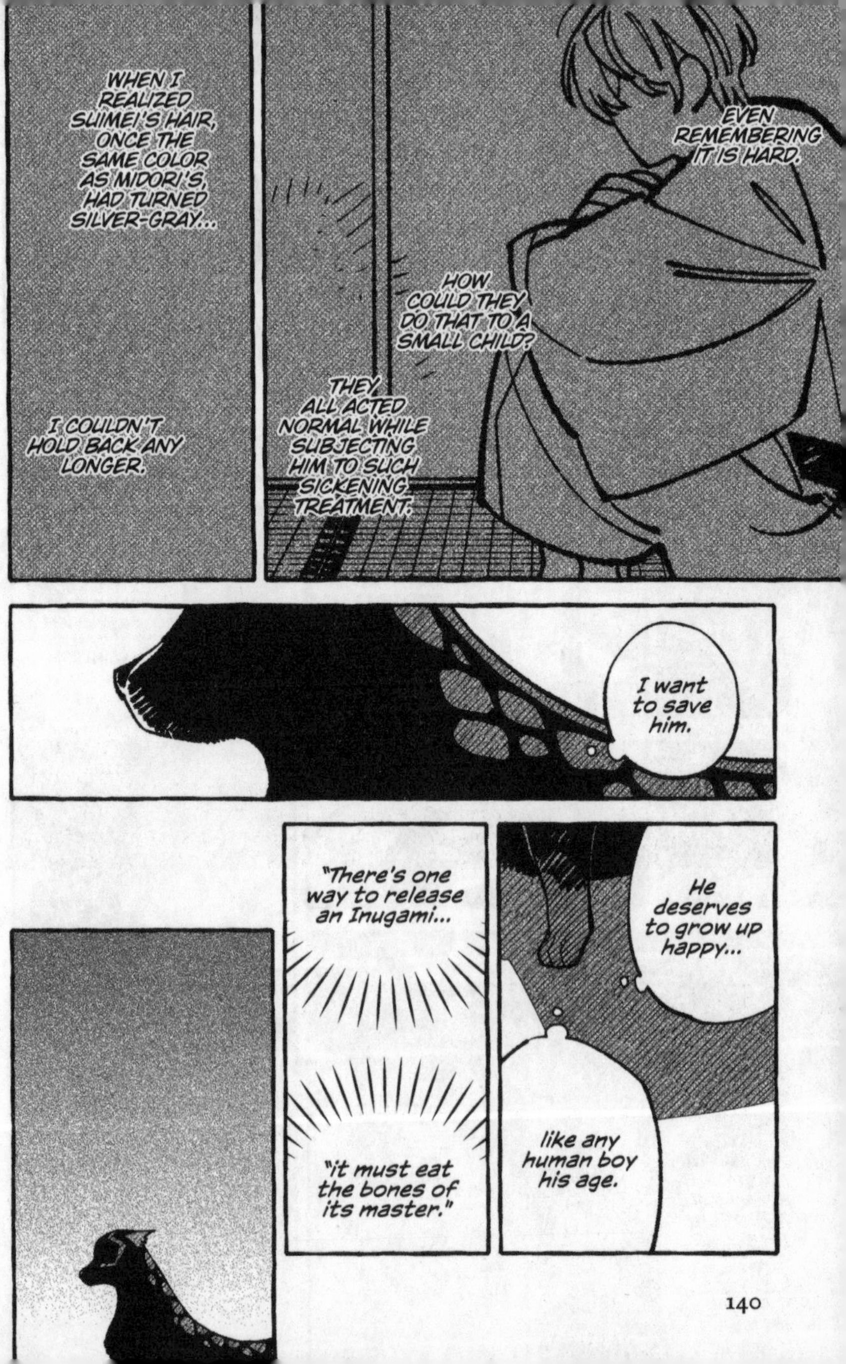
EVEN REMEMBERING IT IS HARD.
HOW COULD THEY DO THAT TO A SMALL CHILD?
THEY ALL ACTED NORMAL WHILE SUBJECTING HIM TO SUCH SICKENING TREATMENT.
WHEN I REALIZED SUIMEI'S HAIR, ONCE THE SAME COLOR AS MIDORI'S, HAD TURNED SILVER-GRAY...
I COULDN'T HOLD BACK ANY LONGER.
I want to save him.
He deserves to grow up happy...
like any human boy his age.
"There's one way to release an Inugami...
"it must eat the bones of its master."

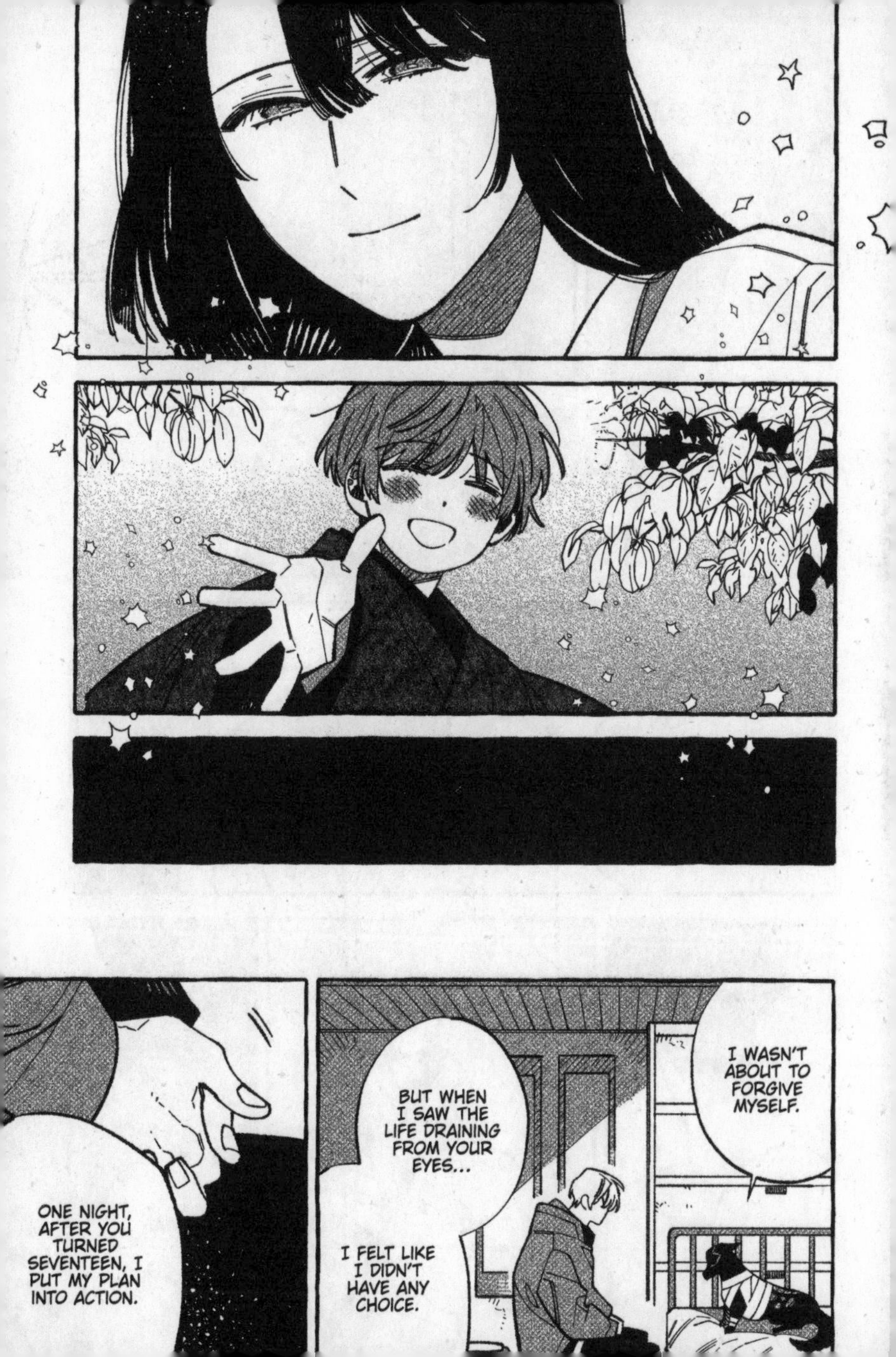
I WASN'T ABOUT TO FORGIVE MYSELF.
BUT WHEN I SAW THE LIFE DRAINING FROM YOUR EYES...
I FELT LIKE I DIDN'T HAVE ANY CHOICE.
ONE NIGHT, AFTER YOU TURNED SEVENTEEN, I PUT MY PLAN INTO ACTION.

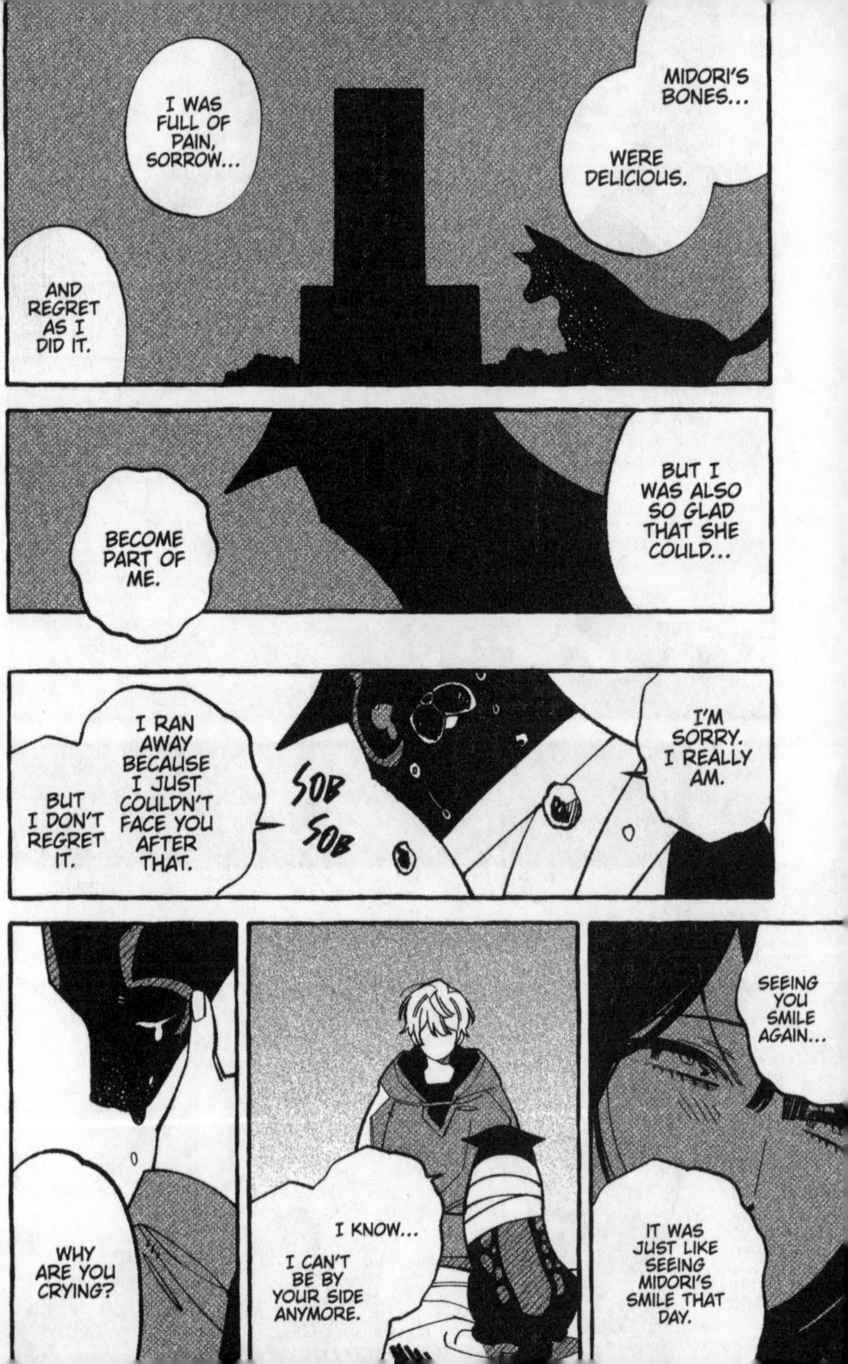
MIDORI'S BONES... WERE DELICIOUS.
I WAS FULL OF PAIN, SORROW...
AND REGRET AS I DID IT.
BUT I WAS ALSO SO GLAD THAT SHE COULD...
BECOME PART OF ME.
I'M SORRY. I REALLY AM.
SOB SOB
I RAN AWAY BECAUSE I JUST COULDN'T FACE YOU AFTER THAT.
BUT I DON'T REGRET IT.
SEEING YOU SMILE AGAIN...
IT WAS JUST LIKE SEEING MIDORI'S SMILE THAT DAY.
I KNOW...
I CAN'T BE BY YOUR SIDE ANYMORE.
WHY ARE YOU CRYING?

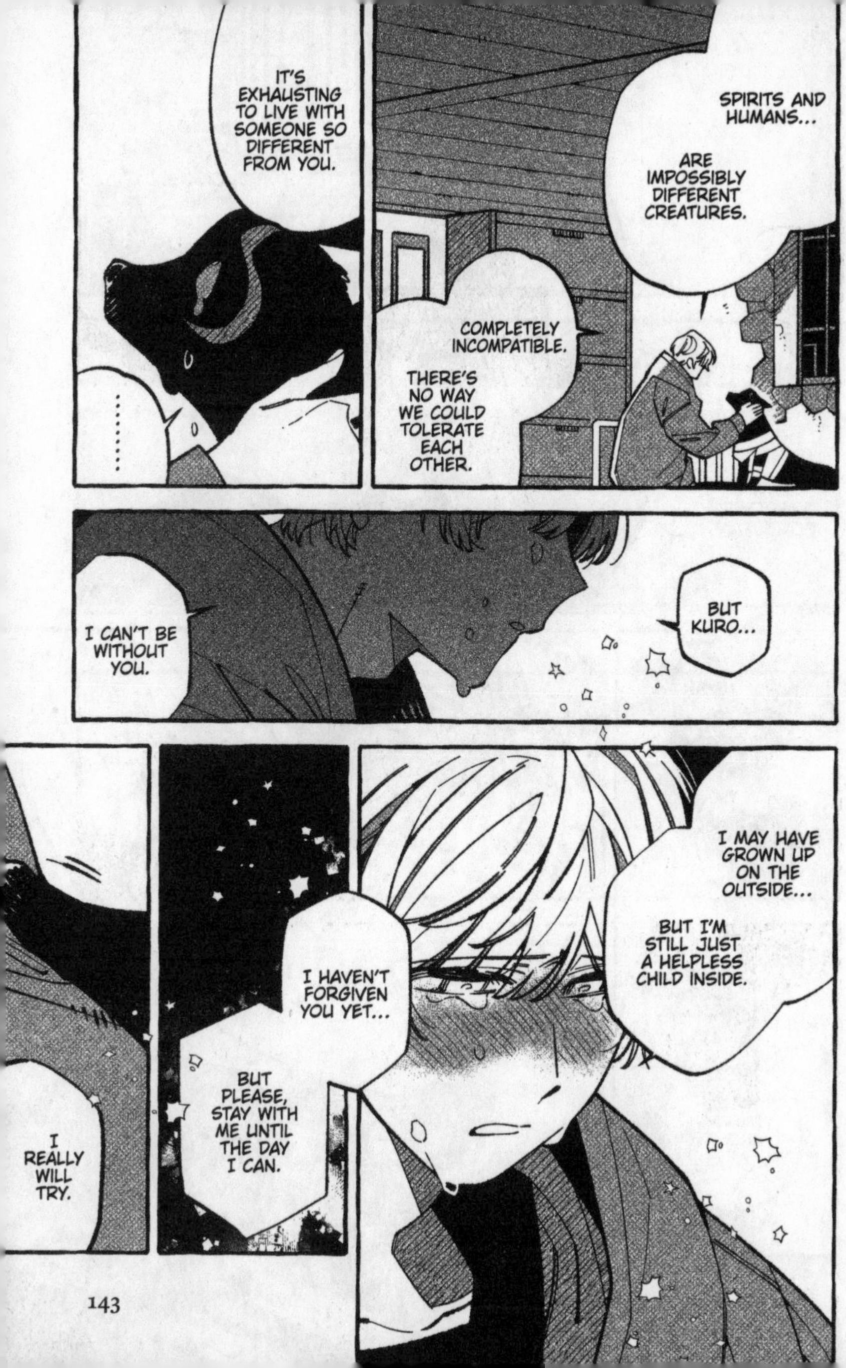
SPIRITS AND HUMANS...
ARE IMPOSSIBLY DIFFERENT CREATURES.
COMPLETELY INCOMPATIBLE.
THERE'S NO WAY WE COULD TOLERATE EACH OTHER.
IT'S EXHAUSTING TO LIVE WITH SOMEONE SO DIFFERENT FROM YOU.
......
BUT KURO...
I CAN'T BE WITHOUT YOU.
I MAY HAVE GROWN UP ON THE OUTSIDE...
BUT I'M STILL JUST A HELPLESS CHILD INSIDE.
I HAVEN'T FORGIVEN YOU YET...
BUT PLEASE, STAY WITH ME UNTIL THE DAY I CAN.
I REALLY WILL TRY.

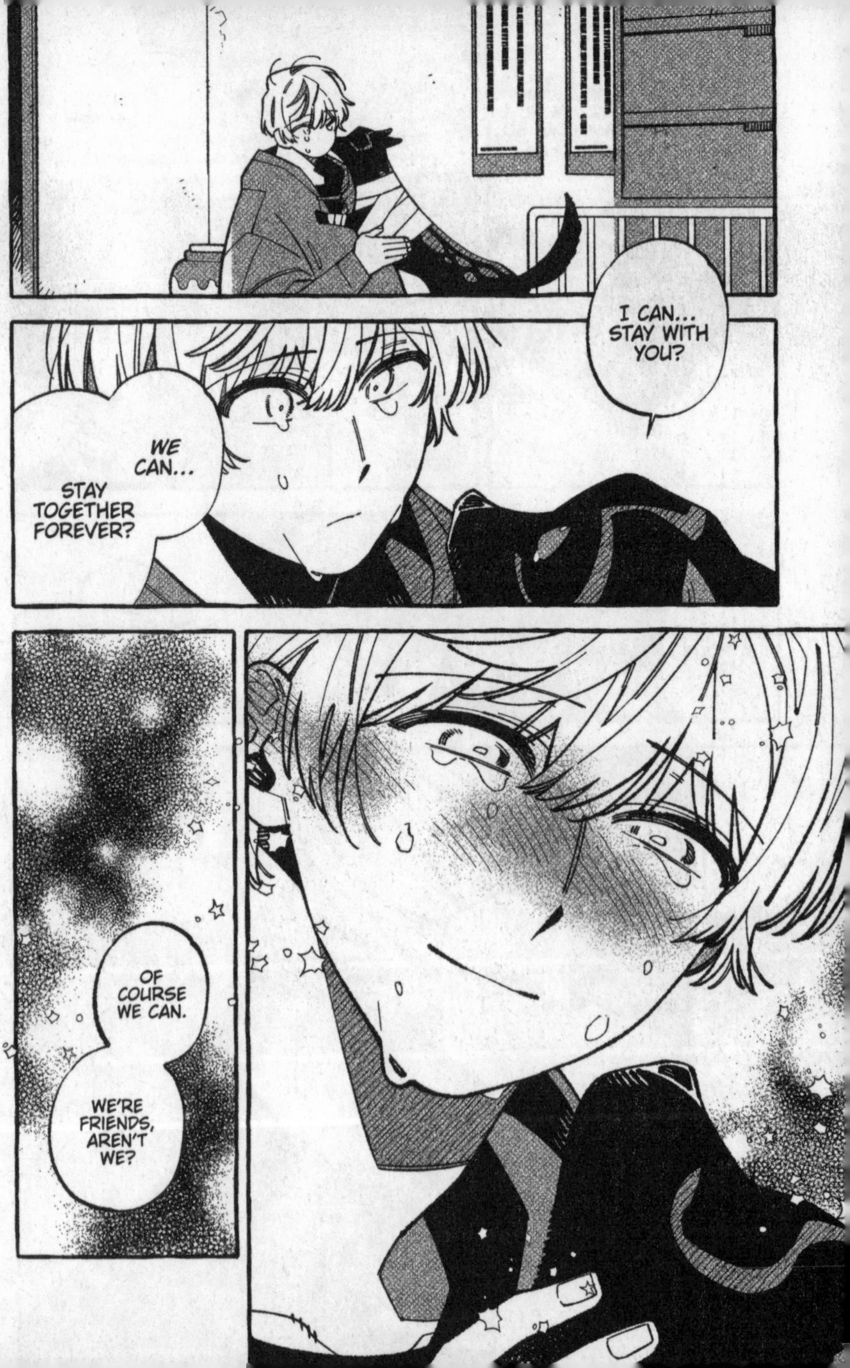
I CAN... STAY WITH YOU?
WE CAN...
STAY TOGETHER FOREVER?
OF COURSE WE CAN.
WE'RE FRIENDS, AREN'T WE?

THE HAUNTED BOOKSTORE

Gateway to a Parallel Universe

THE HAUNTED BOOKSTORE

Gateway to a Parallel Universe

ORIGINAL SHORT STORY

Shirai Midori's
Soliloquy

BY SHINOBUMARU

I had two sons. They were both my pride and joy.

One was a beautiful baby boy named Suimei. He was round and soft and healthy, but he didn't sleep much at night, which worried me. He had the most adorable smile you'll ever see. He'd open his mouth, and two bright white front teeth would poke out. I always imagined they were little pearls when I saw them.

I wanted Suimei to grow up to be happy. The more time I spent with him, the more my wishes for him grew.

My other son was a bit different. He had dark black hair with little splotches of red, his feet were almost too small for his long body, and his eyes were red, like pomegranates. He was always running around energetically.

His name was Kuro, and he was a dog spirit. As an Inugami, he served the Shirai family for many generations.

I might not have given birth to him, but he was my precious son all the same. I'm not sure he'd be very pleased if I told him that, though. He'd probably insist, "You and I are friends, Midori!" And then he'd immediately correct himself, saying, "I-I mean, you're my master, and I'm just your servant. That's all we are," his ears turning down in sadness.

Kuro still has so much to learn about when to hold back and when to let his true feelings out. He's a little clumsy like that, which only makes me love him more. I might be the head of the Shirai family, but that's never changed the way I approach him.

Kuro has been invaluable to me in raising Suimei.

I knew that our family was quite unusual. Normal families don't make their living hunting down the spirits who run rampant in the darkest corners of the world. The training to become an exorcist is ruthless. It doesn't matter how young the child is, they're all forced through the process. Even I had to go through it. I don't like to think about those days. The only memories I have from back then are of pain and sorrow.

To the Shirai family, wielding an Inugami was just another way to make money, a tool of the family business. You had to maintain your tool so that it would work, and so that it wouldn't fail to obey you.

Suimei was the long-awaited heir to the Shirai family. My husband tried to take him away from me as soon as he was born, but I wouldn't stand for it. I told him that if they tried to put Suimei through what they did to me, I'd kill myself, but he didn't listen. He almost succeeded in taking Suimei from me. Thankfully, Kuro protected us. Kuro was the strongest Inugami in our family. If he said "no" to something, there wasn't a single person who could argue with him.

"I'll protect the two of you," he'd say to me. "You just worry about raising Suimei."

What a wonderful son I had. What a protective older brother Suimei had been blessed with.

Once Suimei started learning to walk, things became quite hectic for Kuro and me. The room we lived in was built in the traditional style, and Suimei's favorite game was "break the shoji."

"Eep!" he squealed, as he made bigger and bigger holes with his tiny hands. His baby teeth, which had all grown in now, were dazzlingly bright.

I didn't know whether to scold him or laugh, so I just smiled and shook my head from where I sat on the futon. It was up to his big brother now.

"Suimei! You know better! Putting holes in the door will make me *veeeeery* angry. You don't want me to shout at you and make you cry, right? So don't—" Kuro's scolding was interrupted with a *yip*! "D-don't grab my tail! A-and don't lick that! I was under the floorboards yesterday, so it's dirty—"

"Kuro." I looked at him. "Did you go under the floorboards?"

"N-no! I don't know what you're talking about!"

"Kuuurooo?" I said his name in a sing-song tone.

"I-I *did* play under the floorboards! I'm sorry!"

"Then I hope you're ready for a bath. Because you're getting one."

"But it was Suimei's fault!"

My days with Kuro and Suimei were so lively and fun. Even though we were only one thin wall away from the awful reality waiting outside, we could forget about it for a moment and live our lives in peace.

When Suimei turned three years old, something happened that surprised both Kuro and me.

"Kuro, you know better than to make mischief," Suimei said to his brother.

"I know."

"Why did you hide mom's shoes? She can't go out without them."

"I know."

"Don't just say, 'I know.' Where's your apology?"

"I'm *sooooory!*"

Would you believe it? The younger brother had suddenly become the older brother! I couldn't help but laugh at them.

"Midori! Don't laugh at me! I feel pitiful enough crying as it is."

"I think it's too late to say that when you're already crying."

"Ugh! I know, but..." Kuro sobbed louder, with big, fat tears rolling down his cheeks and nose.

Suimei's hard face didn't crack, but he did take out his handkerchief and dry Kuro's eyes. When I complimented him on taking such good care of his brother, his pale cheeks turned rosy.

I smiled seeing the pride on Suimei's face. "You're such a good boy, Suimei. And a good big brother for Kuro."

Kuro protested, as I knew he would. "B-but *I'm* the oldest, you know!"

"Then you should make sure not to upset your brother, shouldn't you?"

Kuro looked guilty for a moment. "Urgh... But playing tricks is a part of my personality. I can't just quit all of a sudden!"

"Kuro! Bad dog!"

"I-I'm sorry, Suimei."

I laughed loudly, seeing Kuro's ears sink so quickly. There really was no end to the mirth with my two children around. I didn't even care about the family rule that you must never show emotions.

They were such boisterous boys, but there was at least one time each day where they both managed to settle down, and that was when they were sleeping. Each night, the two of them took a spot on either side of me on the futon.

There were even some evenings where I'd find myself staying up late into the night just to watch them sleep so peacefully.

Kuro, in particular, was a mama's boy. He'd always nestle up close to me to sleep. If I rubbed his back, his tail would wag happily, even though he was sleeping. His body would become relaxed—a sign of trust.

On especially quiet nights, I whispered to him, "Kuro, take care of Suimei for me, please." I knew I didn't have long to live, so I placed all my hopes on Suimei's older—though sometimes younger—brother.

"Suimei deserves so much happiness. Make sure you're there by his side whenever he's hurting, all right?" I stroked Kuro's back. His tail wagged, as if in reply.

Smiling, I sang a soft lullaby for my beloved children, to ensure their peaceful dreams.

"Hush-a-bye, hush-a-bye. Sleep, sweet children. May you both find all the happiness in the world."

THE HAUNTED BOOKSTORE
Gateway to a Parallel Universe

Author's Afterword

Thank you so much for purchasing Volume 2 of the manga adaptation of *The Haunted Bookstore*! It still feels like this adaptation just started recently, yet here we are, two volumes in. How is everyone enjoying the story?

I believe we've just about reached the point where Volume 1 of the original novel ends. Volume 1 had everything from Kaori and Suimei meeting each other, to the boisterous Tengu twins, to the surprisingly attractive master of spirits, Nurarihyon, as well as just the tiniest peek at Toochika-san, who runs a general store in the human realm.

So many characters who continue to support the story appeared in this volume. Munashichi-sensei had provided me with character designs for both Nurarihyon and Toochika-san, but this is the first time I'd seen them drawn by Medamayaki-sensei. My heart was racing. They turned out so wonderful!

I like handsome older men quite a bit, so there are always older men in my works. But seeing the images in my head recreated so perfectly on the page really makes me appreciate the qualities of a manga adaptation.

Now, then. It seems the manga is heading into the contents of the original's Volume 2. I hope you'll support the next volume as well. Personally, I'm really looking forward to the appearance of the mysterious "story-seller," Tamaki!

Shinobumaru

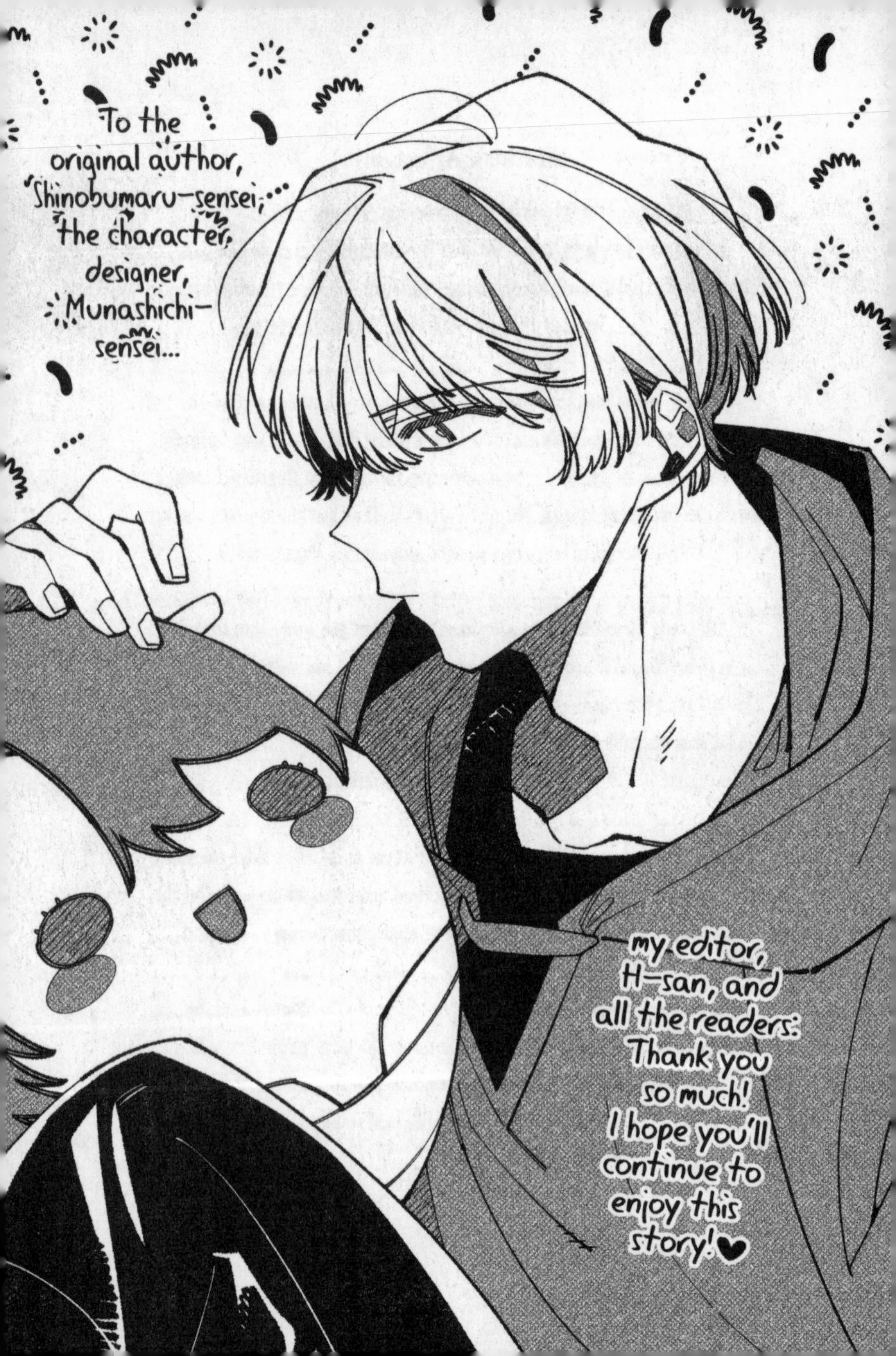
To the original author, Shinobumaru-sensei, the character designer, Munashichi-sensei...
my editor, H-san, and all the readers: Thank you so much! I hope you'll continue to enjoy this story!❤

THE HAUNTED BOOKSTORE

Gateway to a Parallel Universe